# Concepts and society

# International Library of Sociology

Founded by Karl Mannheim

Editor: John Rex, University of Warwick

Arbor Scientiae
Arbor Vitae

A catalogue of the books available in the **International Library of Sociology** and new books in preparation for the Library will be found at the end of this volume.

# Concepts and society

**I. C. Jarvie**

Professor of Philosophy
York University, Toronto

Routledge & Kegan Paul

London and Boston

*First published* 1972
*by Routledge & Kegan Paul Ltd,*
*Broadway House, 68–74 Carter Lane,*
*London EC4V 5EL and*
*9 Park Street,*
*Boston, Mass. 02108, U.S.A.*
*Printed in Great Britain*
*at the St Ann's Press, Park Road,*
*Altrincham, Cheshire WA14 5QQ*

*ISBN* 0 7100 7265 1

# Contents

If men define situations as real, they are real in their consequences.

W. I. Thomas (1928), p. 586

This special difficulty of the social sciences is a result, not merely of the fact that we have to distinguish between the views held by the people which are the object of our study and our views about them, but also of the fact that the people who are our object themselves not only are motivated by ideas but also form ideas about the undesigned results of their actions—popular theories about the various social structures or formations which we share with them and which our study has to revise and improve.

F. A. Hayek (1955), pp. 36–7

The way people think about people, themselves, is part of the reality about which they are trying to think in appropriate ways. The concepts which we employ to grasp what we are become part of what we are; or rather that we use them in this way becomes part of what we are. Thus in social theory we are using concepts to understand beings who define themselves by means of their use of concepts, in some cases the concepts that we are using in trying to understand them.

Alasdair MacIntyre (1962), p. 64

What is meant by 'institution' by any social scientist is no longer a fixed body of rules or visible edifice of bricks and mortar . . . but is the working of some associated set of concepts.

Bernard Crick (1969), p. 155

# Preface

Two problems have been my constant concern in the dozen or so years I have spent studying the philosophy of the social sciences. One is how social change is to be explained. The other is the extent to which beliefs can explain action. One of the most striking features of Popper's philosophy of the social sciences, it has seemed to me, is the link it makes possible between these two problems. For social change, I believe, comes about primarily because people revise their beliefs about the world and society and on that account change the way they act.

Change and belief have become problems because theories put forward by social scientists have not taken adequate account of them. The attempt in sociology and anthropology to explain the workings of society in terms of the functioning of an underlying structure of statuses and roles focused interest on what was unchanging. The attempt in behaviouristic psychology and political science to explain without reference to anything mental was hardly conducive to the serious consideration of beliefs. Both of these attempts, in their different ways, contradict common experience, where change and beliefs are cardinal realities. Popper has recently criticized the ontological parsimony which allows reality only to the world of physics and/or the world of mind. The social world, as he sees it, is neither physical nor mental; nor is it simply a mixture of both. It is also in the realm of objective mind, along with statements, meanings, arguments, scientific theories, works of art, and so on. This 'third world' is what mediates the interaction between the worlds of physical and of mental phenomena, which explains social change and which shows how belief can explain action. Just as many approaches to the social sciences (behaviourism, functionalism) founder precisely because they cannot explain social change, so, frequently, the same approaches also deny any connection between thought and action, between ideas and the world. There is a connection, nevertheless. Popper constantly reiterates that the objects of thought, i.e. ideas, theories, beliefs, values, affect how people act, and thus affect the way the world is. This is the germ of a theory of social change, and an explanation of why denial of the connection between thought and action leads to an inability to explain social change.

My book *The Revolution in Anthropology* was concerned with effecting these connections. What I did not do there, and propose to do here, was explore the thesis that ideas affect the way people act, and hence the way the world is. Many contemporary philosophers are concerned with the relation between thought and action, whether thought can be said to 'cause' action, or merely to give reasons for it. This is not the aspect of the matter I shall be concerned with. I certainly do not believe that thought 'causes' action, since causes are specific, whereas to any thought there would seem to correspond an infinite set of possible implementations in action, depending on a whole host of other factors and how the acting agent appraises them. I would rather speak of people choosing to act on the basis of their beliefs. So, ideas do have some effect on action; we do act in accord with our ideas. My concern shall be how best to explain society and its changes, and what sorts of difficulties we get into, when such a powerful charge of mentalism is injected into the methodology of the social sciences.

In my title, 'concepts' is shorthand for ideas, theories, values, and so on. Some further clarification is necessary to prevent misunderstanding: a title like *Concepts and Society* may portend all sorts of topics. It could take in the problem of how the concepts we use are tied to the social rules for their use, perhaps even constituted by those rules. It could be misread as concepts or, as I would prefer to say, conceptions *of* society and the social process. It has been construed (by Gellner, in a paper under this title [1962]) as including the problem of translating the concepts of one society into terms understandable in other societies. Gellner's problem came to the surface in the work of Winch, who argued for the peculiarity of the concepts necessarily employed in the social sciences from the fact that the concepts are involved in the processes they describe, and hence shape them in decisive ways. In a series of critical papers (1962, 1968a, 1968b) Gellner has exposed the relativism and conceptual conservatism, not to mention Universal Charity, implicit in these ideas. He has countered by illustrating the manifold and often obscure nature of concepts and their use and the necessity of attempting to translate them into our language, rather than accepting them purely on their own terms.

All of these topics will be touched upon in the course of what follows. But they are not themselves the central problem. The central problem to which the book is addressed could be otherwise stated like this. Granted that people act on the basis of the way they see things; granted therefore that the way things subsequently are is to some extent a function of the way they are currently seen by people; granted then that the way people see things affects the way things are; can there then be any objectivity in the social sciences; can they be about the way things are, or must they confine themselves to the way they seem to people? In short, if ideas influence society, are we committed to subjectivism and relativism?

My answer runs as follows. We need to distinguish the way things seem to a single individual from the way things seem to a group which shares an interpretation. A man may fantasize that he is a piece of soap. He may also hold the view shared by others that he is good looking. There is a difference. The world of ideas and theories is not the private world of neuroses. It is a public world, a shared world. Neither physical, nor mental, but elsewhere: what Popper calls the world of objective mind. In attempting to cope with, explain, and perhaps master our world we construct pictures or theories of it. The social world is peculiar in that its entities, processes and relations emerge from, and are constituted by, the actions of its members, and these in turn are predicated on the theories and pictures of it which they entertain from time to time. The social scientist, therefore, has not only his own preconceptions, errors, and distortions to cope with: he has to cope with those of others both in the sense that these enter his mental world, but also in the sense that they are built into the constituents of the world he believes he is studying.

Holding, as I do, that ideas in the form of beliefs influence action in a host of complex as well as obvious ways, I want to press the argument still further. Not only is this philosophically important; is is sociologically important. Reform, change, improvement, modification, if any, seem to me to proceed from the competitive interaction between our private beliefs about the world, and their third world brothers. The struggle of privately held beliefs to realize themselves in the world through the actions of their believers seems to me a fundamental force behind social change. The tension between what people believe and what is, between what they do and what they bring about, is a creative one.

This volume, then, will attempt to articulate the elements of a philosophy of the social and of the social sciences extrapolated from the philosophical ideas of Professor Sir Karl Popper. The word 'extrapolated' is to indicate that much of what is argued here is already contained in Popper's writings. However, one often hears the complaint that Popper nowhere sets out clearly and systematically his total philosophy of the social sciences. Some attribute this to the polemical character of much of his writing on these topics. A better explanation would be that all of Popper's work is intensely problem-oriented; he has never been concerned to outline it as a system or a subject matter. People used to textbook expositions of subjects find it difficult to cope with material that is developed entirely in the context of problems. Yet since Popper's main concern is with solving problems, or at least advancing discussion of them, and hardly at all with spreading his 'system', his neglect of systematic treatments is understandable. He can also appeal to a tradition at least as old as Plato of presenting philosophical results in this dialectical fashion. Even so, there is hardly a dearth of material in his writings: one closely argued book (*The Poverty of Historicism*), substantial sections of two others (*The Open Society and Its Enemies* and *Conjectures and Refutations*), and an untranslated paper 'Die Logik der Sozialwissenschaften', are all devoted to issues in the philosophy of the social sciences.

It would be true to say, however, that problems in the philosophy of the social sciences have never been Popper's primary focus of interest and he has not published as much about them as one could wish. Those of us who have studied with him are especially aware of this as we had access to his further thinking on these matters in lecture courses and seminars. If, then, less than all of the views articulated here can be traced back to Popper's writings, this will probably be because the ideas were otherwise absorbed.

Two doctrines, above all others, are associated with Popper's name by philosophers of the social sciences. These are his anti-historicism and his doctrine of methodological individualism. In the present work, nothing much is said about either. This is because my concern is to emphasize his relatively neglected ideas of situational logic and the third world. As far as historicism is concerned, I think his critique is the last word. But some of the ideas in this book may be thought to be incompatible with methodological individualism, so it is necessary to say something about that now (and in the appendix).

Methodological individualism is often interpreted as a denial of the reality of social wholes, social structures and institutions, and a reduction of these to individuals and their psychology. In denying this interpretation I go along with Agassi, who takes methodological individualism to be the view that the only actors in society are human individuals, and that only human individuals have aims to act upon. This doctrine does not reduce society to the psychology of individuals, since the individual in an explanation is always anonymous and typified, and because psychology is short-circuited by the assumption that the individual is acting (rationally) to realize his aims.

Critics like Mandelbaum, Goldstein and Brodbeck seem to think that methodological individualism takes away the reality of the social or makes it an epiphenomenon of individuals. This is a grave misunderstanding. Methodological individualism is not a reduction at all, but a denial of the possibility of attributing aims and hence actions to non-individuals and especially social wholes like institutions. Shorthand locutions like 'the Government decided', 'the State Department announced', 'Germany's policy was', are perfectly in order so long as the entities named do not become acting agents with aims of their own.

In an important contribution Wisdom (1970) has cleared this up by pointing out that Popper conceives of social institutions as entities resulting from agents' intentions and their consequences, but the resultant aggregate is more than the agents' intentions and their consequences. Social institutions can, as it were, be distributively reduced to the agents' intentions and their consequences, but cannot be collectively so reduced.

A further argument sometimes fastens on the notion of aim or goal-direction action, and the methodological individualist is accused of envisaging the individual in a vacuum, just somehow having these aims or goals. Whereas, the critic wants to claim, in fact his upbringing, education, social origin, and a whole host of other factors can be seen as collectively influencing, if not determining, what aims he has. This is a powerful argument. It can be turned aside with the help of the distinction between distributive reduction and collective reduction used above. No one would deny that distributively a man's beliefs, values, goals, aims or what have you, can be shown to be acquired from this or that source or influence. But the totality of his views cannot be collectively so reduced. It is thus as helpful to insist on the cardinal reality, non-reducibility, of aims or goals, as it is to insist on the cardinal reality, non-reducibility of social institutions themselves. Indeed if, as Diderot and Popper suppose, thought presupposes language, and language is an irreducible social institution, thought, the contents of men's minds, is itself at least partly an irreducible social fact.

Among the cardinal realities facing the individual, then, are his social surroundings, especially institutions. These are as concrete and as real as his physical surroundings, and must play a part in his decisions and actions. What this book endeavours to explain is just how that reality comes to signify.

The argument of the volume is laid out as follows. In chapter 1 Popper's basic model for explanation in the social sciences—the logic of the situation—is expounded in some detail. In chapter 2 this approach is contrasted with Winch's treatment of concepts and society, where an attempt is made to shift the emphasis from a science of society which explains, to a philosophical study of the internal relations between concepts which constitute actions, an enterprise called 'understanding'. This objection overcome, two case studies are introduced to illustrate the importance of beliefs, of the way the actors themselves define the situation they find themselves in, to the explanation of society. In chapter 3 the case study is in the teenage rebellion. Chapter 4 is a lengthy study of the literature on social class, arguing that what is important about class is the importance attributed to it by people. It is real because people believe it to be and act on that belief. Berger and Luckmann's theory of how this social reality is acquired and operated is expounded in chapter 5. Chapter 6 returns to the problems of reality, change, and belief, and explicates them further in terms of Popper's (and Frege's) doctrine of the objective third world of concepts.

# Acknowledgments

This book wrote itself without my being fully aware that it was happening. I found its main themes emerging again and again in papers written for separate occasions. With very little rewriting they made up chapters 1–4. Once the pattern had emerged, the writing of chapters 5 and 6 seemed to flow quite naturally.

To the following editors and publishers I am grateful for permission to re-use some material: to George K. Zollschan, editor, and the Glendessary Press for chapter 1, a shorter version of which is to appear in *Essays on Sociological Explanation;* to Robert Borger and Frank Cioffi, editors, and the Cambridge University Press for chapter 2 which is a revised and expanded version of a paper entitled 'Understanding and Explanation in Sociology and Social Anthropology', which appeared in *Explanation in the Behavioural Sciences,* 1970; and to Mr Richard Hough for kindly permitting me to reproduce the diagram on page 26 from his *Admirals in Collision.*

To my teacher, Sir Karl Popper, I am once again deeply indebted for inspiration and encouragement. It is from his works, and those of Hayek and Gellner, that I have learned most. Two successive classes of undergraduates have helped me grapple with the problems of the subject in a course given under the same title in York University's Division of Social Science. A preliminary draft was commented on by Professors Gellner, Hattiangadi, Sprott and Wisdom, to all of whom my thanks. And, once again, I owe an immense personal debt to Joseph Agassi, ever ready to help and be imposed upon when one descends with manuscript and family and insists on discussing far into the night. I have been trying out the ideas of this book on him since our time together in Hong Kong. He has been very patient, and immensely helpful; I treasure his friendship.

# part one

# Preliminaries

# 1 The logic of the situation[1]

What do the social sciences explain?

> It is a mistake, to which careless expressions by social scientists
> often give countenance, to believe that their aim is to *explain*
> conscious action. This, if it can be done at all, is a different
> task, the task of psychology. . . . The problems [the social
> sciences] try to answer arise only insofar as the conscious actions
> of many men produce undesigned results. . . .
>
> Hayek (1952), p. 39

Human action has consequences, especially unintended consequences,
including patterned structures of relationships which we call institutions, and, while these are the results of human action, they are
not the results of human design. Gellner remarks (1956) that the
proper study of mankind is human groups and institutions.

When human beings act, including speak, there emerges from
their behaviour entities like groups, marriage, morals and knowledge
which transcend them, which are products of their actions but not
necessarily of their intentions. This idea, presaged if not anticipated
by Weber, Cooley, Thomas and Mead, has been worked out most
interestingly by Hayek and Popper. In this chapter, I want to use
it to discuss the question of how the social sciences explain what
they do explain. One might say that the question of what they
explain is one of emphasis: are the social sciences concerned to
explain action or the results of action? By and large action is to
be explained by reasons, and often these are very simple and
straightforward. Those philosophers who identify such giving of
reasons with the activity of doing social science really miss the
whole point. The problems of the social sciences begin where the
giving of reasons ends. For some social events like birth and suicide
rates cannot be explained by giving reasons (whose?) at all. While

other social events, being unintended (traffic accidents, stock market crashes, the breakdown of institutions), have no reasons of an individual kind at all. Sometimes a sociologist or an historian may venture to explain an event for which reasons apparently can be adduced. The outbreak of a war would be an example, as would labour unrest. But here the presumption is that neither one individual's reasons ('Why did you declare war, Mr Chamberlain?' or 'Why are you on strike, Joe?') nor the sum of the reasons of all the individuals concerned suffice to explain the event. This claim amounts to an affirmation of the legitimacy of the social sciences as separate disciplines contributing something novel to the stock of human knowledge.

(The notion of reasons is not one I shall employ much in this volume because it fails to discriminate means from ends, goals from circumstances. A reason for crossing the road may be to go to a shop. This is an aim. A reason for carrying an umbrella may be to avoid a soaking on the way to the shop. While there is no sharp demarcation between means and ends, it is a useful distinction, and I shall therefore employ the terminology of aims and circumstances rather than reasons.)

This chapter contends that the basic explanatory model underlying the social sciences reads as follows.

A man, for the purposes of the social sciences, can be viewed as in pursuit of certain goals or aims, within a framework of natural, social, psychological and ethical circumstances. These circumstances constitute both means of achieving his aims and constraints on that achievement. A man's conscious or unconscious appraisal of how he can achieve his aims within these circumstances might be called sorting out the *logic* of the situation he is in (or his situational logic). 'Logic' because he tries to find out the best and most effective means, within the situation, to realize his aims. There is *no* suggestion that there exists some perfect scrutiny of the situation which yields a uniquely effective move: most often several moves may be indicated, although it is unlikely the actor will be emotionally and morally indifferent between them. The actor's ideas are part of his situation in a complicated way. It is assumed that the situation, if objectively appraised, should favour certain means which are more effective than others and that the measure of rationality consists in the success in approaching such an 'objective' appraisal. The logic of the situation, then, is an empirical description of the procedure of explanation which goes on in the social sciences; it is also a normative prescription for reform of what does not fit the description, particularly holistic and psychologistic social science; it is also, finally, a logical analysis of what underlies plausible social science explanations. The logic of the situation is a special case of the deductive analysis of causal explanation in general and illustrates the unity of method in the sciences.

## Introduction to situational logic

### Description plus examples

This chapter is an attempt systematically to explore what I understand to be the notion of the logic of the situation. It seems to me one of Sir Karl Popper's most powerful yet simple philosophical ideas, and with the help of it one can sort out a great many issues in the methodology of the social sciences. Unfortunately it is nowhere fully explained outside of lectures.[2]

Yet it is not hard to do so. In a nutshell the idea is this. *Situational logic (1) is explanation (2) of human behaviour (3) as attempts to achieve (4) goals or aims (5) with limited means (6).* Each of the numbered key terms in this sentence will have a subsequent section of the chapter devoted to it.[3] Before plunging into this I want to give some illustrative examples of how problems can be tackled in accordance with the logic of the situation. I want to take problems displaying the following characteristics: one stemming from the interaction of an individual quirk and the social situation, involving someone whose aims (or reasons) are clear but who has misappreciated the changing situation; one where the action is unremarkably typical but nevertheless puzzling because it is not clear if conscious aims (or reasons) are involved and if so what; and finally, one where a society-wide problem cannot be explained directly as a result of anyone aiming at the problematic state of affairs or of failing to appreciate what the situation is. The first is satisfied by explaining the case of a cautious driver who has nevertheless caused a multiple collision; the second is satisfied by the problem of explaining why a gentleman raises his hat to a lady; the third is satisfied by explaining the apparent erosion of the social fabric in Libya despite strongly conservative forces—Islam and the monarchy.

*Example 1* How could an otherwise cautious, even blameless, driver suddenly find himself the cause of a serious multiple collision? It was an accident, we say. But is that the best we can do to explain it? Let us try further inquiry. The accident happened on a freeway. Cautious Mr X had never driven on a freeway before and did not realize that it is a completely different driving *situation* from that in a typical urban main street. Let us expand this further.

5

Learning to drive parallels in significant ways learning to live in a society. Traffic and its institutions surround us, but until the statutory age we are not allowed to enter the driving situation and master its logic. One observable consequence of doing so, when we get around to it, is that our behaviour as pedestrians improves. Knowing what it is like to drive a vehicle on a road, we can as pedestrians anticipate some of the dangers and act accordingly. I developed this hypothesis in Hong Kong to explain the apparently careless, even *kamikaze,* behaviour of the pedestrians. Never having sat behind a wheel, therefore trusting naïvely in the ability of cars to stop for them, the pedestrians act as though they were oblivious to danger. It says much for the skill of Hong Kong drivers, and the slow speeds they are forced to go, that the accident rate is as low as it is.

Take now this newish situation on the roads—freeways (called 'motorways' in Britain). Freeways organize traffic somewhat differently from ordinary roads and as a consequence quite new kinds of accidents occur. Cars collide even in cases where, quite clearly, there is no obstruction of vision involved. Multiple collisions occur. Why? For different reasons on different sections. Take first the freeway entry ramp. One is ordinarily trained to enter a transverse traffic stream by stopping the car, waiting for a gap in the oncoming traffic, then swinging out into it. On a freeway one is expected to behave quite differently, in fact to *speed up* and slip into the stream. Why? Because at freeway speeds a gap in the oncoming traffic would have to be very big to give one time to spot it, react to it and then accelerate from rest. In fact, much correct freeway behaviour consists in travelling at a speed comparable to that of the other traffic and then changing lanes when wanting to speed up or to slow down and get off. The cautious driver we are considering who tries to enter the freeway in the same manner that he turns into his local main street would cause a multiple back-up collision if he stopped on the feeder ramp, and another in the oncoming traffic lanes were he to try to accelerate from rest into a gap he has spotted, for this would force oncoming cars drastically to slow down. And yet, in behaving this way he might well imagine he has proceeded with exemplary caution.

Take now exiting from the freeway. Driving along a main street and wanting to exit you proceed slowly, spot the turn you are looking for, then signal, slow down and turn off. On the freeway, slowing down may again cause a multiple back-up collision if the traffic is dense. The problem is that, because of the speed on the freeway, exit signs are posted well in advance of turn-offs, so that, without loss of speed, the driver can anticipate his exit and move across to the inside lane in time to slip into the exit ramp, without slowing down or interfering with through traffic; he slows only when he has been fed off the main traffic lanes.

Take, lastly, simply cruising along. Normally, on a main street cars proceed slowly and bunched together. There is small danger in this, for they can almost stop dead, and at low speeds little harm is done by a rear-end bump. On the freeway, however, bunching is extremely dangerous. It prevents lane-changing, and makes reaction to sudden slow-downs very difficult. Result, more collisions.

Learning about traffic is a model for learning about society. A network of institutions (road signs, lanes, laws), customs (keeping your distance), expectations (that others know the rules), and ideas about all these, and people working together more or less in harmony. In addition to strictly correct driving, there is also courteous, defensive and unselfish driving. There are also vices like over-cautiousness, and competitiveness. The decisive simplification involved in comparing society to traffic is that, whereas in society people and their aims are diverse, on the freeway most people share one aim: to get safely and swiftly from A to B. Special problems arise, like the case of our cautious driver, as unintended consequences of the building of the freeways, and these problems can be understood by contrasting the logic of the freeway situation as experienced by the cautious but experienced driver with that of the cautious but inexperienced driver. Their aims are identical. Their situations are objectively identical. Only their appreciation of the situation, their expectations, their grasp of its logic, are different.

*Example 2* A man raises his hat to a lady. Why? Answer: a ritual gesture of respect observed only by those who know the received ritual and who wish to express their respect. Unlike hand-shaking upon introduction, which seems to have lost any significance it may have had, hat-raising is sufficiently uncommon (decline of hats?) yet known, to be significant. Refusing to shake hands or averting one's face in the street remain significant; not raising the hat is hardly noticeable.

Much of social life turns on arbitrary but significant gestures of this sort. The significance is sometimes clear, sometimes less so. Japanese audiences hiss: it is not at once apparent to the outsider that this is appreciative; many cultures take the burp after a meal as a mandatory gesture of satisfaction, others as rude. Social usages of this kind are peculiar in that most of those performing them could not explain their origin, even tentatively. In the hat-raising example it is unclear whether any aim is involved, except perhaps in the most attenuated sense. Refusing to shake hands upon intro-duction is not problematic in the same way. What, then, are we to make of these apparently aimless social usages? The logic of the situation seems to be this. Those who follow the usages are members of a society who have learned its conventions and who either accept them, or do not feel strongly enough to wish to flout them. Given this attitude they, on occasion, may find themselves wishing to indicate or communicate their respect for a certain woman. Their knowledge of the society tells them that raising the hat, rather than kissing the feet, is the correct gesture. Alternatively, they know it to be *de rigueur* in the society to express respect for women by raising the hat and they do not wish to be regarded as *gauche*; in fact they aim to integrate their behaviour into the society.

*Example 3* 'Libya's Oil Riches Erode Simple Life.'[4] This is a case of the unintended and, it would seem, unwanted consequences of oil wealth. (Subsequently, the monarchy has been overthrown in a *coup d'état*.) Into Libyan society came wealth; then (1) alcohol; (2) shepherds drive fast cars to clandestine bars and get into fatal crashes when driving home drunk; (3) the newly rich, able to afford the pious pilgrimage to Mecca, are also able to seek diversion in the fleshpots of Athens, Rome, and Cairo; (4) the King, as spiritual counsellor, is overwhelmed by citizens asking how to reconcile their dissolute new life with Islam. So the exploitation of oil is having a feedback on religious, social and political *mores*. None of these effects was intended by anyone, and yet no one seems to be able to do anything about it—the King stays out of town and inaccessible, trying to negotiate a middle course.

So the oil producers may not aim to change the society, the King may aim to minimize change, the shepherds aim to enjoy their new wealth *and* to follow their religion of Islam. Into this confusion of aims comes the factor of enormous wealth. The monarch finds it impossible to carry out his religious duty to answer all problems and questions; he has only one wife, although he encourages other men to have more; his wife is not veiled, although most wives of orthodox men are. And the newly wealthy shepherds behave erratically.

Clearly, we are seeing here a certain incompatibility of aims. The aim to have and enjoy wealth is conflicting severely with the aim to be religious, and the latter is suffering. What everyone is avoiding is the making of some sensible choices between these conflicting aims. As a result, what no one is aiming at, the erosion of the simple good life, is happening.

## Sources in economics, Weber and Popper

Popper describes how (Popper, 1957a, historical note), after the original publication in German of his classic, *The Logic of Scientific Discovery,* he turned his attention to the social sciences to see if and how they differed methodologically. In concentrating on economics, he was in fact concerned to see if he could criticize his own theory of science as progressing by means of conjectures and refutations. Economics was, and is, the most developed social science, and he analysed its explanations of, for example, the determination of price in a free market, as involving aims (maximizing profit, minimizing loss), situation (conditions in production and in the market, the nature of their institutions), and the most efficacious means of gaining the former in the latter (pure economic theory). The price in a free market is an unintended outcome of sellers and buyers attempting to minimize their outgoings and maximize their incomings, given the degree of competition, the elasticity of supply, and the 'perfection' of the market. Popper seems to have generalized this analysis to see if it would serve for the social sciences as a whole. Bureaucratic delays, road accidents, train timetables, the rise of philosophical schools, the breakdown of democracy—explanations of all these could be analysed in terms of the same methodological model. Of course, some social phenomena could be explained simply by aims and the fact that the situation did not thwart attempts to achieve them. My being a passenger on a train can be explained by the lack of impediments to my aiming to be such. This sort of case is relatively unproblematic. What is more problematic is when large-scale events, like the breakdown of democracy in Germany, are explained solely by reference to someone, or some group's aim. General recourse to this mode of explanation Popper calls 'the conspiracy theory of society'. In general, while conspiracies do exist, by definition they are dedicated to controversial causes, and it is their success in the face of inertia, complexity and opposition that needs explaining (as, for example, an unintended consequence of the aims and actions of their opponents) by reference to the situation. This is an extremely good sociological insight, because most of us take it for granted that an event is explained when a conspiracy to bring it about is uncovered. Popper rightly contends that that is only the beginning: now the success of the conspiracy has to be explained.[5]

To a large extent, Popper's analysis is far from new. Very similar analyses of social action had previously appeared in the works of Weber (1925, pp. 88–115) and Talcott Parsons—if under different names. The latter certainly makes it explicit enough, but

shares with the former a curiously clotted, even opaque style.[6]
Watkins (1953), who especially contrasts Weber and Popper on
holism and individualism, can with Hayek (1955) be credited with
initiating the currently increasing discussion and application of
Popper's ideas on the methodology of the social sciences.

## The status of situational logic as doctrine

The question arises, is Popper prescribing for the social sciences,
analysing the social sciences or describing the social sciences?

*A normative doctrine*   Normative methodology involves the offering of advice, evaluation, criticism, injunction, etc. Popper is certainly doing this, although it is not his main aim, and the advice
is not moral even where he considers the issues to be moral (for
example, collectivism and historicism). One of his books is called
the *poverty* of historicism, not the *wickedness* of it. He advises
against such holistic doctrines mainly because, he argues, they lead
to a poor methodology. A poor methodology is one which does
not help one to advance the study of problems. Popper does not
claim that any method can help solve problems. That he leaves to
ingenuity. The logic of the situation idea, then, is normative only
in the sense that it is sometimes helpful to be articulate about
method when one is blocked on a problem.[7] Ordinarily, method
is a technique one learns to apply almost without thinking.

*A logical analysis*   It should already be clear that, in addition to
being normative, the logic of the situation can be taken as simply
an analysis of good explanations in the social sciences. 'Good' as
a qualifier because it does not analyse historicist or collectivist
explanations, since they do not refer to individuals and situations
at all. Such explanations as do are analysable in this way. Popper
himself, for example, has given situational analyses both of Plato's
law of the decay of imperfect states, and of Marx's theory of class
struggle (Popper, 1945, ii, pp. 39–45, 111–17). Of course, logic
itself is to a certain extent a normative discipline: it is the theory
of valid inference, the strengths and values of which it indicates—
the drawbacks of invalid inferences being illuminated in the process.

However, while logic is normative, its standards do not come
out of the blue. It begins from inferences that are intuitively in
order, or intuitively not in order. It proceeds to refine our intuitions
of what is in order, what it is to be in order and what is an
inference, to help us discriminate subtle, complicated, or deceptive
cases we had not earlier been able to recognize or handle.

*An empirical doctrine*   In addition to being normative and logical,
the logic of the situation is a shorthand description of what a great

deal of social scientists and historians actually do under other names, or under no name at all. So, not only is the logic of the situation a way explanations are actually made in the social sciences, it is also a standard of explanation to which both logic and the pursuit of truth urge us to turn. Examples: the theory of price in economics explains price as the unintended result of actors acting to minimize their losses and maximize their gains in a situation in which many variables are specified. When Moynihan (1967b) tries to explain the Negro riots, he first indicates that American Negro aims in life are not generally different from those of American whites; what is different is their situation and he isolates factors like the high incidence of families without a male head, the high unemployment rate, the wretched housing conditions. In the end he succeeds in generating empathy in us: showing us how in those conditions we should feel it was the logic of our situation to join in a riot. Kingsley Davis, in his famous article on prostitution (1966), shows how the aims of the prostitute are not special (this renders redundant explanations incorporating assumptions of psychological peculiarities and is a strength of Davis's case) but both her situation, i.e. her gradual drift into 'the life', and her perception of it, *are* special. The service she provides involves a loss of social status, but this is compensated for in monetary terms or in other terms sufficiently liquid to ensure that the compensation does not lead to corrective action to regain status (as contrasted with, say, a kept mistress or second wife).

Evans-Pritchard, too, in his classical study of Azande witchcraft (1937) does not attribute different aims to the Azande than to the rest of mankind; the differences lie in the situation and in the perception of the situation—if you like, the 'reality orientation'. Indeed, Evans-Pritchard endeavours to explain Azande magical practices exclusively with reference to the prosaic aim of avoiding and ameliorating illness and misfortune. In Azande society it is a tradition to consult oracles in cases of disease. It is an Azande belief that witches operate in their society to cause disease. Given all this, their resort to witchcraft is explained (see Jarvie and Agassi, 1967).[8]

*Modification of the doctrine* What look like two modifications have been made in situational logic. The first is more the correction of a mistaken interpretation in regard to psychology; the second looks like an exception in regard to collective behaviour. Firstly, situational logic has been mistakenly identified with psychological reductionism. It is not a reductionism at all—no social or other entities are collectively reduced (see Wisdom, 1970). It is not psychological or subjective, but sociological and objective—it does not refer to feelings but to situations, as in the case of riots, prostitution, and Azande magic. Wisdom has suggested renaming the whole thing 'situational individualism'. Secondly, Watkins had conceded that genuine cases of mass adaptive behaviour, as among bees and ants, may be unamenable to situational-logic explanation. The comparable case in human society may be the mob, mob psychology, and so on.[9] He expresses the hope that these exceptions will turn out not to be such. The analysis of collective human behaviour in Smelser (1962) and Brown (1965) strike me as entirely compatible with situational individualism.

*Loss of the doctrine*   Any doctrine, in addition to being introduced, adopted and modified, can also be rebutted, refuted and lost. Far from being lost, the doctrine of situational logic is subject to vigorous current discussion (see Donagan, 1964; M. Martin, 1968; Leach, 1968).

## Explanation

Before coming to theories of explanation in the social sciences, let us look at the general question of explanation and its role in science. The three principal positions divide over the questions of certainty and truth. The word 'science', after all, comes from the Latin verb *scire,* to know. Hence one may expect a 'scientific explanation' to be one based on knowledge, on *epistēmē* (knowledge) not *doxa* (opinion). But there are arguments, especially from the vagaries of changing ideas in the history of science, which suggest that at best science can be current *doxa.* One reaction to this is to abandon the idea that science explains; another is to accept that scientific knowledge is not certain. The three positions are as follows: (1) The position that the aim of science is to give certain and true explanations. (2) The position that because certain and true explanations are impossible explanations they are outside science, perhaps in religion or metaphysics. Science, it is argued, is not a set of explanations, it is no more than a set of manipulative conventions. (3) The position that agrees with (2) that certainty is beyond science, yet with (1) that the aim of science is explanation, not certain and true, but better and better explanation. Hence, it is argued, explanation is quite possible within a realistic science.[10]

(1) *Explanatory certainty*   The notion that science aims at explanatory certainty includes (*a*) the theory of inductive explanation, (*b*) the theory of *a priori* deductive explanation, and (*c*) the theory of explanation by essences.

(*a*) *Induction*   We need spend little time expounding induction. It is *not* the same as empiricism (Agassi, 1963*b*). It is, rather, the view that we should use observations to back or justify every assertion and explanation we offer. Those we cannot fully justify in this way we can at least render increasingly probable by accumulating instances in their favour. This ideal of unprejudiced, increasingly highly confirmed explanation has been severely criticized for two centuries, but its popularity if anything grows with the years.

(b) *Deductivism*  Apriorists generally wish to proceed from first principles or introspection to the discovery of explanations of the world. The high tide of this tendency in the social sciences is marked by Spencer, who tried to deduce the whole of his theory of super-organic evolution from the principles of the persistence of force and the indestructability of matter [*sic*].[11] Malinowski tried to do it with a set of basic needs, although he would no doubt have been horrified to have them labelled *a priori* (see Piddington, 1957). A straightforward logical problem confronts the apriorists: how can we explain the *world* unless we inject some information about the world into our premises? How can we inject information about the world into our premises *prior* to our experience of the world? And how can we proceed the better to understand the world unless we check our premises against the world? (It is interesting that Spencer solved this problem by a kind of collective mind theory. He says that *a priori* knowledge is the product of immense accumulations of experiences of countless of man's ancestors transmitted through the inheritance of the nervous system (1900, final footnote to chap. IV of part II).)[12]

(c) *Essentialism*  Essentialism is the doctrine that explanatory certainty can only be attained when we are sure we have penetrated to the true essence of things. This can be regarded as a further specification of both inductivism and deductivism. Bacon, an inductivist, thought his method would lead to axioms stating the ultimate essence of such phenomena as heat. Descartes, a deductivist, believed that physics started with attempts to capture the essence of things like matter. The belief that things have essences or essential properties which make them what they are and thus explain what they are has been savaged by philosophers as different as Popper (1945) and Wittgenstein (1954), although the latter never uses the term (see Pitcher, 1964, section entitled 'The Critique of Essentialism').

(2) *Explanation as manipulative conventions*  Conventionalism is the doctrine that science does not explain: it is simply a set of extremely useful conventions. On the basis provided by them, we can predict and control events. Any claim that this predicting system is an ultimate or certain explanation is quite mistaken.

Again, conventionalism has been severely criticized on the grounds that science does sometimes adopt new theories that are unsuccessful as predictors and goes on using old theories which are successful predictors. Thus, to a strict conventionalist, the progress of science from theory to theory becomes unintelligible.

(3) *Hypothetico-deductive explanation* This is an attempt to give an account of scientific explanation that neither demands an unattainable certainty, nor uses induction, nor proceeds entirely *a priori,* nor abandons the concept of truth as part of the scientific quest. Explanations are conceived of as hypothetical, not making claims to certainty. When it is called deductive, that does not mean that it proceeds deductively from axioms, it means that the only logic used is deductive.[13]

Of late, the thesis that hypothetico-deductive explanation applies *mutatis mutandis* to human behaviour has been repeatedly challenged. At first the attack came from those concerned with the philosophy of history. Later, it has been argued that human actions are to be explained in terms of the reasons given for doing them, these reasons specifying the meaning the actions have for the actors. Bartley (1962a), Hempel (1962 and 1965), White (1965), and Danto (1966) have pitched in to reply vigorously enough, but mainly on technical matters. To show that the critics tilt at windmills or make elementary logical errors is not enough.

All this may be ignored for the present. Here it will be shown first, that the principal existing means of successful explanation of human action is the logic of the situation (in which the meaning of certain actions to the actors is of course part of the situation as they see it). And second, that the logic of the situation is a form of hypothetico-deductive explanation and that therefore all explanation of human behaviour is to be explicated deductively. The hypothetico-deductive explication of all explanation is presented here as utilizing deductive logic, which is trivial (Popper, 1948), and in particular the principle that, in a valid inference, a false conclusion indicates that one or more premises are false. That an explanation can be a valid inference is no more than minimal, i.e. it is necessary but not sufficient for an explanation to be satisfactory.

First of all, we note that 'explain', like 'true', is a metalinguistic word—strictly speaking, then, we do not explain facts or events, but statements describing these facts or events. So, when we say a statement is explained by another, we mean that the explaining statements (*explicans, explanans*) stand in some relationship to the explained statement (*explicandum, explanandum*).[14] The best relationship to postulate between these sets of statements is that of ordinary logical deduction. This is not always obvious; for example, if we ask why King Charles I of England died (*explicandum*), and we are told that he had his head cut off (*explicans* I), it is not a satisfactory deductive explanation. However, we may claim it is if we know that all men die when their heads are cut off (*explicans* II)—with this premise in mind, we may feel the *explicandum* has in fact been explained. In other words, 'King Charles I died' is not explained by and it does not follow from 'King Charles I had his head cut off', but it is explained by and it does follow from the latter statement together with 'all men die when their heads are cut off' (and, perhaps, the rider 'King Charles I was a man' [*explicans* III]). This is to add something to the letter of an historical explanation, which is in the spirit of the hypothetico-deductive model, and in line with the fact that deductions are never formally complete (outside of formal logical work), i.e. missing premises are a routine matter in all explanations and not ghastly lacunae which the methodologists are demanding be filled (Agassi, 1963a, especially section 18).

So far we have only the logical bare bones of an explanation of the death of King Charles I. We could now go further and discuss not the physiology of his death, but, for example, the historical question, 'why did King Charles I get his head cut off?' or, the sociological question, 'under what social conditions is it possible for a ruling monarch to get his head cut off?' or, the political question, 'what are the constitutional and political consequences of a king's getting his head cut off?' All these further questions take the fact of the physiological beheading and give it an extra dimension, either historical, sociological, or political. No one claims that these three realms are wholly distinct or distinguishable. It might even be reasonable to say they are all aspects of the question, 'why did King Charles I of England die?' However, the question should not be treated colloquially for purposes of logical analysis, and logically the word 'die' is primarily a physiological one, hence the initial explanation by appeal to beheading and the law that all men die when beheaded. But of course death, and especially the sudden death of a monarch, is not exclusively a physiological fact, hence the, so to speak, 'logical room' or 'logical space' left for the historian, sociologist, and political scientist. It becomes clear that the logical bare bones of physiology, while necessary, are nowhere near sufficient to yield a satisfactory explanation.

The distinction is sometimes made between historical and generalizing sciences, in that the one explains particular facts, the other general, or repeatable facts. Plausible enough to start with, this distinction is not easy to maintain. The death of King Charles I is an instance of the socio-political phenomenon of regicide. It is also an instance of human death. Is it also a particular, unique,

15

occurrence? Yes, but no one tries to explain that. Even to describe the phenomenon, one must use general or universal words, and it is these with which the historian explains by reference to general laws and especially the logic of the situation. The death of this unique king at this unique instant is inexplicable—only what we choose to see as general, as an instance of a universal, can we explain by universal laws (Agassi, 1968).

While whether an explanation or a derivation is valid can be established by a purely formal definition of validity, satisfactoriness cannot. In his classic work on the subject, Popper (1957b) indicates that to be satisfactory it must be capable of being tested, neither circular nor *ad hoc*, and capable of being tested independently; moreover it should have survived being tested (corroborated).

(Incidentally, it might be worth noting at this point a slight ambiguity in our usage of the word 'explanation'. Sometimes we speak of a theory explaining a fact; at other times we speak of analysing an explanation where clearly we mean *all* the premises of the deduction—the several theories involved together with the initial conditions. Strictly, what explains, the explanation, is the *set* of theoretical and factual premises which yield the deductive conclusion. Looser usage should always be read as shorthand for this strict interpretation.)

As we have already seen with the logic of the situation itself, the deductive explication of explanation can be regarded as to some extent normative, to some extent logical analysis or rational reconstruction,[15] and to some extent a factual description of explanations. There is the added complication of whether deductive explanation is psychologically satisfactory; that is, whether a valid and methodologically satisfactory derivation of the statement describing the problem resolves the sense of psychological puzzlement, leads to feelings like understanding and enlightenment (see chapter 2). This will partly depend on what the phenomenon is validly derived from, and whether that in turn is puzzling. If someone is puzzled by the prosperity of America relative to Great Britain and they are answered by reference to resources-base, high rates of capital formation, fiercer competition, and so on, whether their puzzlement evaporates will certainly partly depend on whether these ideas are familiar to them and tested and accepted as relatively unproblematic compared to the original question of relative prosperity. In other words, to ask this question is to enter into the further problem of the satisfactoriness of an explanation, which we have already reviewed. Be that as it may, and before showing that situational logic is only a special case of deductive explanation in general, it should be stressed that the normative element in this analysis is not great. No one seriously suggests

16

explanations in any scientific work should be *set out* in a deductive pattern. The exceptions to this are the formalists, who thrive in mathematics, and who bemuse their students and avoid all the awkward questions by the simple device of axiomatizing everything they can (Lakatos, 1962; see also Rudner, 1966, and my review, 1967*b*; and Kyburg, 1968, and Howson's review, 1969). However, there is a *use* which recommends this deductive analysis on occasion, as when trying to pin down the source of an intuitive sense of dissatisfaction with an explanation—then might be the time to trace out its deductive logical structure before going on to the more general question of its satisfactoriness.

A simple way to indicate that situational logic is a special case of deductive explanation is to expose the deductive logical skeleton beneath the three examples I used at the beginning of this chapter. The traffic accident, the hat-raising, and the erosion of Libyan society. The statement to be explained in the traffic accident concerns a careful driver who is the cause of a collision. The explaining statements consist of statements about the driver's aims, and especially his caution (an aim or a means?), statements about his situation as it objectively is (freeway), and about his knowledge of the situation (thinks it is a road like any other). The upshot is that we can make an inference of this kind: given his aims and caution, given his situation, and given his appreciation of the situation, that he would cause a collision *follows*. Or, if you like, his getting away with no collision would in those circumstances itself require explanation, for example, colossal luck (=highly unexpected modification in the conditions assumed to prevail). The hat-raising, too, is a simple enough inference: this man is someone who among other things aims to conform to certain social practices and the intention is followed by the action with no difficulty at all. (It might be better to call conformity a limit on aims rather than an aim. A phrase such as 'aiming to conform' ascribes intention where there probably is none. Conformity is less something a person aims at, much more a social boundary or marker, circumscribing the aims and means which are socially acceptable. It is in not adopting aims or employing means that are not socially acceptable that conformity consists. See Merton, 1957, pp. 132ff.) 'This man raised his hat' follows from, 'For these and these reasons this man wanted to raise his hat and moreover there was no impediment to his turning wish into action.' 'These and these reasons' could be internalized and intentional, such that he could if asked articulate them, or they could be simply an account of more or less automatic behaviour on his part in situations of this kind. In the latter case, his acquisition of such automatic habits could perhaps be explained also. In both cases we would need to outline his situation, and the significance or meaning of hat-raising in the situation, and add to it in the case of its being intentional some account of his appreciation of the situation; in the case of it being automatic, some account of how and why the society (to speak metaphorically) accomplishes training in such behaviour, and why.

Analysis of the Libyan case is no more difficult. Here the emphasis is very much on the situation and its interlocking features. Islam prohibits alcohol, gambling, profligacy, and so on. Among those with little money for these things, the prohibitions do not weigh heavily. Once the supply of money to those unused to it appears, they experience grave conflicts of aims and values. They wish to enjoy their money and to remain pious. The deduction is something of this order. Give wealth to those unused to it and some will spend it in ways they themselves in sober moments consider unwise. If this is done in a society where the unwise spending is religiously as well as socially condemned, it follows that the result will be to create conflicts between the society which permits the wealth to intrude and the religion which suffers from it. Other institutions buttressed by the religion, such as the family, the monarchy, may also be put under a strain.

More generally, then, we could say this. Sociological explanation is deductive because the logic of the situation is deductive. Where the behaviour is regular and repeatable we search for laws governing it like 'all social changes create vested interests which resist further social changes'.[16] These laws in turn we explain by exposing the logic of the typical vested interest individual's situation and why it would be rational for him to act against further change. Where an action is of a rare or unique kind, we seek no sociological laws of it; we simply see how close an approximation to it we can deduce from the assumption of rationality. Asked why that worker is boarding that bus half an hour before his office starts work, we should seek explanations in overall sociological laws of traffic movement in large cities. Confronted with the same worker abruptly insulting his boss, we should assume he had a reason, and reconstruct the situation as he saw it to try and find it. Explanation of repeatable or unique actions by means of the logic of the situation might be classed as part of the material requirements for an explanation to be *satisfactory*—along with the requirement of independent testability.

### Human behaviour

*Demarcation of human behaviour*

What is human? What is behaviour? It has been argued at least since Hobbes that there is no special category 'human behaviour' which requires demarcation of 'human' and demarcation of 'behaviour'. For Hobbes, the human was a machine of pulleys, levers, pumps and pipes like any other, and was to be explained in these terms.[17] The twentieth-century movements of behaviourism and cybernetics are more sophisticated and more philosophical, but of the same ilk. Behaviourism trusts that behaviour, unlike intentions, institutions, consciousness, etc., is unproblematically observable. Cybernetics simply goes on to focus especially on the servo-mechanism, or on aspects of behaviour of systems governed by feedback. Clearly the logic of the situation cuts against all this since it concerns itself with aims and with the individual's perceptions of his situation. To the situational logician, that behaviourist who trains rats to push bars to get food-pellets merely narrows his studies to cases involving one aim, food, under very artificial circumstances. Further, such a behaviourist will interpret any evidence that the rat is *thinking* about its situation (for example, if it begins to behave as if it 'thought' its behaviour was causing the shocks it gets) as 'superstitious'. This is not the place to enter a discussion of the naïveté of behaviourism.[18] One might mention the logical point that explanation is deductive and it is an iron rule of deduction that 'nothing in the conclusion is not already contained in the premises'. This ensures the autonomy of sociology and the failure of reductionism. Where the question utilizes terms at the sociological level, so must the answers, otherwise there will be illicit importation. The logic of the situation operates on the level of the social.

### Borderline problems

Clearly, as we have seen, not all human behaviour is to be explained by the logic of the situation. Panic, for example, takes on something like a life of its own which can only partly be explained by this method.[19] Doubtless jealousy and other 'irrational' behaviour are no different. Watkins (1953) brings up an interesting point when he discusses apparently holistic behaviour of bees. This too is way beyond the logic of the situation, although ethological research on higher animals shows them to be remarkably amenable to situational reconstructions. One does not want to render the discussion circular and say that human behaviour equals that phenomenon tackled by situational logic. But one can point out that irrational behaviour, so-called, need not be situationally inexplicable. Freud's method of explanation is to show how, given the situation as it is perceived by the neurotic, the irrational or neurotic behaviour constitutes a defence against hurt, namely is goal-oriented and effective, at the cost of other things. Someone whose identity crisis prevents him from signing his name pays the price of being unable to operate a chequing account, and must suffer the inconveniences of making all transactions in cash.

There are phenomena which look collective, not individual-situational, for example, demographic phenomena, like the birth rate. The birth rate looks as though it cannot be explained situationally: for example, the steady growth of population—although a generalized or typical-situational account (people like children, in more prosperous times they will tend to decide to have them) may give a plausible explanation. But such explanations, appealing to prosperity or medical advances, are false. The population seems to grow fast precisely where conditions are bad or worsening. The unprecedentedly stable period between the wars showed a decline in the birth rates in Britain and France, not reversed by the economic climb out of the depression. Rich countries have a lower birth rate generally than poor ones. At a certain level of economic development, population growth is governed by natural conditions, which include ignorance of birth control and of the latest methods of combating disease. At a higher level, when the link between prosperity and small families is established, small family size can well come to seem a sensible choice. At another level again, when prosperity is all around, population can again grow, but in a controlled way as people's resources allow it. Similarly, we can explain the large numbers of couples who marry just before the tax year ends by the 'typical' situation that most people aim to minimize their tax payments, and to marry at the end of the year is to have to pay the higher rates for a married couple's joint income for a short period of the year, at the small cost of manipulating such a non-commercial matter as the date of marriage.

## The conventionalist approach to human behaviour

In sum, what is human, and what is behaviour, are not 'natural' categories named by universal words. 'Human behaviour' has its borderline cases, both of humanity, and of behaviour. The problem is not where to draw the line. It is, that situational logic is the only method we have of explaining human behaviour, and that we would do well, therefore, to keep trying in an 'imperialistic' fashion to push at the vague borderlines of 'human' and 'behaviour'. The use of situational logic in primate and other animal ethology is fascinating, and has a terrific feedback on explanation of human behaviour—including such wild but stimulating ideas as Lorenz's that species' intra-specific aggression is controlled, Lorenz's and Ardrey's that we have an inbuilt defence mechanism where territory is concerned. Unfortunately, both authors put their ideas in psychologistic form; the territorial imperative is seen as an attribute of 'human nature', whatever that may be. It is easy to avoid this by regarding the aggressive rituals, for example, of submission, as social mannerisms which are transmitted in the socialization process of the animal society and which constitute behaviour preferred by natural selection, since they curb the self-destructive tendencies of aggression and are thus conducive to survival.

Postulating an aim, and attempts to achieve it, as explaining action is to make human behaviour appear rational. Something of the power of this method is indicated, not only by its subsumption of Freud's explanation of neurotic irrationality, or its use in ethology, but also in that it can be a model for rational thought too. Rational thought can be viewed as merely a special case of rational action.[20] In this case, the aim is to solve an intellectual *problem*, the means are to manufacture hypotheses and criticize them, and so on—to the limits of one's ability to invent and to criticize. Feyerabend (1961, 1963, 1965) has christened this 'critical pluralism'. It is only a special case of situational logic, and one of his key arguments makes this clear. The ultimate aim (Feyerabend would make this a hypothesis too) is the truth. Multiplying theories, unlike multiplying entities, is good because only by exploring many possibilities can we have any sense of not missing some obvious possibility (even though we may have missed it nevertheless), and, more strongly, criticism comes from a point of view, therefore the more points of view one can produce, the more directions one can criticize from, the better or more severe one's criticisms can be.

## Levels of simplicity and complexity

It will be worthwhile to indicate the complexities in problems around human behaviour. Many philosophers, in talking of action, believe that the explanation of the act of raising an arm is simpler than the explanation of a salute. This view is terribly puzzling until it is recalled that the same philosophers usually think the epistemology of 'I am seeing red now' is simpler than the epistemology of 'bodies attract each other with a force in inverse proportion to the square of the distance between them'. The intuitive notion of simplicity being employed here demands scrutiny. Of course, there are those who think that laws of attraction rest on, are built on or out of, or otherwise presuppose, 'simpler' perception statements. This is an inductivist error. That disposed of, we can ask which statement is better testable: the counter-intuitive answer is that the perception-statement, apparently incorrigible, *is not in fact testable at all.* It is private and in a sense mysterious and inaccessible. The law of attraction, however, is public, unmysterious and testable. As to which statement has the greater paucity of assumptions, the answer is not easy. As to which has the greater paucity of untested assumptions—clearly the law of attraction.[21]

The point about assumptions being testable is that some at least of the infinite class of theories which fit the facts are ruled out. Thus the explanatory task confronting one with laws of attraction or a salute is simpler than with a perception or an arm-raising. A salute, it seems clear, can be explained in a straightforward way as a goal-directed action in a certain social situation. An uninterpreted arm-raising, however, raises hosts of possibilities of explanation, including neurophysiological ones which completely fail to include its significance as a salute at all. In other words, 'he saluted' is a statement testable by reference to all kinds of circumscribed evidence. 'He raised his arm' seems much more impoverished, taken by itself, and anyway, devoid of interpretation, it is devoid of interest.

To begin epistemology with sense-experience seems a bit like beginning the study of language with babies' gurgles. To ask questions like 'what are intentions?' or 'are there intentions?' seems to be futile essentialism. What an action or an intention is, or involves, or trying to get clear about the concept of intention is little more than a fiddling with words, disguised as conceptual enquiry, disguised as serious discussion. Actions or intentions are, for our purposes, categories of explanation in situational logic.

Let us return now to survey with examples the scope of human behaviour as it is studied in the social sciences. Quirkish individual behaviour is by and large not their concern. Typical or standard behaviour, or the typified aspects of quirky behaviour are their concern. To begin with, four individual events and the sorts of scientific explanation applicable to them; then, four large-scale events and their explanation. Our list proceeds from simplest to most complex in a way that has nothing to do with epistemological notions as they are usually conceived these days.

Why does John wear spectacles? This calls for an individual *physiological* explanation (although social and psychological factors lurk behind).

Why did John raise his hat? This calls for a typified individual *sociological* explanation.

Why was this (cautious) driver in a freeway collision? This again involves individual factors—although his *psychological* caution disposes him to act in typical ways—to which must be added his typified *social* situation on the freeway.

Why did Oswald assassinate Kennedy? Such a problem calls for an *individual* phychological explanation (the exact pattern of Oswald's neurosis), with some sociological typification of Oswald

22

and of who Kennedy was in Oswald's *social* as well as *psycho-logical* universe.

Why were there riots in Hong Kong in 1966 and 1967? This collective behaviour calls for two unique *historical-sociological* explanations, always provided it is granted that riots are social not psychological phenomena. The general history and sociology of Hong Kong are involved, so that the situation confronting those who rioted can be typified.

Why for a time were there riots in the Negro ghettoes in the USA every summer? This calls for a *broad sociological* explanation of a general pattern of behaviour in the USA, which would refer to the overall social structure of American cities. The pattern and the structure are, of course, unintended effects, not holistic causes.

Why do Arab countries constantly threaten to annihilate Israel? In sober moments they deny saying so. They also are probably aware that they cannot. What we are dealing with are statements made to the world that are really for internal consumption, to boost morale, distract, and reinforce the position of dictators and demagogues. The phenomenon that a radical must always avoid being out-radicalized by his rivals is also involved. The explanation involves both *sociological* and *social-psychological* ideas, since there would seem to be a special psychological state behind such threats, although this in turn could no doubt be explained sociologically.

Why are there wars? This might seem to call for a generalized explanation, as when Russell suggests there is an aggressive side to human nature (Russell, 1955, part II, chap. II). It seems to me it calls for individual explanations of each war, taking in *sociological, political, social-psychological* and *psychological factors* in each case as one tries to explain the sociological question: why, despite their aims, have men failed to build institutions which would stop wars? However, much of the answer would be made up, I believe, of sociological accounts of how immensely complex the task of building such institutions is. How, in other words, declared common aims do not make situations or their logic, or, especially, perceptions of situations, common.

These are only a few examples of the many kinds of problems and the many layers in each.

## Attempting and achieving

In this section, I wish to compare and contrast theories of how we attempt with theories of how we achieve. After explaining the importance of the issue, I shall discuss some alternative theories that say we do these two things by having knowledge, by being rational, by being irrational, by using the best estimate, and by trial and error, respectively.

## Collingwood versus Watkins

R. G. Collingwood (1939, pp. 50–1) has argued that we should not bother with trying to explain attempts to achieve which in fact failed of their achievement: unsuccessful attempts to achieve cannot be explained.

> How can we discover what the tactical problem was that Nelson set himself at Trafalgar? Only by studying the tactics he pursued in the battle. We argue back from the solution to the problem. What else could we do? Even if we had the original typescript of the coded orders issued by wireless to his captains a few hours before the battle began, this would not tell us that he had not changed his mind at the last moment, extemporized a new plan on seeing some new factor in the situation. . . . Naval historians think it worthwhile to argue about Nelson's tactical plan at Trafalgar because he won the battle. It is not worthwhile arguing about Villeneuve's plan. He did not succeed in carrying it out, and therefore no one will ever know what it was. We can only guess. And guessing is not history.

Unless we know what the action achieved is, we cannot know what was attempted, and of failed attempts we obviously do not know the achievement, since it was not achieved. We cannnot explain what Villeneuve did at Trafalgar because he failed, and thus, we cannot know what he planned to do, how he saw the situation. What is reported, or what he said, is only hearsay; we need concrete achievements, or outcomes, to be able to decide. The situation is, after all, the *problem* the actor confronts. From his solution to that problem (his answer), we can work out what the problem was (his question): no solution, then problem unknown.

This is to reduce attempts to achievements, and to say that at best situational logic is the attempt to explain by showing how particular actions have been conducive to the achievement. Actions which fail are inexplicable. This is like arguing that until a theatre performance is finished you cannot know what interpretation an actor is giving to the role: this seems absurd: one can learn *that* without ever seeing the performance.

In two places (1963, 1970) J. W. N. Watkins takes issue with this. He challenges Collingwood by citing a case where the principal actor died during the performance, and left no direct testimony of any kind. This is the case of the British Vice-Admiral Tryon who, in 1893, ordered two parallel columns of ships to turn in on each other, even though they were so close that this made collision inevitable unless one column turned inside the other (see Fig. 1). A collision occurred, despite the querying of the order by the leading ship in the other column, and the Admiral went down with his ship having signalled that rescue boats were not to be launched by the other ships. Until recently, Tryon's behaviour, at the climax of a brilliant career, had been regarded as inexplicable, mad, or drunken. Watkins, however, basing himself on Hough (1959) shows how if the attempt is made to reconstruct the problem-situation as Tryon saw it, and as it developed step by step, his planned manoeuvre is easily explained, as are his orders about the boats and his last comment, 'It was all my fault'. The story seems to be this: the two lines of ships were approaching shallow water. Tryon ordered the inward turns and that the order of the fleet be preserved. This latter implied that the columns were to turn, one inside the other. But which? The rule of the road at sea is that ships pass port side to port side. After hesitating and querying the order, Rear-Admiral Markham leading his column in HMS *Camperdown* executed hard-a-starboard, trying to turn *inside* Tryon's column according to the rule of the road instead of outside, as he should have, when he saw Tryon had the *Victoria* hard-a-port, since it was a Queen's Regulation that in collision situations, the ship which has the other on her starboard side is to make the avoidance manoeuvre. Despite attempts to manoeuvre, *Camperdown* rammed *Victoria*. Tryon then apparently tried to run his ship aground, for when it suddenly sank, the engines were going full tilt, causing further loss of life but explaining why he ordered no boats lowered. But if Tryon was waiting for the other column to turn wide before beginning his own hard turn inside them, their incompetence was to blame. Why then did he say, 'It was all my fault'? His apparent acceptance of responsibility, Watkins argues, is a classic case of an officer taking responsibility for the errors of a subordinate. Watkins sums it all up by saying that here was a clear attempt to achieve something, which failed, and yet which is entirely satisfactorily explained without *ad hoc* hypotheses of sudden madness or undetectable drunkenness.

Here, then, a clear issue is joined. Collingwood, of course, was worried that we cannot *know* all of this sort of explanation to be true, whilst we can *know* what Montgomery's plan for a pivotal manoeuvre in the break-out in Normandy was because he did it (Ellis, 1962, pp. 365ff., 404ff.). One answer to this would be that it ignores the possibility that achievements are the unintended outcomes of something else, are even improvisations rather than

25

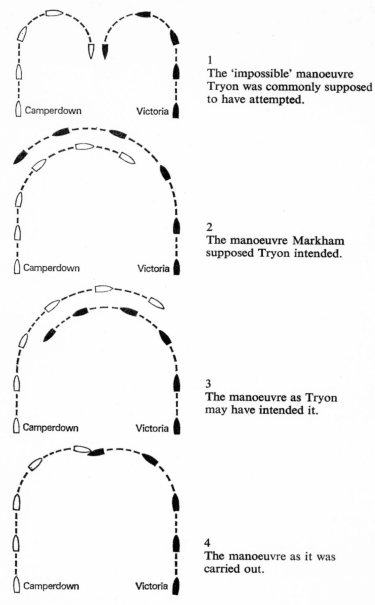

1
The 'impossible' manoeuvre Tryon was commonly supposed to have attempted.

2
The manoeuvre Markham supposed Tryon intended.

3
The manoeuvre as Tryon may have intended it.

4
The manoeuvre as it was carried out.

*Figure 1* The Fatal Manoeuvre

26

things attempted and gained. Moreover, the evidence one would look to to discover whether the achievement was an attempted outcome or not, would be the same sort of evidence one would look to to reconstruct the plans or failed attempts, namely, talks, writing, maps, etc. So Montgomery's success has not stifled controversy about what he was attempting, his competence, boldness, etc.

I conclude, then, that we can discuss attempts and achievements separately, in the sense that the latter is not a necessary condition for the former to be interesting. I now proceed to outline five theories of how we attempt and how we achieve.

*Attempts and achievements as knowledge-based*   This theory says that we make an *attempt* to achieve something only when we *know how* to do it and *that we can* do it. Anything else is not a serious attempt. When we are in this position we have perfect knowledge and it would be irrational to attempt things we don't know the how or wherefore of. We achieve things because we set out with perfect knowledge. If we fail, then we obviously acted irrationally in trying, since if failure was possible we must have *known* it. This position may appear absurd. It can be defended by saying that success that is not due to knowledge is fortuitous and not properly an achievement (which one could take credit for, etc.). Bacon's theory of how we achieve scientific knowledge proceeds somewhat on these lines. We achieve it only if we systematically eliminate all possibility of error: then we know we will gain the truth. We can occasionally gain it by luck, but that is no credit to us.

In my view, the theory that attempts and achievements must be knowledge-based is absurd perfectionism: there is a large element of risk, known risk, in most of our endeavours. If we only attempted to do what we know how to do, we would never begin.

*Attempting and achieving as rational*   This theory would distinguish silly attempts from attempts which are undertaken calmly, with detachment, and which do not involve hastily drawn conclusions out of ignorance. It seems to suggest that if we are rational beings, things will work out well because nature and phenomena are amenable to our rational approach, because nature and phenomena are not deceivers and frustrators. Bacon also gave us a rational way to achieve science: not his *false method* of simple induction but his *true method* of a cautious and optimistic procedure. ('Knowledge-based' and 'rational' are the same in a Baconian theory.) Historians have been trying to fit the history of science to Bacon's rational model ever since, with conspicuous lack of success (Agassi, 1963*a*). This theory of attempts and achievements as rational rules out bold tries at something which seems

27

impossible, it rules out guesses, wild and otherwise, and it rules out the use of imagination in our attempts and our achievements.

*Attempting and achieving as irrational*  It can be argued that we attempt things when we really have no information to go on; we gamble, or hope. This can hardly be true of all attempts unless we describe successful attempts as accidents not attempts. Luck or chance or fluke in a wayward and perhaps chaotic world can be used to explain our achievements. But there is more to be said. Darwinian evolution is for example a non-rational theory of achievement, though not of attempting. The individual attempts to ensure his own survival, but nature regulates his 'achievement' on her estimate of his fitness as a member of a species. So survival is not related to rational action, although on a global scale it may be rational. Functionalism, too, allows that people may act for unsuitable reasons, but interprets achievement as dependent on survival factors which are not rational.

*Attempting and achieving as partial knowledge*  If we decide to attempt something in the face of partial knowledge, the question is less how much we need—the answer is subjective, some of us are more prepared to chance our arm than others—and more a matter of what the partial knowledge is partial of. That is, is it that we cannot get complete knowledge and must approximate because of the nature of the beast, or is it that inadequacy, ignorance, or premature need for knowledge forces us to use approximations?[22] Whatever the answer, it cannot provide an adequate guideline for the estimate of achievement.

For achieving we have no sensible parallel. One either achieves or one does not, and to say 'I tried, acting on the best estimate', may be an explanation of why you did what you did; it is not an explanation of the outcome. Here the contrast between subjectivism, Collingwoodianism and Popper's approach is very sharp. Whether the partial knowledge is partial ignorance, or indeterminacy in the facts, the explanation of the outcome must be in terms of the objective situation and the interaction of that with the attempt. Again, attempts based on partial knowledge would be inexplicable to Collingwood if they failed. Here we see instead that the actor's partial knowledge, i.e. his partial misperception of the situation as it is, must be introduced to explain the outcome, given his aims.

*Attempting and achieving as trial and error*  Partial knowledge, partial misperception, seems an inescapable fact of the human situation. We are not, it so happens, omniscient (*even in hindsight*; and this also explains why our explanations in science are constantly revised). But there is no way we can guarantee 'good estimates' of the situation we confront; all we can do is grope forward by means of trial and error. In this kind of a theory, aims are given as part of the explanation. Our knowledge of the means to our aims is partial. We improve it only by attempting one avenue and then another. But the quest does not end when we achieve our aims, because they will turn out to be subordinate to continuing aims, and so on.

The successful achievement of aims can have several results. One is the loss of those aims, the feeling that they were not after all worthwhile (once rich and powerful a man may find he really wants a happiness he does not have). Another is the modification of those aims in the light of the means which apparently must be used to achieve them (the road to riches may involve unpleasant means). Yet a third is the search for alternate means of achieving them (how many ways there are to get rich). So we not only learn from achievement that the achievement is possible, we also learn about the aims themselves, the means and alternate means.

The emphasis thus shifts from the apparently ultimate or 'given' character of the aims to the aims as devices for our acquisition of knowledge about the society and the aims realizable within it, including modification of our initial partial knowledge and mis-perceptions. Social action can thus be seen as a constant process of exploring and learning about the social universe, very much in parallel to exploring and learning about the physical universe.

Collingwood's ideas now have to be completely rejected in this respect (whatever else of value they contain), because his success-philosophy is not only totally rejected, it is practically reversed. We can say failure to achieve, far from being irrational (if your knowledge was partial, why did you do it?), still farther from being inexplicable, turns out to be at least as interesting from the point of view of understanding society as successful action *and possibly more so*. This latter is analogous with confirmation of a theory in science: these are not so hard to come by (Popper, 1934, section 28; Hempel, 1965, chap. 1) and enlighten us little unless they are—on the face of it—counter-examples. Similarly, actions which lead to success can become routinized and uninteresting. Struggle to achieve, like struggle to learn, is challenging to actor and social scientist alike.

## Aims: their acquisition and modification

### Sources of aims

Trying, striving, attempting, aiming, seem to be fundamental characteristics or dispositions of the human being in which he is both quantitatively and qualitatively different from his neighbour-

29

ing and possibly ancestral species. In particular, of course, his very possession of language is a way of articulating, discussing and ranking aims—as well as preserving and communicating them—which are much more sophisticated than anything else in the animal world.

From his very first moment, it seems, the human infant probes and explores his world. Here the aim to find out is closer to an instinct. This is clearly an invaluable characteristic, since it enables him rapidly to learn about that world and thus to use and manipulate it, as well as to defend himself against its more hostile traits. One cannot go further than this. Curiosity may be something evolution has favoured; no particular set of conscious or derived aims is so favoured. While it is true that most people aim to stay alive, to enjoy it, to eat, to make love, to have some prosperity, and to behave decently, it is not true that we *all* pursue *all* these aims, or that we pursue them with the same vigour. Our aims also range from the self-destructive/world-destructive, right through to the power-maniac who wants to control every aspect of everything and repopulate the world to his own specifications, regardless of human cost.

*Status of aims: social and psychological*

How aims are acquired, then, apart from the very few which are near-universal and basic, is very much an individual matter, and no doubt family and social influences are here paramount. The working-class conservative, the millionaire communist, have no doubt acquired their aims in an explicable way. The aims are not, I would say, usefully explained psychologically. Apart from the complication that our psyche develops in a social framework, which is thus somehow prior, even if not determining, aims are not equivalent to *desires* (or *needs*). The distinction is parallel to that drawn in economics between *wants* and *demands*. No one denies that a lust for chocolate may lead to one demanding (i.e. offering money in exchange for) it, but there is no need to confuse the two. Many of us harbour desires (secret or otherwise) which we in no way convert into actively pursued aims, and which we certainly do not attempt to achieve by, for example, entering the market. Just as we may say a desire becomes a demand when we enter the market and compete to purchase it, so we may generalize this and declare a desire (or need) to be an aim when we act in society in an attempt to achieve it.

This raises another possibility, namely, that a person's ostensible or declared aims may differ from his objective aims. When a parent is inconsistent in disciplining a child, that parent may have the aim to be firm yet warm. If the outsider points out that inconsistency produces confusion, i.e. failure to learn or to modify expectations and thus frustration and neurosis, the parent may be outraged if this 'aim' is 'read off' from his inconsistent disciplining. Whether he has reason to be enraged is a moot point. In ethics the question of responsibility is very often answered not by saying one is responsible only if one acted in full foreknowledge, but that one is responsible if one could have foreseen what would happen had one taken the matter seriously enough to think it out. To say, 'I never meant to make my child neurotic' is to say what usually goes without saying. It is not quite like saying after pulling the trigger, 'I never meant to kill him', but it is close. Thoughtless and irresponsible behaviour does not excuse responsibility in law or in morality; nor need it in social science. One has to be careful, though, in putting such a construction on action, not to attribute a conscious aim where it is not warranted. This is especially tempting in political matters, where it can merge over into the conspiracy theory of society very quickly. For example, one of the phenomena of the years 1965–7 was the discrediting, in the eyes of American radicals, of the liberals who surrounded and supported President Kennedy. When, as a class, their financial support of civil rights shrank as militancy and then riot arose, they were accused of being against Negro emancipation. This is an odd suggestion, in view of their earlier support. When the Moynihan Report leaked out, its author, a fighter for civil rights of the most obvious stripe, was accused of 'subtle racism'.[23] Even President Johnson, perhaps the most effective liberal President since Roosevelt, has been accused, on the basis of the escalation of the Vietnam War, of actively or 'objectively' aiming at a confrontation with China.[24] When it is argued that this could hardly be anyone's aim, since it is insane, the accusers draw that conclusion with equanimity and in the teeth of all the evidence. Thus, we have to proceed with caution when we deal with people who act without appreciating the aims or outcomes of what they do, even if they are in a position to ascertain them if they tried.

Objectivity and conspiracy raise the question of whether there is such a thing as a group aim. Here we have a key test case, because the conspiracy is the bridge: a conspiracy is usually a group, and it is usually dedicated to an aim. However, it is not unique in this; any statutory body, like the Hong Kong Government's Resettlement Department, set up to rehouse squatters, is also a group, even an institution, with a presumed aim. In some cases political parties, and in all cases parliamentary lobbies, are groups dedicated to an aim. However, it is inherent in the idea of an aim that it can be articulated, criticized, modified and abandoned. But such activities cannot be attributed to a group or institution, only to people. It thus might seem to serve clarity if we reserve 'aim' for individuals, and use other words for aims ascribed to social wholes (perhaps 'quasi-aim' and 'quasi-intention').[25] This is especially important when the difference between manifest and latent aims is concerned. Our school system, for example, may well be an 'instrument of class oppression', but that is not what those who built and man it aim at. If one believes otherwise, one is a paranoid surrounded by evil forces and conspiracies of oppression. In fact, on this sort of thing, Marx was a follower of Smith: capitalists do not conspire together to oppress workers; indeed capitalists aim to cut each other's throats. The oppression is an unintended effect of their rational action, i.e. maximizing gain, in a capitalist institutional framework.

The position that only individuals have aims is the doctrine of methodological individualism, which is not identical with situational logic, but is part of it. Groups, institutions and other social wholes have effects, if one wants to speak loosely, or the actions of individuals comprising (or constituting, as Hayek would say) them have effects. For Popper, institutions are intermediate between persons: they serve as means of co-ordination between the diverse aims of diverse people.

The opponent of methodological individualism (Professor Gellner reminds me) can argue that it is not so much a matter of social wholes having aims, as of the formation of language and concepts only being possible within the context of social wholes, and that without these concepts the individual cannot articulate any aims, or regard his behaviour as 'meaningful action'. The questions of precedence here are partly logical and partly temporal. For what it is worth, I suggest in chapter 5 (following Berger and Luckmann) that social relationships, institutions including language, and the concept of a human self, an individual agent, arise together.

## Changes of aims

The main ways in which aims change are by interacting with each other, or by inhibiting each other. The difference will, I hope, become clear. Aims can either interact or be inhibited, both in our heads and in the group.

*Interaction in the head*  The simplest case of an interaction of aims in the head is the exercise of choice. When we contemplate an array of aims, we know that we can act to achieve only a limited number, and that thus we must rank the aims in order of preference. We may, in doing this, also discover that the achievement of one aim incorporates or leads to the achievement of another, which is thus automatically ranked subordinately. But in addition to ranking, there is direct choice where one may choose to abandon an aim for practical, or moral, or other reasons. In this case, one aim (to be practical or moral) is interacting with other aims and replacing them.

*Interaction in the group*   We act to achieve our aims in a social context where others are also doing the same. However, their aims are likely to be diverse. If this is true, we can expect that some aims will reinforce or inhibit others (see below), while others will interact. My aim to get educated in a well-paying profession may interact with my teacher's aim to get me to think, and we both may modify our actions—for example I may cease interpreting education so narrowly, he may cease to brush aside vocational interests.

*Inhibition in the head*   Aims can be inhibited in the head by fears or neuroses. We may, for example, aim to stay healthy yet dread medical examination. We may aim to get rich but loathe personal contacts and the role of salesman. Clearly, the greater our self-knowledge here, the better. Only if we have a map of our own neuroses can we pursue our ends (getting rich, for example) while avoiding those paths which make us feel neurotic. (But 'paths' are perhaps means, not aims. True, but what is an aim and what is a means is completely relative to the problem at hand. There is no absolute in this. Even aims like 'to live the moral life' can be means to, for example, the saving of your soul, or social harmony, etc.) However, let us look at aims inhibited regardless of means. Perhaps the aim to get rich can be vitiated by insupportable guilt accompanying wealth, however obtained. Here again, clearly, the problem is not of ranking—one may have no aim higher than getting rich—and yet the inhibition is so strong that it paralyzes the attempt to go beyond a certain point.

*Inhibition in the group*   Strong inhibition can also happen in a group. It seems especially common in fields of government policy and social action. Many drastic actions like the aim of destroying an enemy in war throw up extraordinarily violent inhibitions, not only about the means, but also about the ends—namely, inhibiting questions like: what makes us so sure that our aims are right and good: maybe the enemy's view of us is the correct one. Much criticism has been directed at the Allied aim in World War II of unconditional surrender by the Axis. Can one really be so sure of one's rightness and one's duty? If these doubts had been aired in high places, we might well have seen the will to pursue the chosen aim inhibited. In general, self-doubt plagues political action and the doubt is very often that the aims are unworthy or that they are unclear.

Then, of course, one aim can interfere with another. For example, a terrorized civil service might obey orders without question, trying desperately to please the authorities. But it might well also, for the same reason, convey false information because it has reason to fear the consequences of the authorities finding out what the real situation is, and hence its inadequacies. This in turn leads the authorities to base their actions on false premises and to give orders which cannot be carried out, and so on.[26]

### Changes of aims and loss of aims

Aims, then, can be changed—they are 'given' only for the explanatory purpose to hand. Their loss or abandonment we have already indicated can be from choice or inhibition. Besides these, there is disillusion. Take an attainable aim, say wealth, which requires a certain effort to sustain, for example, not spending too much. It is quite possible that a person strives to achieve this aim constantly, but finds it turns to ashes in his mouth. He may lose that aim and *not* act to keep his wealth (the dissipation syndrome in the scions of rich families). There is also confusion of aims in that someone may want happiness, but confuse it with wealth. Only when he gains wealth may he discover it is happiness he really wanted and then abandon his aim to sustain his wealth. The Libyan example shows all this: wealth has without decision or intention induced loss of certain aims connected with the good life.

The only other way aims are lost is with death. But since groups and societies do not have a life that terminates in a normal way, the other means of loss, inhibition, and expulsion are what is important.

### Means: their modifiers and limiters

Since we have investigated the interaction, inhibition, changes and loss of aims, we can perhaps read this section as parallel to the previous one. Let us review the picture of situational logic up to this point: actions are explained as goal-directed within a framework or situation which consists of (a) the material circumstances, (b) the social circumstances, (c) the psychological circumstances, (d) the moral and ethical views which bear on the proposed means as well as the intended goals, and finally, (e) other aims of the same person and of other people. Let us now consider how the situation interacts with the aims. Usually the circumstances are treated as means only, but this is to ignore a huge area of the history of ideas in which the situation has been taken to be the determinant of only apparently freely chosen aims. Let us now review these first four (a), (b), (c), and (d) and their combinations.

## (a) Material circumstances as means, limits and modifiers

Of course, any action we take is taken within physical circumstances we cannot escape—we cannot jump twenty feet in the air. A Libyan king can only see a limited number of people in a day. Our technology is our means to try to master these physical limitations.[27] Some philosophers have thought that these limits to our action deeply influence or render superfluous our aims. Heraclitus seems to suggest that, since all is flux, the search for certainty and permanence is in vain. All laws of universal progress or universal decay uttered by other philosophers would eliminate many possible aims we might have: if things are inevitably getting worse, we cannot reasonably aim to make them better, only to stop them or slow them down; if they are inevitably getting better again, only slowing down or stopping the process is allowable. Extreme materialists would no doubt argue that concrete circumstances determine the society man builds, that the society in turn creates psychological states, which in turn give rise to the moral ideas, all predictable without aims at all. Another theory might be that circumstances are productive of psychology, which in turn produces morals and society—this is a form of mechanism to be found in McDougall, Wiener, Watson, and Skinner.

## (b) Social circumstances as means, limits and modifiers

Again, it is obvious that our actions are hedged around by social constraints—by our not being omnipotent, by our inability to foresee all the consequences of our actions, by the interference with our achievements by other people and their actions, whether deliberate or not. The laws and by-laws structure the situation of driving; informal traditions and conventions govern even casual relations between the sexes (hat-doffing, rising when a woman enters the room, etc.).

The most obvious attempts to explain aims with the help of society have been made by the collectivists, such as Durkheim. He suggested that suicide is connected with social conditions, whether it is egoistic, altruistic or anomic. It is society which allows, induces or causes the suicidal thoughts, which are productive of suicidal acts.[28] In his extreme organicism we can see the tendency to explain even moral ideas, for example, within religions, as serving a social end. Certainly this extreme is developed in places in Malinowski's writings.

35

### (c) Psychological circumstances as means, limits and modifiers

Any action we take will be affected by our neuroses—lusts as well as phobias, and also by our misperceptions of the world. We may do things we should not; we may fail to do things we should. Some people catch on to freeway driving faster than others; others refuse to doff their hats to anyone. We may try to do things which our imperfection prevents.

Psychological reductionism is also quite well known as a way of explaining aims. Its strongest expressions are in Hume and Mill. The idea is that the fundamental laws of man are psychological laws concerning his perceiving, learning, and thinking, and that these interacting psyches are what throw up society and moral ideas. This doctrine is sometimes called individualism because it is the one attempt at reduction of aims that goes to individuals and not to the society as a whole, or to the impersonal circumstances. It is, nevertheless, strongly pitted against the methodological individualism mentioned above in not being merely methodological reduction but reduction *tout court*, going in a way to a sub-individual level—a person is not a disembodied psyche.

Be all this as it may, the view I discuss last of all denies all the reductions hitherto and perhaps most vehemently the reductions of ethics—the materialist reduction, the social reduction and the psychological reduction.

### (d) The dualism of facts and decisions as means, limits and modifiers

This is Popper's view, and of course Hayek, von Mises, not to mention Kant, are predecessors. This doctrine treats aims as on a par with circumstances, material, social and psychological—all are facts. It allows to morals the special role of judging actions and aims in their effects on those circumstances. Moreover, these aims can themselves, as we saw, set limits on each other as well as on means. But morals, while factual (people do have them), cannot be derived from facts. Decisions, standards, and choices are not reducible to facts. The logic of the situation is a logic of choice, decision, and action in the light both of circumstances and of standards. On our mastery of that logic will turn our ability to explain, predict, and perhaps even understand, people's social behaviour.

# 2 Understanding and explaining in the social sciences

## Introduction

What it is to explain something and what it is to understand something are matters it is easy to conflate. Ordinary usage may mislead us here, because the words 'explanation' and 'understanding' are used almost interchangeably.[1] But it will not do to identify them, for it is perfectly possible that you fail to understand an explanation of something which nevertheless does not at all fail on that account to be an explanation (and even a good or satisfactory one). Were the two the same this would not be possible. So it would seem that your understanding of an explanation is something additional to the fact of that explanation itself. It is, among other things, a psychological event in you. (An explanation declared to be understandable or not understandable is having thereby a non-psychological property attributed to it, namely the dispositions as the case may be to allow or to resist psychological acts of understanding.) An explanation, though, is not even in part a psychological event, but an event (or state of affairs) in the world of ideas (see chapter 6).

In the philosophy of science we may keep explanation and understanding separate by adopting a deductive explication of the former, and thus serve clarity. Whatever understanding is, we take explanation to be the process of deducing one statement from others in accordance with some formal and some material requirements.[2] Hopefully, while it may be that what one man understands another can be puzzled by, it cannot be that what obeys the rules of valid deduction also does not obey them (which is not to say there will be no disputes about whether something obeys them or not). The act of understanding may or may not accompany such deductive explanations. Perhaps it too can be analysed now

37

that explanation is separated out. Understanding (or grasping or making sense of), like perceiving, would seem to be an interplay between expectation and feedback; the attempt to 'impose' a mental set on the flux of experience and at the same time the use of experience to correct that set. Our preconceptions are thus essentially involved in the process of understanding: and among these preconceptions are what appear to resemble standards, for example, we find not understandable those explanations of human behaviour which do not render it 'reasonable'; just as we do not understand theories attributing lack of symmetry to nature (for example, parity is not conserved and 'strangeness'). The analogy between the rationality of actions and symmetry in nature may not be close, but their roles as standards of understandability are: understanding a human being and understanding an atom are not totally different processes.

That our preconceptions are involved in that act of understanding might seem no more than an uncontroversial platitude, until it is recalled that in the standard (inductivist-empiricist) view we should approach the study of alien societies without prejudice, i.e. without preconceptions. It becomes my counter-contention that we *cannot but* approach alien societies with preconceptions formed in our society; we therefore look at other societies in terms of ours, and as a first approximation try to understand them on analogy with us. Only where there occur breakdowns and inconsistencies in our translation do we scrutinize the preconceptions in terms of which we are operating and change them.

We cannot perceive, understand, operate at all without preconceptions. It makes no sense to jettison our preconceptions until something has gone wrong on account of them. Besides, the notion of jettisoning them *in toto* makes no sense: what would take their place, what would our starting point be?

A serious problem arises here. The contention is that preconceptions are inescapable in intellectual inquiry. Indeed, it seems as though they are essentially involved in what it means to come to an intellectual understanding of something. It means in part either fitting the thing into one's preconceptions, or coming to grasp where and why those preconceptions are inadequate and modifying them. What, then, becomes of the aim of studying societies objectively; that is to say, of trying to eliminate bias and error in the search for a true picture?[3] How precisely can we be critical of our preconceptions, how can we test for their truth-values? Does not this simply amount to invoking other preconceptions or standards?

This self-doubt, even diffidence, about our own standards and preconceptions is a new phenomenon. It results from arguments anthropologists developed in the course of their self-discovery of prejudice, bias, misunderstanding. Indeed, serious anthropology is thought to be possible only once the easy confidence in one's own culture and intellectual standards has been shaken.

In the heyday of intellectualist anthropology the scholar took it for granted that he and his society were models of rationality and understandability—if not of virtue. He was thus led quickly into misunderstanding and misjudging alien societies simply because they operated with entirely different preconceptions. In the more liberal climate of this century it has been argued that we can avoid misjudgment by making no judgments at all—since moral value systems are incommensurable—but it seems as though we should not avoid misunderstanding by making no stabs at understanding at all. The doctrine here is slightly different. We are told to avoid misunderstanding by not invoking our preconceptions; instead we should try to understand entirely in terms of the indigenous preconceptions of the people under study. The logic of this is odd, since we cannot simply plug-in on other people's preconceptions; or rather, if we did, our account should be unintelligible to our potential audience, namely one which shares *our* preconceptions. (We shall not straighten out all these questions until chapter 6.)

Intellectualist anthropology was being challenged by arguments presupposing a species of moral and intellectual relativism. Whether something is moral or immoral, true or false, depends on the standards of morality and truth being applied. From this true premise, relativists invalidly infer that only indigenous standards can be applied. The morality or immorality of an action, the truth or falsity of a statement, can only be judged relative to the standards of morality or truth—the preconceptions—of the culture under discussion.

Like the liberal critics of intellectualist anthropology, I find myself against both misunderstandings and misjudgments. However, I do not regard relativism as either the only respectable, or even as a satisfactory, alternative.[4] Indeed, my argument above leads me to conclude that *all* our efforts to understand—relativist or not— will involve misunderstandings, misjudgments and over-simplifications. The most we can do about it is face the fact and be as critical as possible of our efforts.

Recently, there has appeared a new and plausible doctrine which concedes many of the relativist points but seemingly avoids total commitment to it. Its author is Peter Winch, and he has published it in a paper, 'Understanding a Primitive Society' (1964b), which is a follow-up to his controversial and intriguing book *The Idea of a Social Science* (1958). Winch argues elsewhere (1960) that there are certain universally necessary conditions, social and moral, for there to be any social life at all: thus he is not a complete relativist. He also argues, if I may indulge a crude first approximation to his 1964 position, that cross-cultural value-judgments will always be misjudgments—and therefore should be avoided—because there is no language game in which cross-cultural value-judgments could be legitimate moves. The conflict between his position as I have stated it and my previous contention about the inescapability of our preconceptions in the very enterprise of understanding itself, is obvious. I therefore wish to bring out my ideas on explanation and understanding in the course of showing that Winch yields too much to relativism, that there are language games in which cross-cultural value-judgments are legitimate moves, and that these moves are made in all cultures including the sociologists' sub-culture. Indeed such cross-cultural value-judgments, such use of one's own society and preconceptions as a measuring instrument or a sounding board, is the principal way sociological understanding of an alien society is reached.

## Winch's position in outline

Winch's concern in 'Understanding a Primitive Society' is the broad problem of how we can understand the customs of an alien primitive society. He focuses his discussion not on understanding primitive customs in general, but on understanding those special cases of primitive customs which involve beliefs—like beliefs about how reproduction occurs—which conflict with beliefs taken for granted in our society. Thus we have two problems, a narrower problem of understanding and a broader one. The broader one is of understanding primitive customs in general; the narrower one is of understanding those customs involving ideas which conflict with our ideas. Winch apparently regards this narrower problem of understanding as crucial to the broader problem of understanding, and concentrates on it presumably in the belief that if we can understand the special cases, understanding primitive customs in general will be facilitated.[5]

Winch opens up his problem by discussing a remark in Evans-Pritchard's book on Azande magic (1937) to the effect that Azande magical beliefs not only run counter to beliefs of ours, but do not themselves 'accord with objective reality'. In dealing with Azande witchcraft, Evans-Pritchard asserts that not only do some of its component beliefs contradict some of ours (which is not so serious, since both could be false), but also that ours are true and theirs are false.

Winch's central argument is that in saying that the beliefs of primitives do not accord with objective reality we are talking in terms of reality seemingly conceived of outside language and culture. This, however, Winch believes we cannot legitimately do. Even if there is such a thing as objective reality outside language, to conceive of it outside of language and culture is impossible. In saying that primitive beliefs are false we are saying they do not accord with *our* conceptions of reality; with reality as *conceived* by us, if you prefer. But imposing our conceptions in this way is no way to come to understand primitive society. It is no way to understand it because magical beliefs, for example, may well be tied into a whole system of other beliefs, a veritable world-view in which the disputed beliefs play an essential social and theoretical role. This system constitutes an on-going way of life and it shows grave lack of understanding (in several senses) to single out elements of it and attempt to adjudge them not in accord with objective reality. They may not accord with reality as seen from the standpoint of our language and culture, but they can hardly be said not to accord with the same reality as they themselves conceive it—even the reality, linguistic and cultural, they themselves embody.

Winch, it seems, holds that in certain ways our society's beliefs and primitive beliefs are incommensurable; they cannot be compared. The road to understanding is nevertheless to seek out the universal problems of human life; but not to give them universal solutions, since these would be outside language and culture, which is impossible. Rather, we have to try to show how the primitive society solves them in its own way. Here Winch has skilfully pulled back from the relativist precipice by asserting that all societies do have something in common, the problem of human life in general and its general root in universal facts, i.e. birth, sex, and death.[6] So if we begin social studies with these universal facts and their ensuing universal problems, we have some bases of comparison, some universals in terms of which we can begin to make sense of any society: namely, how each society handles the universal facts of birth, sex, and death.[7]

### An alternative to Winch

Before expanding on and discussing[8] what I take Winch's position to be, I should like to contrast it with the admittedly not very sympathetic position from which my criticisms will come.[9]

I have no quarrel with the suggestion that in the social sciences we aim to understand other societies. But I would go further: the social sciences also aim to *explain* and *appraise* societies, their institutions, and beliefs. The social sciences, like any other sciences, use language in attempts to make true universal statements about the world, which will explain the world. We have these aims because of something like an innate curiosity which drives us to ask questions, formulate problems, seek answers which will improve our knowledge and understanding. The phylogenetic explanation of our curiosity and concern with problems sees it as an adaptive mechanism, a means to survive, that is to say, to get food, give birth, avoid death. The ontogenesis of problems seems to be something like disappointed expectations, i.e. refuted beliefs and theories.[10] The (conscious and unconscious) expectations and theories we hold are clearly deeply influenced by the upbringing and education—the culture, in fact—of which we are products; thus expectations, especially disappointed expectations, are the links between culture and the universal facts of birth, sex, death (and food).

It follows from all this that the entire activity of social science involves, and necessarily involves, bringing the ideas, standards and concepts of our language and culture—in short, our preconceptions—to bear on those of other cultures, seeking to find correspondences and trying them out, then following through on the feedback and modifying both our concepts and the correspondences. Social science, then, examines the survival value of cultures, allegedly from an absolute standard but in fact parochially. And this is *the* problem of social methodology. What we find problematic will at first be a result of our culture and expectations (knowledge). What we find good and bad, true and false, will depend at first on our culture and knowledge. In striving within these limits to understand other peoples we have resort to something rather resembling the act of translation from one language to another (cf. Gellner, 1962). We do our best to find equivalents when translating but must also rely on analogy, similarity, metaphor and the occasional directly appropriated, then explicated, untranslatable concept—such as litter the anthropological literature. This act of translation fails if it leaves us unable to appraise the truth of the beliefs of the other culture, or to discuss the values of that culture as we can our own. It would fail in the same way as a translation from a French or Russian science or religion or ethics text would fail if it left us in no position to appraise the finished product.

'One curious phenomenon to which I will return below at pp. 54 ff., is how constant exposure in anthropology to alternative sets of concepts and ways of classifying the world tends to shatter a lot of preconceptions. The bizarre ceases to be bizarre, and a degree of self-awareness about one's own culture and society is gained which only the greatest of imaginative leaps can otherwise obtain.)

Whether the social sciences are concerned to explain from the position of the outsider, as it were, or empathetically to understand from the position of the insider, thus becomes a false contrast. The questions an Azande asks about his society are not the questions a social scientist asks. Confusion may arise because of failure to note the point, made in chapter 1, that the social sciences are not out to explain why people do things, to understand or explain in that sense. Primarily they are concerned to explain typical, repeatable and unintended phenomena and hence to gain an understanding of the society in many ways totally different from the understanding we would attribute to its members. An infantry man's account of the war, and a general's account of the strategy, tactics, victories and defeats, are altogether different, although each may be useful in illuminating the other. But battles are rarely unintentional; Nelson and Villeneuve were in charge. Events in society are by and large unintentional and so the social scientist is like a scholar trying to grasp the battle from the fragmentary accounts of the infantry.

Crucially, explanation and understanding in the social sciences, as opposed to social living, involve bringing to bear on the phenomena preconceptions, models, theories, guesses variously arrived at. The explanation and understanding sought has nothing to do with answers to such questions as, 'Do you understand what you are doing?', 'How do you explain yourself?' These are individual, even psychological questions, according to Hayek. In a sense, only the individual who is already an amateur social scientist ever asks the level of question we are after, when unreflective social living is not the concern, but abstract and theoretical grasp of the working of social structures and institutions.

## Winch's position developed

Winch has produced a plausible, even a beguiling, argument. I am uneasy about more than I can coherently criticize; I can criticize more than I have space for. In particular, I shall not criticize the general Wittgensteinian underlay to Winch's philosophy as it has been discussed elsewhere,[11] and, moreover, it is irrelevant to my present aim. My aim is to come to a fuller understanding of what is involved in explaining and understanding alien societies, and to proceed to do so via a detour through Winch's pretty flower-bed of arguments.

My account of understanding in the first and previous sections would seem to beg the very questions Winch wants to raise. The entire enterprise of attempting to map the ideas and actions of alien people on to our conceptual scheme is regarded as futile. How he comes to this might be reconstructed thus. Take the problem of

43

some idea that is universally held in another society. How do we decide if it is true or false? Whether a statement is true or false will depend upon what it means. What it means, in Winch's view, will depend upon how it is being used, how it functions as part of the form of life it belongs to. The notion, then, of translating one form of life into the terms, concepts, preconceptions of another, does not make much sense. The way beliefs operate in a form of life is peculiar to that form of life. In particular, there is no reason to suppose that a statement true-to-them is translatable into a statement true-to-us; but if it is translatable into a statement false-to-us that does not show that it is false-to-them. One way or another, it makes no sense to talk of true or false *tout court*.

It would not hurt Winch's case for him to agree that anthropologists have always struggled to make beliefs we cannot share, held by others, such as magical beliefs, understandable. It is a simple matter of fact, anyway, that often anthropologists find themselves studying beliefs that they report as not true, yet as believed to be true by all informants belonging to the culture they study. It is also a simple matter of fact that in most such cases plausible translation accompanies such reports. Plausible translation involves giving an account of what is true-to-them which, though false-to-us, at least satisfies our 'scientific' culture's criteria of rationality[12] or intelligibility. Winch would contend that the last sentence refers to an illegitimate activity: that it is justified by claiming that what is true-to-them but false-to-us is simply false. But this claim cannot be uttered intelligibly because the words 'not true' and 'true' belong to two quite separate universes of discourse (ours and theirs), or they both belong to ours and are not found used of the beliefs in question in theirs. But our universe of discourse cannot appraise other universes of discourse, or appraise itself as the only true universe of discourse. Reality is built into a universe of discourse, and the outcome of a question about it in another cannot be appraised in the first. Winch gives an example from religion (p. 309): 'What [God's] reality amounts to can only be seen from the religious tradition in which the concept of God is used. . . .' Winch is not here quite repeating the hoary old chestnut that only the religious can handle and discuss religious concepts. Unlike those religious people who claim this, Winch nowhere says there is anything to stop the non-believer coming fully to grasp and being able to play the religious language game. (It can hardly be a rule of the game that sincerity of belief is required, even though display of sincerity may be required in ritual fashion.) But the ability properly to play it, and only this, shows true understanding of it. 'Reality is not what gives language sense. What is real and what is unreal shows itself *in* the sense that language has' (p. 309).

There are then for Winch no agreed transcultural criteria for what is externally or objectively real against which to measure a culture's universe of discourse. Not that Winch denies the existence of that objective reality; rather, assuming that he thinks there is an objective reality, we must understand him to be claiming that discussion about it takes place within a universe of discourse, but discussion about measuring the success of the universe of discourse in capturing objective reality cannot take place within that universe of discourse. (The opacity of Winch's argument on these points may be a consequence of the classical difficulty of trying to express the ineffable; like Wittgenstein of the *Tractatus* he is trying, within a universe of discourse, to point beyond that universe of discourse, to indicate its limitations.)[13] What is true of the universe of discourse of magic, according to Winch, apparently also holds for that of science. Science exists in a cultural context outside of which the actions and statements which constitute it would not make sense. Those who do not play its game can hardly appraise, for example, its theories or experiments; those who can play that game cannot use the game to appraise itself.

The question then about Azande magic is simply whether it is a coherent game, universe of discourse, world-view, form of life. Yet Winch denies that a 'yes' in answer to this question commits him to endorsing all magic. It only commits him to that which is 'one of the principal foundations of their whole social life' (p. 310). Magic in our culture is *not* foundational, it is parasitic as the black mass is on the mass. The former is not understandable without reference to the latter; but not vice versa. This aside, then, is Winch's answer 'yes': does he think Azande beliefs a coherent system? To begin with some difficulties, not only do Azande beliefs lead to inconsistencies, but the Azande use *ad hoc* devices to evade these. Azande, however, Winch notes, do not themselves press beliefs until they yield contradictions; and they showed no theoretical interest if these were pressed on them by the outsider. In their game, so to speak, they do not press; if we press them we are trying to force them to play our (scientific) culture's game. Azande do not regard the revelations of the oracle as hypotheses open to discussion and criticism: 'Oracular revelations are not treated as hypotheses and, since their sense derives from the way they are treated in their context, they therefore are not hypotheses' (p. 312). Indeed, 'to say of a society that it has a language is also to say that it has a concept of rationality' (or intelligibility?, p. 318) and that standard may involve not bothering about *ad hoc*-ness, or about checking inconsistency; in fact, what is to *count* as consistency depends on the wider context of life (p. 318).

Are there then any universals on which the social sciences can get a purchase so that other forms of life can be understood without living them through? Winch isolates T. S. Eliot's trio of 'Birth, copulation, and death' as points every society has to be organized around. From motherhood, marriage and funerals, social science can start.

## Critical discussion of Winch on understanding

Many kinds of criticism have been levelled against Winch's ideas. One is that his conclusions fly in the face of what social scientists constantly and successfully do (Gellner, 1968). This is a particularly strong criticism, since Winch believes in leaving every game to its players with no interference, whereas the criticism is that Winch unwittingly interferes with the game of the social scientists. Another is to show that his methodological conclusions do not follow from his philosophical premises (Cohen, 1968). That is to say, even if magic is the game he says it is, within our game of science we need not deny that it is wrong. Convincing as these are, they by no means exhaust what is to be said. For my part, I shall criticize certain philosophical ideas Winch holds which seem to me to lead to totally mistaken views about what can and cannot be truly said about societies other than our own. Let me start where Winch is surely in the right: there is no point in defending Evans-Pritchard's unqualified statement that Azande magical beliefs do not accord with objective reality. On Evans-Pritchard's own evidence, Azande magic is irrefutable, quite metaphysical. It asserts that there is a presence in the world causing things to happen. Whatever happens can be made to fit this theory. For this reason it is questionable whether we can justify the claim that our (culture's) physiological explanation of a man's death is nearer to the truth than the Zande magical one. Certainly any conceivable crucial experiment could be interpreted to fit the magical theory.[14]

What can be said—and surely Winch will agree (he even makes use of it)—is that whereas on the one hand, our explanation of death comes from an open and critical intellectual system in which ideas about the world are constantly scrutinized, criticized, and revised to meet these criticisms; on the other hand, Zande magic is part of a closed and unrevisable system of beliefs which may have been frozen that way for a long time. The issue then is not whether magic or physiology truly explain the death, but whether the choice between an open and a closed world-view can be rationally argued. And here Winch's view seems to be, roughly, that the choice cannot be rationally argued because there are different standards of rationality embedded in each position, and we could only decide the issue if one side was allowed to impose its standards on the other. If this happened it would indeed settle the argument before it started—as Winch himself tries to do by suggesting the outcome will be inconclusive.

It is at this point that my agreement with Winch stops. I would deny the different standards of rationality doctrine and hold that there is something like a community of rationality shared by all men, but recognized or fostered by different societies in varying degrees (none being perfect). This rationality consists at the very least in changing and improving our ideas, i.e. learning from experience, and especially from mistakes. All the ethnography I have ever read turns up no people, however primitive, who do not in some matters learn from their mistakes. The minimum standard is thus ever present even though seldom acknowledged. Those unaware of having it could have it disclosed to them that they possessed it by outsiders, like white men. But self-discovery is also possible. This could come about in the following way. Their closed system of ideas comes into contact with another closed system of different ideas. Suddenly for the first time there is the shock of choice: another view of the world is possible. Once this is realized, to accept either becomes difficult, since what if there is a third, fourth, etc.? Of course I am idealizing and simplifying, but all I seek to establish is the possibility of indigenous change. It would not then be an unreasonable conclusion on the part of these newly enlightened people to decide that whatever world-view is chosen it had better be held tentatively in case something better comes along. The first culture we know to have broken through to this stage is that of Ionia and its intellectual heirs, including ourselves.[15] That it is something of a feat to get so far should not be forgotten, since other reactions to culture clash are possible, especially dogmatism (we just know we are right); mysticism (truth surpasses understanding); and scepticism (all world-views are equally doubtful and thus equally arbitrary).

Having suggested there is a community of rationality recognizing at least learning from mistakes; and having also shown how awareness of choice of world-views could lead to a more tentative attitude, a more rational attitude, one that recognizes and seeks to avoid the possibility of making mistakes; I shall now discuss certain *consequences* of Winch's view that different societies have different standards of rationality and that therefore there can be no mutual appraisal between those standards. I shall argue that, in contradiction to Winch's view that standards of rationality are culture-bound and hence incommensurable, rational argument is possible between open and closed systems: indeed the way we discover intellectual problems and make intellectual progress (both ontogenetically and phylogenetically, so to speak) depends on such argument being carried out (not only between primitives and primitives, primitives and westerners, but even between Einsteins and Bohrs).[16] Winch's view seems to: (i) deny universal standards to other societies which they in fact possess; (ii) suggest that we are our own best interpreters, that a society's own view of itself is the best possible; (iii) postulate a metaphysical distinction between the core of a culture and what is parasitic on it; (iv) presuppose that societies are demarcatable and seamless; (v) deny empirical content to the beliefs of primitive peoples.

(i) If, when we say that there are inconsistencies within Azande ideas we are, in doing so, imposing our standards on them, then a curious situation is created. Do the Azande recognize this inconsistency as a problem? If they get contradictory advice from their oracles what do they do? They cannot do both things; they must choose. How do Azande choose? They certainly do not allow that their oracles are in any way discredited by the contradictions. What they do is what we could call resorting to *ad hoc* re-interpretations which resolve the inconsistencies—indeed Evans-Pritchard tells us of *standard* techniques to this end; they show no theoretical interest in exposing and extirpating these inconsistencies: in fact the standard techniques make them unaware of the problem as it makes them solve it all too readily. But the problem confronting them—inconsistency of prescriptions—is there and cannot be evaded. In whatever way Azande reach decisions in such cases we can report truthfully that Azande ideas sometimes yield contradictions which they resolve by *ad hoc* measures. A contradiction exists whether or not someone faced with it fails to see it, refuses to see it, or is indifferent to whether he sees it or not. Its objectivity—if you like its reality—is affected by none of these attitudes. In fact with Azande it is not that they cannot see any problem when they get contradictory advice, but that they possess a poor strategy for dealing with it. Yet one should also acknowledge that *ad hoc* defence is common in our culture.[17] This only goes to show that the standard which invokes consistency is by no means universally accepted in our society: but at least our culture has argued the issue.

Thus the Azande do possess some standard of rationality recognizable in the west as rational, though as rather poor. This contradicts Winch's claim (p. 315) that 'the context from which the suggestion about the contradiction is made, the context of our scientific culture, is not on the same level as the context in which the beliefs about witchcraft operate'.

(ii) The above quotation from Winch already indicates what his probable reply would be: not that Zande have no standards, nor that they have different and inferior standards, but that they have different and non-comparable standards. Even if I have shown that there is overlap between our standards and theirs, I have not shown that the non-overlap makes no difference in all cases. Winch insists that it does not make sense to say that Azande magic is inconsistent, only: by our standards of consistency Azande magic is inconsistent. My claim is that overlap of standards is more important because in overlap may lie the seeds of appraisal and even if the appraisal is not complementary, because it belongs to the overlap, it may be accepted by the Zande and thus lead to change. Winch's view somehow freezes the Azande within their contemporary standards, unable to appraise and revise them. All cultures will, I agree with Winch, take some of their current beliefs as obviously true; but this is a mere matter of regrettable fact; in freezing current views Winch intellectualizes this fact; he accepts the claim that the current beliefs are (obviously) true; and thus he freezes them beyond the desirable and even the factual. Assuming the alternative view for a moment, namely that a culture does not have to accept its own appraisal of itself, we would wonder why Winch thinks social anthropologists have to. Even in closed systems the *possibility* of rational discussion of current beliefs exists. Winch's view is based on a picture he seems to have of primitive society as clearly bordered, internally coherent and interlocking, all the parts reinforcing each other; he seems to think that Azande live by their magic and never sit around saying 'this is what we believe and it is true', for to say this they would have to have some conception of what it would mean if it were false. Winch claims their beliefs are not hypotheses and not therefore dubitable in this way. This amounts to the claim that a culture accepts its own appraisal of its own beliefs. It is a false claim, and empirically refuted every time any society reappraises itself—whether from the inside or as the result of outside intrusions. To this Winch may say, from the inside never and from the outside only accompanied by violence of sorts which thus does not count. This answer, be it good or bad, cannot be seriously considered except on the view that societies are seamless and coherent, and especially that their systems of ideas are closed and cut off in some clear-cut sense. But consider the following argument.

An idealized model of Azande magic would be one of an isolated group of people bowling happily on their way in a social system heavily dependent on magic. Not being aware of alternative views they never consider the truth or falsity of their magical beliefs. They are just a part of their way of life and it makes no sense for us to declare some arbitrary part of that way of life false. But what then do they make of their own member who one day announces: 'it says in your book of laws . . . but verily I say unto you . . .'? Reforming kings and priests and prophets can change societies. They sometimes condemn previous beliefs not just as wicked, but as false, and previous deities and demons as false gods. So even within closed societies a monolithic world-view can come to be undermined.[18]

Then of course if we look at culture clash we see other ways in which the Azande might come to doubt their own appraisal. Those Azande who have been educated abroad and have come back, what shall they believe? They can live as Azande half-believing in the old ways. Trying not to press the issue, under pressure they will usually hold to what their education has taught them. Consider the case of a member of a primitive society who has become a western doctor and returned to his society. He might turn a blind eye to local remedies or minor disorders; he will be more concerned to interfere in serious cases, or where the local remedy is harmful; when the case is hopeless he will again turn a blind eye to traditional practices.[19] What could be more reasonable? For minor matters and for hopeless matters it medically does not much matter what you do, so long as it is not positively harmful. Whereas in terms of public relations for when western medicine *can* do something, or culturally where the practices are intricately interlaced into the social system, it may matter a great deal not to interfere with custom. Yet there is a large class of serious but curable cases where traditional practices and modern medicine come into direct conflict and the former is to be rejected as false. It is a matter of empirical fact that in most parts of the world when this is put to practical test the population opts for the western magic (Gellner, 1965). This may be because the westerners can often propose and then carry out crucial experiments. These have great power to impress—which also suggests that standards of rationality have universal components. Chinese in Hong Kong know that western medicine, given a chance, can cure most cases of TB: traditionally, to catch it was to be doomed, as the folk-tradition and the many fictional characters who die of it testify. Of course, viewing western medicine as magic is not in conflict with Winch's view. But the preference for western magic by local standards is a refutation of Winch's thesis that a culture accepts its own ideas as true; cannot but operate with them; would be 'utterly lost and bewildered' (p. 311) without them; and therefore cannot judge them against others. Whenever a culture can adapt itself to new ideas, and implement them into its way of life, Winch's view does not hold.

(iii) In the light of Winch's assertion, quoted immediately above, and his approval of Wittgenstein's saying, *'The limits of my language mean the limits of my world'*, and his citation of Evans-Pritchard's view that,

> In this web of belief every strand depends on every other strand, and a Zande cannot get outside its meshes because this is the only world he knows. The web . . . is the texture of his thought and he cannot think that his thought is wrong

(both quotes in Winch at p. 313), it is not easy to reconstruct what Winch's reply to point (ii) would be. Perhaps, that culture clash is a special case unrelated to the case of widely separated societies trying to come to terms with one another. This raises the question of whether there is a Zande 'web' of thought in the required sense: whether there is a Zande culture utterly different from those it comes into contact with, and having at its core certain fundamental meanings or conventions in terms of which it organizes experience. Or whether it is not rather typically the case that societies interact constantly both with their neighbours and, so to speak, with themselves, with their history, and that no demarcatable system of ideas or meanings ever is fixed and permanent.

Winch says he avoids relativism and is able to say magic in our society is false because it is parasitic on the main ideas of our society—i.e. religion—and therefore can rightly be judged false in terms of, and by the standards of, the dominant beliefs. This cannot be done with Azande magic because it is not parasitic but fundamental to their way of life. In other words, he is unwilling to separate Azande magic from Azande culture, but insists on separating Azande culture from English culture. Is this not arbitrary? Let us go slowly here. Not separating Azande magic from Azande culture involves not separating it from any other Azande aspect. Now the Azande have a 'scientific' (in our sense) technology as well: can they then judge the one in terms, and by the standards, of the other? If Zande technology is parasitic on Zande magic then it should be judged in terms of Zande magic. If Zande magic is parasitic on Zande technology then it should be judged by the standards of Zande technology. Should Zande technology be judged in terms of Zande magic or vice versa? Or both in terms of both?

What is parasitic exactly? Winch's claim that magic in our society is parasitic is based on his view that it is a parody: the black mass parodies and distorts the idea of the mass. The mass, however, is a parody of Jewish synagogue practices. These in their turn may be parodies of Egyptian, Babylonian and other ceremonies. Here internal reform makes Winch's idea of a parody a parody of the real situation. What goes on in present day witches' covens probably antedates the mass (cf. Lethbridge, 1962; Hughes,

1952; Mair, 1969). What is parasitic on what? When does the parasitic parody become a principal foundation for a whole social life? Moreover, our society contains science and religion, and these two clash constantly, or at least they did—rightly or wrongly—at times in the past. That is, they did try to judge each other false, despite frequent attempts to avoid these clashes by *ad hoc* re-definitions of the scope and nature of religion (tending on the whole to make it ever more vacuous and metaphysical).[20] Which of these is parasitic? Or is neither? Is it not pure metaphysics to seek a core of a culture which makes it what it is?[21] Are not now most societies pluralistic; and is not pluralism constant interaction, often violent, rather than non-comparability; and do not such empirical facts refute Winch's attempt to escape relativism?

(iv) Winch's response to this might be that we are trying to impose our pluralistic standard of rationality on the Azande. My reply is the much more radical view that we and the Azande are all parts of one pluralistic world culture. Winch's whole view pre-supposes separate ways of life which enable their members to live untroubled within their existing system of ideas and brush off all contact with the rest of the world. Once upon a time, in small isolated Pacific island societies, this might have been the case (although Kon-Tiki and later investigations of Thor Heyerdahl [1950, 1958] and others showed that even isolation was not complete). Now it is not. No culture really is a closed system, and any that fancies it is tends to get awakened rudely. In other words, Popper's model of the closed society probably never was actualized, and certainly is not now.[22] There are only different degrees of openness. And since they are not seamless the possibility for contrast and self-appraisal is always there. Azande differ from our society mainly in not having a tradition of self-reappraisal, and institutions to carry that tradition. They are *capable* of both things. And they certainly do not have our metatheory that self-appraisal and criticism are positive goods. The differences between us are ones of empirical fact. But still there is a break-point. And that is when the conscious idea of critical appraisal and discussion is introduced.

This break-point may have much to do with the acquisition of literacy. For until there is literacy the past is in no way 'fixed' as a standard of comparison, the notion of learning is thus much less rich and definite. Indeed a very great strengthening of rationality in our sense of learning from experience seems to turn on literacy.[23] Moreover, our world-view seems more powerful because literacy enables us to incorporate and discuss other world-views.[24]

Thus Winch's thesis (p. 315) that 'The concepts used by primitive peoples can only be interpreted in the context of the way of

52

life of those peoples', founders because no such utterly cut-off and circumscribed 'way of life' exists.

(v) My last critical point is that Winch's curious view that primitive beliefs cannot be critically discussed along western lines empties them of empirical content. Western science is realistic. We believe it makes assertions about the world which are true or false. The reality of that world is extra-linguistic. Winch denies this last (p. 315) and thus denies realism. For Winch there is no linguistically external reality against which to match a dispute between our essential or fundamental beliefs and such primitive beliefs. However, this realism is presupposed by our western science, to which Winch confesses no hostility. Science, in other words, sees itself as exploring reality, not a reality, and therefore allows criticism not only within a framework but also of a framework itself (cf. Wisdom, 1971). Winch would presumably hold that this is a misconception. I have already argued that primitive peoples can come to appraise their own fundamental beliefs about why things happen against our competing suggestions. What is happening in such cases? Are the primitives revising their conception of reality? How do they do that? For Winch reality is not what gives sense or meaning to language, but shows itself in the sense that language has. But how can one adopt another's conception of reality without judging it better, without claiming it is a truer conception of what is? If reality (or the world) shows itself *in the sense that language has* then there is no such thing as a truth independent of the ideas and wishes of man. Provided a culture is coherent, and one works within its well entrenched beliefs, then there is no way of saying that these are false. They must be true. Only beliefs which run against the general grain of the culture, while accepting its terms of reference, can be false. Indeed (if I am right) for Winch all beliefs of a society become tautologies, and all 'outside' assertions self-contradictions.

Does Winch want to deny that there exist primitive people who have beliefs some of which make factual assertions about the world of existing things? Does he believe that factual assertions about the world can be true or false regardless of the language or culture in which they are formulated? If he does not then he is the sort of Protagorean relativist he strives to convince us he is not. A non-relativist would hold that the world is not altered by the language in which it is being discussed. Therefore its reality is in some sense extra-linguistic. Truth and consistency are qualities we attribute to statements apropos their relationship to this 'external world'. Inconsistent statements cannot possibly be true together of any world; true statements are true of this world; false statements are false of this world. That the Azande do not have explicit notions corresponding to these, show little interest in them, etc., is simply an empirical fact. These ideas are great discoveries in the history of mankind. They are accepted in a wide diversity of cultures, from Ancient Greek and Jewish, to modern European and American. They are not some special and weird peculiarity. They are at the core of what I earlier referred to as a universal standard of rationality.[25] Diffusion is not perfect and so they are not to be found everywhere yet. But I predict that, like industrialization, they will be.

This fact in itself must give Winch some discomfort. For how and why can two incommensurable belief-systems like that of the west and that of the Azande lead to one completely ousting and replacing the other? Did it just happen, or was there some process of rational discussion?

## Sociological problems and the inescapability of mutual and self-appraisal

Because of the existence of the universal standards of truth and consistency it seems to me that no two belief-systems are incommensurable. My conviction is reinforced by Bartley's argument (1962b) to the effect that there are no logical difficulties in maintaining that all elements of a belief-system can be held tentatively, open to criticism. What he calls the checks of the problem, logic, and the facts are available, as well as the check of other components of the belief-system. Since criticism is always possible, it cannot be dismissed as peculiar to one system and out of place in others. Those others may suppress it or ignore it, but it can erupt, and, since it can, it 'belongs' there as much as anywhere. Thus it is my conclusion that there is nothing extraneous about our standards of truth and consistency and that, provided they are manipulated with sympathy, and provided we do not make them an excuse for condescension, we are at liberty to discuss whether other people's beliefs have these properties.

However, I wish to claim more in this final section of the chapter. It seems to me that if evaluative standards of different societies were incommensurable, there would be and could be no social science, indeed no history. After all, history is the attempt to explain the past in terms of the present—what we nowadays regard as satisfactory explanation is a matter of on-going debate and thus very much a product of current ideas. We have to explain historical events, such as why a man did something apparently stupid. One explanation would be that he happened to hold a false belief. The falseness is not a contingent fact that can be ignored, since from it may stem the consequences we are trying to explain.

We cannot explain medieval plagues without reference to medieval ideas of disease and hygiene *and their falsity.* We no longer accept that race explains behaviour; few will get away with explaining wars by an aggressive instinct; theories that say societies degenerate are not much used. But in history we are in a way looking at, explaining, and evaluating the beliefs of, another society. As one explores further into the past of one's culture, or country, the gap becomes larger between them and us. Do we stop ourselves at some point and say we cannot criticize, for example, witch- and heretic-burning because, as Winch might have it, 'what a witch's or a heretic's reality amounts to can be seen only from the (religious) tradition in which the concepts of witch and heretic are used . . .'? There is something absurd about this. We do it, and there is nothing wrong, philosophically or otherwise, with it. Similarly, in our contemporary society, we may not be able to explain actions without pointing out the falsity of the beliefs on which they were based. If we can appraise a past state of affairs of our own society and segments of our own society today, then we can do it to others.

As to social science in general: my thesis would be that there is very unlikely to be any social science in a smoothly working, closed society; that the social sciences are in fact a product of the impact of other cultures on our own. What happens is that when other possible ways of ordering social arrangements are seen, one's own ways come into question—if only in the sense that they have to be explained and defended to oneself. If our system of monogamy is better than, say, polygyny, what sociological and other arguments can we produce that it is? First we question our own society. Then others raise puzzles. It is intriguing how many social scientists are themselves marginal to their society. They are refugees, foreigners, from minority groups, or otherwise 'loners'— perhaps they are trying to explain to themselves what others unthinkingly belong to. Thus my remark about ontogeny and phylogeny. Curiosity about sociological questions as it has grown in the course of time and its growth in individual men, seems to me to be connected with contact, culture shock, disruption, which lead one into evaluative and comparative questions.

All this seems obvious enough, yet Winch flies in the face of it. He maintains in his book that understanding a society is a kind of conceptual empathy which imprisons you in a universe of discourse that cannot evaluate itself. He thus attacks Popper for saying that sociological concepts are explanatory models.[26] Since Winch holds sociological concepts play a role in the actions themselves, they somehow cannot explain it. There is some vacillation here in the use of 'understanding' and 'explanation' (see Rudner,

1966). True, participants in a war hold a concept or model of war. But this is purely conventional—it is *their* explanatory model of what they are doing. Whether it is a war or not is not decided by them or explained by their use of the concept. They may understand that they are in a war but be mistaken. War is a label that cannot be strictly applied and which is useful only if it satisfies someone asking for an explanation of what is going on.

Among the main problems of economics, sociology and social anthropology are the explanation of certain events, especially large-scale events like depressions, suicide of democracy, disintegration in circumstances of contact. Problems of this kind are not easy to handle. Unlike smaller-scale problems they cannot be put down to someone or some people aiming to bring them about (as can orderly traffic flow, or social security payments). On the contrary, these are events which everyone wants not to happen, they are unintended and unwanted. They are also inter-societal, not confined to one social system either in their occurrence or in the scope of their explanation. Social scientists can neither come face to face with them nor solve them without indulging in some evaluation of beliefs. However long an economy has been depressed (or underdeveloped), the economist can say that this needs explanation. He may find himself saying: 'the British have to learn that their twin desires to support an international reserve currency, and have a high growth rate, are inconsistent with each other.' Or that 'the Indians have to see that their desire for economic development is being vitiated partly by their religious attitude to cows.' Sociologists may in all conscience have to point out that 'total freedom for everyone and the *maintenance* of democratic systems are not simultaneously realizable in this unhappy world.' Anthropologists may say to missionaries: 'your declared love of this people and their way of life makes you blind to the fact that you will destroy it by your proselytizing and interference.' All these could be made logical inconsistencies by different formulations. But also, the British are being told their values are in conflict, so are the Indians, lovers of freedom, and missionaries. Such evaluations of evaluative systems are not the result of illegitimate straying by the social scientists, but what the social sciences are all about.

## Appendix: discussion of Winch's reply

In a reply to the original published version of this chapter Winch answered some of the criticisms made above. In my own reply some new points emerged which make me wish to include this as an appendix to the chapter. To a considerable extent I summarize

Winch's counter-argument in what follows, and the additional argument and clarification seem important.

Consider the following claim:

Certain social institutions (including ways of conducting argument and of using language) impede attempts to discover what the world is like.

An unexceptionable enough piece of sociology, one would think. Yet, unless I continue to get Winch's ideas wrong, his position should lead him to discover grave difficulties in saying just what sense this claim makes. Winch has argued that what the world is like (what is real and unreal) is a distinction of language, i.e. a social usage. The activity of discovering what there is would seem to go together with the question of what is real and unreal and become a linguistic matter. My counter to Winch is to ask whether it is a social usage to say the sun rises and falls every day. Perhaps it is; it is also a grave error. Now, maybe geocentrism stands at the centre of a complex, satisfying, even beautiful social system. Well and good, but nothing to get sentimental about: that social system is predicated on a mistake. The question is, do its members know it, and—if they do not—were it brought home to them, would it make any difference?

Is this 'scientific' example fair? Are not the cases of witchcraft or of God different? In what ways? Well, unlike geocentrism, they allegedly concern non-empirical, metaphysical matters.[27] Even if that is true, have they not also been used to account for empirical phenomena? Yes. Insofar as witches and God are used to account for disease, disaster, crop failure, success in life, health, etc., we are entitled to appraise them as explanations, perhaps note the logical lacunae in the deductions and, in that case, the incorrectness of any claim that they have explanatory power. Like atomism, they may one day graduate to empirical testability, but critical appraisal of them need not stop in the meantime. Especially as some who accept witch-beliefs and God-beliefs indicate how they can be efficacious, this opens up the possibility of comparison with the more efficacious western explanations. (Efficacious both in the practical and in the intellectual sense.)

I contend, then, that my opening claim *makes sense*. It could be unpacked to mean, for example, that magical and tabooistic attitudes to things are inimical to intellectual progress; that oracular and authoritarian traditions of education inhibit learning; that entrenched metaphysical systems are inimical to progress; that witchcraft is wasteful and redundant as a treatment of disease, though it may be useful when combined with western remedies— not useful medically, but as a means to overcome prejudice, induce calm, etc.; and so on.

If the claim I have made is true, then it is reasonable to remove or alter those social institutions which impede discovery. It seems to me that Winch's views on languages and their limits, and on the institutions of rationalty, are inimical to my initial claim, and therefore, inasmuch as they are proposals for institutional reform of the social sciences, are themselves to be rejected or altered because they impede attempts to discover what the world is like. In what follows I should like to look only at a handful of the points in his 'Reply' to me which are relevant to the aforementioned claim.

Winch considers a very interesting hypothetical case of a tribe with no concept of height, and none of the ancillary concepts that might be used to describe it indirectly. Winch holds that to say that Azande magic has no reality may be 'very analogous' to the heightless society saying height has no reality, which in turn is like the philosopher saying 'time has no reality'. To argue against the latter, 'before I had breakfast I washed myself' is a reminder about the language game into which the concepts of time enters, and does not constitute a straightforward refutation. The problem may be in talking of beliefs, with the invited question, 'are they true or false?' rather than of concepts. Winch is not saying 'there are witches' but rather that, if I say there are not, he holds I shall be 'betraying . . . lack of comprehension of the institution in the context of which we do affirm those propositions' in question (about witches).

Before coming to beliefs, some remarks on concepts. Here I find myself in very strong disagreement with Winch—I think *his* confusion is connected with his misplaced interest in *concepts* rather than theories (or beliefs). Little purpose is served, I would say, by discussing concepts—what is interesting is what the concepts are used to *say*. Indeed I incline to think that almost any interesting doctrine can be reformulated so as not to use a disputed concept. This view may have grave difficulties, but Winch's view that concepts, like institutions, depend on agreement in their use, has equally grave ones. Winch quotes Wittgenstein in the *Philosophical Investigations* as saying that: for statements to communicate, there must be agreement in definitions *and in judgments*. Not, of course, in any particular judgment but, at least, in standards for judging such judgments.

241. 'So you are saying that human agreement decides what is true and what is false?' It is what human beings *say* that is true and false; and they agree in the *language* they use. That is not agreement in opinions but in form of life.

242. If language is to be a form of communication there must be agreement not only in definitions but also (queer as this may sound) in judgments. This seems to abolish logic, but does not do so. It is one thing to describe methods of measurement, and another to obtain and state results of measurement. But what we call 'measuring' is partly determined by a certain constancy in results of measurement.

This is a key passage in Wittgenstein; I for one am grateful to Winch for drawing attention to it. The idea it expresses might be called Wittgenstein's theory of language as a social institution, and in language he includes both concepts and standards of judgment. It is a theory which deserves close critical scrutiny. I consider it open to several serious objections.

For one thing, when using concepts and statements which employ them, we attempt to do with them what we do not attempt to do with most institutions, i.e. to *say* something about the world. Some are used to describe, some to explain, some to evaluate, some to perform, and so on. Concepts are simply tools for performing these specific acts; and they are in this sense unique as well. We use institutions for various purposes, but these are seldom substitutable within the same social context. Rituals like applause cannot be altered (for example, to hissing as in Japan) without losing their significance altogether. Even magic words are not allowed much variation ('abracadabra', or 'open Sesame', must be pronounced just so). But ordinary concepts and words are all too easily substitutable.

Some of the statements we use make truth-claims. Whether or not any particular statement *is true* does not depend only on an agreement in the use of the concepts. Even whether or not we can *agree* on whether what is said is true does not depend only on an agreement in the use of concepts. Such agreement depends on whether we can agree on the truth or falsity of other statements which they contradict. How can we agree on the truth or falsity of statements which contradict them: if we can falsify them by agreeing on the non-falsity of statements which contradict them; or, if we cannot falsify them, then by continuing the discussion; and so on. Agreement, in a strict or tight or wide or comprehensive sense, is *never* reached: all we have is partial and temporary; tentative acceptance with the possibility of revision any time. This is true of the standards of judgment and the rules of the discussion, as well as of truth-claims and meanings. Disputes over all these are regular, inescapable, fruitful and conducive to progress. So if we must 'agree in the language we use', that is, in the form of life, we never do.

Revisability is a matter of correction-cum-expansion. Correction is often changes in the language, and thus of shifts of concepts; these can be easily explained in specific cases. Now when one grasps a new use of an old concept—say the new hippie use of 'bag'—one sometimes does it before general agreement has been given to the concept. And to say of someone, 'man, he can't get out of that folk-rock bag' can be true despite the fact that most people in the society would not be able to face the question of whether it is true or not because they cannot handle the concept. And hence, Wittgenstein seems to be in error. Wittgenstein himself perhaps noticed this and tried to cover it by his idea of *loose,* expandable conventions, of language games involving family resemblances. So let us pursue this idea.

Consider, then, the doctrine that the one 'given' in language is not words, or rules, or meanings, but the form of life of which the language is a part. The language games of the building trade are adapted to the building trade form of life. Now, the building trade is a role, or a complex of roles we call an institution. A person often finds that his different roles conflict. Is there an analogue where we can see persons involved in different language games that conflict with each other? People who have changed their social class sometimes can play the language games both of their class of procreation and of their class of orientation. Which form of life does their double language game belong to? Or are there two? Bilinguals are an extreme case of this—is their form of life and two-language game *sui generis*? How are we to demarcate forms of life that contain persons who play different language games simultaneously? Ah, but they never do it at the same time! What then of double spies such as Philby (see Page, Leitch and Knightly, 1968)? They never *reveal* the other game they play, so how do we know they play it correctly—either one? Not by asking! What is the problem? The double spy has no 'given' form of life—so what is his language game?[28]

As there is violation of game rules, so there is the question of misuse of concepts; but if the rules are loose, is there violation, and how? Wittgenstein thinks that philosophers violate the rules. There are non-philosophical violations too and I think Wittgenstein cannot account for them because of his loose conventions. Compare the two cases, first the permissible use of 'rises' in 'the sun rises', or 'bag' in 'man, he can't get out of that folk-rock bag'; second, a vicious misuse. Popper (1945) has a passage where he imagines someone reversing the concepts of democracy and tyranny: Popper's strategy—not to be deflected from the point by playing with concepts—seems to me sensible and sound. Wittgenstein's theory leaves us helpless. Within Communist language games 'democracy', 'formal democracy', 'dictatorship of the proletariat', all have well defined usages which are viciously parasitic on their usages in ordinary language (see Carew Hunt, 1957). The pro-feelings aroused by their ordinary use are transferred to their perverted use, which certainly bears a family resemblance to their normal use.

Let me come back sharply now to the issue of whether or not there are witches. Winch grants that it is possible to raise doubts about the whole institution, to argue against a whole way of speaking. But when I say there are no witches I am doing much more than attacking a way of speaking. I am also attacking an Azande claim about the furniture of the universe. Winch agrees that people like the Azande make factual claims (for example, witchcraft-substance exists and can be detected in autopsies, and by administering medicines to chickens); he also agrees that the world is not changed by the claims made about it. So : we cannot conclude that there are witches *because* Azande believe and act as though there are; the Azande happen to be mistaken, just as were the followers of Galen—i.e. almost all medieval and Renaissance doctors—who for so long believed there was a hole in the wall between the two sides of the heart were mistaken. To be mistaken is not to be stupid, unthinking, primitive, immoral or anything else. It is to be honestly, decently, and yet hopelessly wrong. I cannot show that the Azande are wrong directly by a refutation, because not only is their doctrine of *benge* hedged around so much as to make it virtually irrefutable, but also, when the post-mortem that is supposed to discover it fails to, they have a barrage of *ad hoc* devices for handling this, and one can always defend any claim infinitely long if *ad hoc* devices are freely to hand. Rather would I argue with them that if, as Evans-Pritchard suggests, the problem their magic comes to solve is mainly the explanation of disaster, there exists a much more powerful explanatory scheme in my culture. For example, we can wipe out termites so that they do not pick on anyone's granary; we can immunize people from diseases witches cause altogether. We cannot do everything and we cannot convince all doubters, and we cannot answer the allegation that what we are offering is merely a more powerful magic. But we can in all integrity peddle our notions in the belief that they accomplish aims the Azande already have, better than the means indigenous to them.

Winch's hint that my endorsement of all this is to affect superiority or to be historicist seems to me baseless. I do think that Azande adoption of western ways might be an improvement and also that it need not involve much changing of their ways of speaking. We in our culture still speak, with complete justice, of the sun rising and setting, of the land around airports as 'flat', of the sky being 'up', the earth 'down', etc. Even though these ways of speaking force our educators to spend time confuting them, they are still in order. But using the language of medicine or of science as a sort of mumbo-jumbo is highly reprehensible. If this is condescending to magic, so be it; if viewing science as a higher order activity than magic is historicism, I concede the charge.

Let me return to Winch's problems with concepts, namely, their close connection with the institution in the context of which the statements employing them are asserted. We remember it came out sharply in his discussion of witches, time, and height. I maintain that witchcraft is, aside from all else, certain beliefs about the world, and that whether or not there are witches is a fact outside of language. This leads Winch to pose the very curious question: is whether or not there is height a fact outside of language, or is the reality of height extra-linguistic?

I do not know what 'the reality of height' can mean. Winch is surely right that operationist logical positivists could not possibly reduce 'height' to measuring operations language games. Then he says, 'the reality of height shows itself in the sense that these language games have'. What can this mean? Can a language game have a sense? What kind of sense? A move in a game can make sense; but chess, for example, does not possess 'sense'. To a non-player it may seem a meaningless waste of time—nonsense. Does Winch mean that the reality of height shows itself in the sense that language games involving the word 'height' make when they are played? But games do not 'make sense' when they are played. What would it mean to say this game of soccer does not make sense when played (or when not played)? When one says 'there are no witches' one is *not* saying that witch-talk makes no sense, anymore than the man without a concept of height who has learned our concept could think of it as mumbo-jumbo (*pace* Winch). We can, since Evans-Pritchard, very well distinguish 'making sense of' and 'understanding'. The point being that 'there are no witches' says not that 'witches' has no *sense,* but that it has no *reference,* in the same way as 'phlogiston' has no reference, or perhaps 'God'. Of course, to claim that phlogiston exists is to make a different *kind* of claim than that God exists. However, when I deny them both there is a strong similarity: I am denying existence, on one level or another, to putative entities, of one kind or another (hitherto believed in by man).[29] But I cannot really say how great or small this similarity is because, after all, the difference between a difference in kind and a difference in degree is itself a difference of degree. This applies even to the very abstract difference referred to by 'height'.

Winch thinks we cannot analyse very far the case of a people with no concept of height because height is so fundamental. He says that a visitor from Britain would have great trouble because he would have to teach the heightless society new techniques and new ways of speaking. For my part, I think this is a typical, not a special case. I think that Newton and Faraday and Einstein and Planck and Bohr (and Jesus, and Buddha, and Luther) all taught the human race new techniques and new ways of speaking. Einstein argued against certain views or beliefs, not against certain ways of speaking or a certain form of life. Indeed, Koestler (1959) has said rightly that the Newtonian ways of speaking still dominate our form of life. And our forms of life still use Newtonian concepts— even centrally, for example, the National Aeronautics and Space Administration. Winch is drawing attention to a genuine problem, but I think his views make it insoluble: the whole problem when someone like these great figures, the Einsteins, Buddhas, etc., comes along is just 'is he a genius or a crank?', very much the reaction of the heightless ones to Winch's Briton. And indeed the solution is very difficult, for reasons noticed by Winch. But that we do, regularly, solve these problems is undeniable. Winch's theory, however, is this: when we speak or accept the genius's language we have decided he is a genius, and vice versa. This is true, but irrelevant: the problem is by what criteria *do* we decide to accept or speak? On Winch's theory this is inexplicable: as long as we use an older language game that game *a priori* excludes all other language games, old or new. This corollary of Winch comes out most clearly when Winch argues that a businessman who fails to grasp a moral criticism can be said to be 'imprisoned' within his viewpoint. Winch allows that we can criticize the businessman on moral grounds because we possess moral concepts he does not. The question is, does Winch think the only way out of the limitations of the businessman's moral conceptual scheme is through being taught by those possessing concepts he does not? Then, who teaches the teachers? Are we not all imprisoned? Winch agrees that to say *we* were imprisoned someone would have to show that we, too, are being blind to a certain possibility, as the businessman was blind to our different moral concepts. But then he must specify this possibility. Then we could ask him, how come he can show us what we cannot show the businessman! We may agree in principle —Winch will join me, I think—that all conceptual schemes are limited: how else could they and their forms of life grow and develop? To refuse to concede this, as Winch does, until the areas they can grow into can be specified—before they have grown there—is having it both ways. 'We won't agree we are limited until you show us how; if you can show us how we are no longer so limited.' Few of us doubt that our scientific knowledge is limited, but not only because we can see where, but also because of a general metaphysics which holds open the possibility that our horizons could be radically expanded tomorrow. But now, here is precisely this metaphysics we do not share with the Azande. And I would not baulk at the idea that this metaphysics makes sense because of its place in the life of the society it and we inhabit. The Azande do not live it, and to grasp it they may have to; but the way the Azande live is captured and made intelligible by *our* conceptual apparatus as well as theirs.

Thus, Winch's argument about the people with no conception of height is a beautiful one, for it boomerangs nicely: *we,* who lack witchcraft, are, when we discuss witchcraft, like the heightless people trying to discuss height with us. Those without height, witches, or God, inhabit, so to say, the same world, but they 'see' it in different ways: the reality of it is different for each of them since the reality is constituted by their conception of it, their concepts. The radical conventionalism of this view is striking for it might lead one to conclude that any possible conceptual scheme is viable. This, however, is not Winch's view. He believes that all viable conceptual schemes must have the central events of forms of *life*—without which life still does not go on—central to *them*. I do not follow this myself, since a radical materialistic conceptual scheme without the concept of life would seem possible and even viable—because if forms of life with no conceptual scheme at all are possible as in the animal, fish, insect and plant kingdoms, then can we possibly say things must be different for man?

So far I have tried to show where there is a clash between the claim I made at the beginning of this appendix and Winch's views on language and its limits. Now I turn to the problem of rationality and consistency where I think both Azande views (*ad hoc* evasion), and Winch-type views (the Azande know what they are doing), disastrous. But first there is a minor misunderstanding to be cleared up. Winch contends that my crude first approximation to his position is the contrary of what he holds. I wrote in paraphrase of him: 'cross-cultural value-judgments will always be misjudgments —and therefore should be avoided—because there is no language game in which cross-cultural value-judgments could be legitimate moves.' Winch claims that in 'Understanding a Primitive Society' he *was making* cross-cultural comparisons—although not value-judgments, which he treats elsewhere. I confess to using 'value-judgment' to include cross-cultural comparisons (evaluations?) of the rationality of actions and the truth of claims. However, even if we now write 'comparisons' for 'value-judgments', I cannot grasp what the contrary position is that Winch was arguing for, since I am sure he would not want to assert either of these contraries:

'cross-cultural comparisons will *never* be miscomparisons—and therefore need not be avoided—because there *is* a language game in which cross-cultural comparisons can be legitimate moves', or 'cross-cultural comparisons will not be miscomparisons—and therefore need not be avoided—because in *every* language game cross-cultural comparisons can be legitimate moves'. That aside, it is unclear in what language game Winch permits or forbids comparisons. He is ostensibly using our language to explain that it is not possible for us to pass judgment on whether Azande witch-talk corresponds to reality. Holding that what is real and unreal is a distinction belonging to each language or form of life, and that in the Azande form of life, where the witch-talk occurs, witchcraft is not treated as a hypothesis subject to such a question, the question makes no sense. Here then is our language being used by Winch to teach us about another language and its contrasts with our own. Winch's discourse, then, is at least second-order, or metalinguistic. (He is not speaking the English of the English magician, priest, or scientist, but of an English anthropologist or philosopher.) We do then have a way, either anthropological or philosophical, of discussing the adequacy of Azande language—such as their real/unreal distinction—the *adequacy of their form of life* (as compared and contrasted with western ways of life or not). To some extent the whole point of this chapter is that the form of life is not a 'given'—unquestionable and basic. Not only is it that our form of life permits consideration of other forms of life and our own, but that the whole 'justificationist' belief that there can be a 'given', is a fundamental mistake. A 'given' form of life is open to precisely the same objections as a 'given' sense-datum, a 'given' protocol-sentence, or whatever.[30]

What does Winch say about rationality? It seemed to me he said that 'standards of rationality are incomparable'. Yet he writes that he has 'never held any view of which' he would be willing to regard this as 'a proper paraphrase'. But he writes elsewhere (p. 317): 'MacIntyre seems to be saying that certain standards are taken as criteria of rationality because they are criteria of rationality. But whose?' In his unexplained question Winch here seemed to me to be denying that criteria of rationality can be compared to the extent that they are criteria of rationality. Q.E.D. To ask 'whose?', is to relativize the whole question and beg it. If he was not denying it, then Winch and I are agreed, since I hold that standards of rationality *are* comparable and western ones are *better* than Zande. Does Winch agree? If so, no quarrel; if not, my paraphrase is quite in order.

As an example of why I rate western standards of rationality as better, I used Winch's own example of the Azande attitude to contradictions. Zande standards of rationality which are indifferent to certain contradictions can only seem 'rather poor', Winch thinks, depending on the point of the activity in which the contradictions grow up. But why cannot standards of rationality seem rather poor as standards of rationality? What purpose do standards of rationality serve? As a minimum requirement they must serve the acquisition of knowledge. Now, if our knowledge is greater than Azande knowledge (as it is in at least one way: we know how to go to them and make sense of their way of life, they do not know how to reciprocate) we would seem to have a prima facie argument that our standards do the job their standards try to do, and do it better. Therefore, might they not well come to agree that ours should be theirs, and that theirs are rather poor?

Claiming that western standards of rationality are better, I instanced science. Winch then says, 'Our own conception of what it is to be rational is certainly not exhausted by the practices of science.' Quite. I should only claim (see refs 12 and 16) that science is *a* paradigm of human rationality—for us and *tout court*. I should go further than Winch and say that the *rationality of science* is not exhausted by the *practices of science*—why else is there continuing methodological debate? Yet *the* paradigm of rationality is action taken with full knowledge; *the* paradigm of full knowledge is scientific knowledge; therefore action taken to gain scientific knowledge is at the heart of any idea of rationality (see Jarvie and Agassi, 1967).

In the two chapters just concluded, I have tried to show several things: how the fundamental model for explanation in the social sciences is the logic of the situation. The logic of the situation has deeply embedded in it the rationality principle, the methodological rule that we attribute rationality—goal-directedness—to human actions in need of explanation, unless we have good grounds for not doing so. What we find problematic, and what we find rational, are tied in essential ways to our own society and its outlook. Thus, when we set out to explain and understand the deeds and societies of others, we have to be clear that this cannot but be performed in terms of the categories and preconceptions we operate with. These are not fixed or uncriticizable, but they are quite basic.

Part 2 will consist of two case studies exemplifying the logic of the situation and the unintended consequences of actions, but will also open up the topic not so much of the categories and preconceptions brought by the investigator to the articulation of his problems, but rather the categories and preconceptions in terms of which the actors themselves are operating and the relevance of these to the social sciences. In Part 3 that relevance will be directly discussed.

66

# part two

# Case studies

# 3 Between adult and child: notes on the teenage problem

Another psychological fact which is significant for sociology, and which raises grave political and institutional problems, is that to live in the haven of the tribe, or of a 'community' approaching a tribe, is for many men an emotional necessity (especially for young people, who perhaps in accordance with a parallelism between ontogenetic and phylogenetic development, seem to have to pass through a tribal or 'American-Indian' stage).

Popper (1945, 1962), ii, p. 98

The older generation of any group teaches the younger how it ought to behave. Though the elders may have lost confidence in some of their doctrines, they cannot go so far as to leave the young alone. True, the argument that the socialization process automatically prepares the young to take just those rôles society is ready to offer them is a facile solution to the problem of social continuity. A society may teach its young men values subversive to its own stability. Let a boy learn at his mother's knee such impeccable social values as independence and achievement; and he may, when he grows up and if he finds the opportunity, take action that will change the society radically, not maintain it. Still, some initial tendency for the young to learn, and thus perpetuate, the customs of the past will undoubtedly be there.

Homans (1967), p. 91

In the following two chapters case studies will be used to exemplify the idea that how society is *conceived to be* by its members considerably influences how it *is*. Chapter 3 tries to explain the mutual hostility on both sides of the generation gap. The ideas and expectations about society and social behaviour which underlie the hostility are shown to be inadequate and unrealistic. Physical and social facts connected with growing up are not allowed for. The result is the generation gap.

## Introduction

Why do successive generations of teenagers fail to conform to the standards adults expect of them? Why do adults persistently strike attitudes of shock, incomprehension and censure when faced with these deviations?

To answer these questions I shall suggest (pp. 70–2) that myths about teenagers are popular among the adults of our society, and that these myths rationalize diametrically opposed attitudes: (*a*) a complacent omnitolerance towards all that teenagers do; and (*b*) a hypercritical intolerance no matter what they do. Stating the myths will be enough to expose them and undermine the corresponding attitudes (pp. 72–6). Teenage behaviour can be better explained when it is seen that our society provides so poorly for the teens that it could easily seem to be intending to disorient and confuse. To grasp the importance of the disorientation it is necessary to invoke a trivial sociological theory (pp. 76–9) about the need for orderliness in social life, including the life of teenagers. It transpires that (pp. 79–84), while all teenagers are somehow left in-between, teenagers in our society are left chronically so, this in comparison (pp. 84–7) with 'primitive' societies. The behaviour of contemporary western teenagers can, to a considerable extent, be explained (pp. 87–9) as attempts on their part to solve the problem of social living in an in-between age group. Probably the problem is universal: all adolescents have to improvise. Some societies, however, give more help and direction than others. Our society is one of the others. Yet each generation of teenagers has to get by. 'Problematic' teenage behaviour can be explained as attempts to get by. This is a riposte to those who are inclined to dismiss these teenage attempts to solve the problem of their own status as evidence of the worthlessness of this particular generation. My interpretation of events allows us to be more optimistic.

## The teenager in adult myth

The main thesis of the chapter is that adult attitudes to teenagers are a consequence of the adults' belief in certain superficial myths about teenage behaviour and attitudes. The content of these two myths is, roughly, that teenagers are either just sowing their wild oats and will soon settle down, or that this particular generation of teenagers (it does not matter which one) is especially deviant and irresponsible and must be curbed if it is not to destroy the fabric of society. These myths are superficial because they ignore the underlying causes of teenage behaviour and attitudes; they are myths because they bear only a fanciful resemblance to what teenagers are like or how they see themselves. The superficiality and mythical quality of adult views being exposed, might enable us to get a little nearer the truth and also to be more understanding and tolerant.

Of course, all societies possess any number of social myths: some superficial, some not; some serving some function, some not. Clearly, it would be impossible to expose all of them. And indeed, if they serve some function, might one not have second thoughts about exposing them at all? One might consider them ripe for exposure, I suppose, when their pernicious effects seem to be greater than the benefits conferred by any function they might conceivably serve. It is difficult to offer a conjecture as to the function in our society of adult myths about teenagers. They are perhaps ways adults have of insulating themselves against, and of controlling, certain criticisms of their accepted standards which are implicit in the rebellious behaviour so characteristic of the teens. The 'wild oats' myth encourages the comforting idea that adolescent criticisms of the society of their seniors are not serious and that the criticism and rebellion will be silenced by time. After sowing wild oats they will settle down to the *status quo*. The myth encourages an attitude of smug condescension. The 'irresponsible and deviant' myth sees adolescent criticism and rebellion as destructive and to be resisted at all costs. Condescension is replaced by hostility, sometimes savagery.

If these attitudes are consequences of the myths, then they provide a second argument for exploding them. On the one hand, the myths lead to teenagers being treated badly—either indifferently or harshly; and on the other hand, the myths insulate the society against possibly quite valid criticism.

There is a third argument for exposing the myths. Myths about teenagers cloud the understanding even of adults who are striving to come to terms with the younger generation. The myths mislead them about why teenagers behave the way they do. Bemused by these stereotyping myths, adults get trapped into either omnitolerant or hypercritical attitudes. Even if the melodramatic nineteenth-century cry of 'never darken my door again' is uncharacteristic of our time, there is still a wealth of unnecessary tension and mutual misunderstanding between teenagers and adults. The explanation is not the simple one that adults have 'forgotten what it is like' to be young. Often, adults who remember their own teenage quite well strike the same attitudes. Even when an adult remembers his own teenage, he does not necessarily understand it, or know how to ease tense relations with teenage offspring. This process of mutual misunderstanding between the generations is not only unpleasant: it looks set to go on perpetuating itself for a long time. Unless one generation of adults is helped towards an understanding of what they themselves went through, and what their teenage children are going through, then our present teenagers will as likely be as intolerant of, or indifferent to, teenagers when they are adult as are today's adults. That the job falls to sociology, rather than taking place spontaneously, is perhaps a measure of how the increasing size and complexity of society requires more self-consciousness if it is to be operated smoothly.

## Criticism of the myths

For the purpose of simplifying our discussion we will continue to distinguish only two extreme myths about teenagers. As we have seen, one is naïvely optimistic, suggesting that youth will have its fling and that rebellious teenagers will 'settle down' one day. Let us call this 'the settling down myth' or the theory that 'teenagers will settle down one day'. Despite the naïve optimism this myth embodies and gives rise to, it is admirable to the extent that it enjoins tolerance, if not approval, of teenage behaviour. An obvious criticism is that the line between sowing wild oats and criminal delinquency is not drawn. Some conduct, such as juvenile delinquency, cannot be seen simply as part of youth having its fling before settling down. The tolerant must guard against omnitolerance, against renouncing all standards. The second myth, which incorporates and encourages a very pessimistic attitude, sees teenage behaviour as a threat to standards. So far from tolerating too much, the tendency is to view all rebellious teenage behaviour, however mild, as being on the slippery slope to delinquency and hence indistinguishable from it. We could call this the myth that 'present teenagers are a bad lot'. It encourages the view that teenage rebellion requires sharp corrective action if standards are to be prevented from falling further. Of course, this theory incorporates the assumption that previous generations behaved better (else there has been no deterioration). An obvious criticism of this myth is that it can become intolerant of any modification of standards of behaviour since it holds the past up as a model.

Having characterized two extreme myths and the attitudes that accompany them, they should now be recognizably present in Britain and North America. There are those parents who seem indifferent to the rebellion of their children and there are many cases of this tolerance becoming indifference (or perhaps stemming from it) as witness the astonished or diffident parents of juvenile thieves, prostitutes, thugs, etc., who appear in the courts. There are also parents who nag, bully and agitate against their teenage children and who insist that things like teenage smoking (not just pot smoking) and dancing to rock music must be suppressed if the rot is to be halted. Professor Carstairs in his Reith Lectures (1962) suggested that often the tougher attitude goes with indifferent behaviour and belief that the necessary corrective should be administered by the State.

Clearly both the settling down myth of teenagers and the sharp corrective myth are unsatisfactory. Both omnitolerance and intolerance are better avoided, although intolerance in thought plus inaction in deed (leave it to the State) strike me as the worst combination. Apathy about the aspirations and problems of the young is not easily forgivable either. Clearly what is wanted is some sort of sensible balance of tolerance with standards. There has been very little discussion of how we can rationally maintain the two in our attitudes to teenagers. Indeed, most discussion is carried on on the primitive level of the black-or-white myths. Professor Carstairs countered this with some intelligent and perceptive remarks in his third Reith Lecture. However, he deliberately concerned himself with the trends towards juvenile delinquency and greater sexual freedom. While these are no doubt important, my sociological interests cover the whole range of teenage *mores*. While there may be some excuse for the heat generated by Professor Carstairs's remarks, I believe his ideas and the problems I am discussing here deserve far more serious discussion than they have yet received.

Hitherto, I have characterized popular social theories to explain teenage behaviour as 'myths'. 'Folk knowledge' or 'folk wisdom' would have been alternative terms, but they conceal the fancifulness of the beliefs concerned. It hardly needs saying that teenage rebellion is not all innocent or all evil. The sociologist must attempt to replace folk myths, stereotypes, and attitudes, with theories which better explain what is happening. It helps if such theories are testable. It further helps if those theories lead to practical suggestions as to how the social problem being explained can be tackled.

My theory of teenage rebellion is easily summarized. (1) Human life tends to be organized in stages in all societies, for example, the stages of infancy, childhood, adolescence, adulthood (young adult, middle-age, old age). Of these, we are interested here in childhood, adolescence (teenage), and adulthood. (2) Adolescence or teenage has become in our society more a residual category, a transitional stage with few independent roles, and those poorly defined. (3) This in-between character of the teens has certain consequences, like lack of clear rules for behaviour. (4*a*) Our society has failed to provide ways for teenagers to cope with the problems of living without clear rules. (4*b*) Other societies have failed with these problems in different ways. (5) Some societies, especially some primitive societies, seem to have avoided all this. (6) In our society, teenagers are tackling the problem by forming themselves into a sub-cultural group with its own roles and rules. (7) These roles and rules are new, that is, they are different from the received wisdom as well as from the roles and rules appropriate to the neighbouring stages of childhood and adulthood. (8) Not being children, teenagers reject the roles and rules of childhood; not being adults they reject those roles and rules too. Permitted by default to devise their own roles and rules ever more freely, they seem deliberately to choose roles and rules that will affront adults. I presume there is an element of resentment and defiance in this. Faced with incomprehension, indifference, or censure, and an (unforgivable) failure to see their point of view, it might almost be expected that teenagers would favour *mores* which actively annoy, rather than being simply distinctive. Thus, despite increasing tolerance and permissiveness in the society, teenage roles and rules get ever more diametrically opposed to adult standards.

After working out this, I read Erikson's illuminating *Young Man Luther* (1959), where he employs his fascinating idea of the 'identity crisis'. In the course of this Erikson comments (p. 252):

> Whoever is hard put to feel identical with one set of people and ideas must that much more violently repudiate another set; and whenever an identity, once established, meets further crises, the danger of irrational repudiation of otherness and temporarily even of one's own identity increases.

This is rather striking. My view can be seen as an application of it. The teenager is hard put to identify with his group because it is a group which is nebulous until brought together by the repudiation of the adult group and its ideas. But the parallel then breaks down, for it is of the nature of adolescence that the identity *qua* adolescent is transitory.

We might find it useful to distinguish, at this stage, physiological and psychological childhood from sociological childhood. Physiological and psychological childhood are involved and partly naturalistic concepts. The concepts of physical and mental maturity are not entirely conventional. Sociological childhood, though, is entirely conventional, varies widely between societies, and seems very often to have quite arbitrary boundaries. Moreover, in our own society the boundaries of childhood are far from clear cut. Legal childhood is one thing; childhood for purposes of soldiering, marrying, driving, and being seduced, are all different. And there is great individual variation over the point where an adult begins to treat a child as an adult. Sociological childhood, like human society itself, is the unintended outcome of the operation of institutions and traditions. Comparison shows that other societies have more social stages based on age alone than we do; but, more important, they have much clearer and sharper dividing lines between these sociological stages than we do. Our informal criteria for childhood, and adulthood, are much discussed ('grow up', etc.) and yet remain vague. After all, how much does it convey to a teenager to tell him to grow up? He may not find the admonishing adult's behaviour at all attractive. In a primitive society, as we shall see later on, you cannot admonish a person to grow up unless he has already done so. Put it like this, perhaps: growing up is a function of (*a*) your age (a natural fact) and (*b*) which *rites de passage* you have passed through (a social convention). There can of course be criticism of one who has passed the adult rites yet still behaves 'childishly'. But that is somewhat different; his social status is not in doubt.

A teenager in our society is no longer a physical or psychological child and yet is also not a sociological adult. A person in his teens requires a different social life with different standards of independence, etc., from that of a child, one commensurate with his greater biological and psychological maturity. Yet he is not considered quite ready, biologically and psychologically, for the social life and responsibilities of adulthood. But what will not do is a mishmash of both: a teenager is in-between and needs something distinctively in-between, something in which he can find an identity.

In my view, while permissiveness and tolerance of teenagers are increasing, understanding is not. Thus teenage rebellion seems to be intensifying.[1] I shall argue below that teenagers act the way they do because that is the logic of their in-between situation; and it is the failure of the wider society to realize that their behaviour will not change unless their situation is changed which maintains the situation. My thesis is that teenagers are in a situation which disorients them without, on the one hand, any clear received standards or norms for their in-between age, and, on the other hand, they are at the receiving end of propaganda which castigates them for being rebellious (not good, docile, little children) and irresponsible (not good adults). While as children or adults they might accept these

75

standards, as teenagers they will not; and as logical people they could hardly accept both. Thus both adults and teenagers get frustrated and tense and we have the present state of affairs.

## The stability of social expectations

My further development of these ideas rests on the following very straightforward sociological theory.

Human beings need a degree of stability in their social lives; they need to know 'where they are', *vis-à-vis* their society and other people, in order to be able to live their lives. The basis of this theory is not a psychological need for security, although doubtless that enters into it; the basis rather is sociological. Without some social stability it becomes difficult for people to live comfortably or even to survive. Of course it is easy to imagine a prisoner in a cell being reduced to insanity by not knowing whether he would be fed or tortured the next time the door opened. What especially interests me, however, is that probably he would also be unable to perform any tasks. He would be so upset by the uncertainty he would be unable to sleep, to eat, to shave, to sweep his cell. The point of this illustration is not to compare social life to prison, but to draw attention to what can happen when all stability begins to disappear. The example will also serve to distinguish the psychological consequences (say, madness) from the social consequence or even the effect on the survival of the person (cell unswept, inability to eat).

Almost every social action we take, it seems to me, is based on our expectation that there will be stability in social life. When we walk to work we do not expect passers-by to attack us, else we would have gone by car; when we go by car we do not expect people systematically to abandon all the rules of the road else we would not venture forth (see chapter 1). When we post letters we expect them to arrive; when we speak to people we expect them to mean what they say and to stick to what they promise; when we buy and sell we expect money to have a certain value. Without a certain amount of confidence in this sort of thing we obviously could not carry out very successful social lives or, possibly, survive at all. Of course, we are flexible: the Highway Code can be altered, people's manners can deteriorate, but not much. Think of the social panic caused by galloping inflation; of the fury one feels when others violate the Highway Code; of the terrible fear and uncertainty felt when, suddenly, Negro and Caucasian strangers regard each other with hatred on the street. How these events can cause a rapid disruption of social life, including economic life, is possibly one of the semi-inherent factors which make for resistance to change in any society, a resistance especially strong among those for whom the disruption causes a monetary loss.

Having given extreme illustrations of the theory, I want now to suggest that even a slight loss of stability or expectation causes social disruption. A touch of inflation very rapidly preoccupies some people and alters their behaviour (for example, their cash savings). A proposal to ease the divorce or homosexuality laws brings to the fore all sorts of groups who oppose the changes almost as if they meant the collapse of the world. Similarly, when teenagers are cocky rather than respectful, promiscuous rather than chaste, some in the wider society can be heard predicting doom.

Among the things which we expect to be stable are standards of behaviour. Standards which tell us how we should act if we are to be accepted by our peers. Adults know that if they obey the law, are kind and decent, observe basic social niceties, they are doing very well by the standards of their peers. Children know that they are powerless and without rights and that if they do what adults want they are living up to the highest standards. Children and adults have the advantage of fairly well-defined roles and rules.

Teenagers do not have (a) the roles and (b) the clear rules that adults want them to have. But this is partly because adults try to foist inappropriate roles and rules on teenagers, failing to take into account the fact that teenagers, unlike children, do have some rights and some power (especially economic) and, unlike adults, do not piously subscribe to norms of decency and social nicety that correspond to those endorsed by adults. To exemplify all this, let us look at how the situation might look to a teenager.

As a child he looked up to adults, was controlled by them to a large extent, and knew that there would be penalties for not behaving as they demanded. Almost overnight, the teenager finds he has ceased to be a child. He is tall, strong, and he begins to feel the adult plateau is within his grasp. Simultaneously with this development, adults partly recognize his new status by revoking his licence to indulge in childish behaviour and constantly calling on him to grow up. This latter demand, however, he distrusts, since he is still denied many of the privileges of adulthood—such as independence of adult control, and economic independence. What incentive has he to accept what he sees as the dull peers and the heavy and responsible standards of adult life, when he feels young, wants to be free of constraints suffered through childhood and school, and is denied any genuine equality with the adults even if he accepts their standards?

Imagine how we would react if overnight all the standards we had been living by were revoked and we had thrust towards us unpleasant and conflicting standards. First of all, we would be confused and unsure; secondly, we would be rebellious and resentful of the new standard; and finally, the confusion of standards would frustrate us because we would not know when we were rebelling and when conforming.

Yet does not precisely this happen to teenagers? Time passes quickly in adolescence. Are they not children one minute, the next minute going through puberty and leaving school? (I do not think I need spend much time on who the teenagers are. I agree with Terence Morris [1963] that the thirteen to twenty age group is not homogeneous. I also accept his point that school leaving is a vital division in teenage life. But I disagree with him when he says that the pop culture is not homogeneous. One of the things which links those at work with those who have stayed on at school is precisely the shared pop culture. There seems to me to be a growing homogeneity in teenage *mores,* which seem now to begin taking hold around the age of eleven and to end only with marriage in the twenties. Certainly the ages of twenty-one or eighteen are no magic dividers.) Are they not on pocket money one day and drawing a wage packet the next? Are they not contemptuous of girls one day and chasing them the next? Are they not under their parents' thumb one day and conscious of their independence the next?

At the same time, the teenager has not made a smooth changeover from one stage to the next, because the new standards thrust at him are a disconcerting mixture of childish and adult ones. He is expected to be deferential to adults (especially school teachers), as children are; he is expected to be responsible, like adults are; he is slanged as children are when he fools around and plays jokes; he is condemned as too young if he starts an *affaire* or wants to get married. As Morris (1962) points out, there are also anomalies in the teenager's legal position: technically an infant until he is aged eighteen: he can marry at sixteen (with consent); drive at seventeen (in the UK); be conscripted and vote at eighteen.

Confronted with roles and rules partly a hang-over from childhood and partly an anticipation of adulthood, the adolescent is, understandably, disoriented. Our society seems singularly unable to tolerate too many stages and standards. It is as though the adult world found it difficult to be flexible and was trying to allocate everyone into two simple categories: child and adult. That things are a little more complicated than this, it seems determined to ignore. Much the same story can be told about the status of old age. Past the stage of being like working adults, it is well known how much old people resent the fact that all of a sudden they are treated as helpless, senile, old fogeys. They have been led to expect old age will be a period of dignity and respect. In fact, there is often the attitude that they should be seen and not heard. Their comments and advice are brushed off as would be the questions of a child. Understandably they get frustrated and become cantankerous: 'be good little children and don't get in the way while you die' is hardly an acceptable standard for living by. Here again there seems to be a rigidity or failure of imagination on the part of the mass of adult society. Of course it is difficult and unpleasant, but old people have to face the reality of the drawing to a close of their useful lives and, inevitably, of their lives, period. My initial suggestion that folk myths cloud attempts to understand will have to be changed if it is to apply, *mutatis mutandis,* to the elderly. Primarily, this is because adults less frequently stand in judgment on the morality of the behaviour of the elderly, and therefore do not look to an improvement in their behaviour. But the attitude adopted towards the elderly is certainly partly a way of evading their often well-founded criticism of the way they are treated. It is here that I would pinpoint my explanation of the refusal to use sympathetic understanding on the teenager or the elderly person: their criticisms of adult society are felt to be a threat to social stability. Adults want to stick to what is simple, straightforward and well known. This makes it easy to live their lives, even if teenagers and the elderly suffer as side effects. Changing things would be a great strain and one would not know where one is or what one ought and ought not to do. The desire to remain self-righteous may also be present.

The teenage problem is more urgent than that of the elderly because it can warp those as yet unwarped, and because it is less a problem of callous lack of understanding in individuals than is the problem of old people.

## Teenage as in-between

Part of the socialization process every child goes through in every society is learning what standards of behaviour he must live up to. These standards, imposed by adult sanction, are both proscriptive and prescriptive: the child learns that he must not do certain things (for example, in toilet training) and, on the other hand, that he is expected to do other things. He is expected in our present-day society to be good, i.e. not troublesome, to do as he is told, to observe his table manners, to go to bed early, to work hard at school. Some of these standards are preparation for adult life; but others are not. It is no preparation for life to learn to take orders without question, always to defer to the authority of one's elders. However, children do differ from adults in many obvious ways: physiologically, psychologically, and in their economic and social roles. Physiologically children are weak and small; psychologically they are not fully matured and therefore vulnerable; socially and economically they are a class without rights, without means to sustain themselves and thus utterly dependent upon, even at the mercy of (within the law), their parents. Consequently, it is not surprising that their range of behaviour, permitted, forbidden, and expected, should differ considerably from that of adults. Children these days are not, for example, expected to make polite conversation with anyone they are introduced to; they are not expected to do a full day's work (even at school).

When a child becomes a teenager, however, he is still physiologically, psychologically, and socially and economically different from adults, and from children as well. He is of more comparable physical and mental stature now to adults, he is capable of fending for himself, yet facing the startling new experience of puberty (both social and physical);[2] puberty and his approach towards adulthood create a very complicated psychological situation; and socially and economically he is in a curious limbo. Food, clothing and accommodation on an adult scale are needed, while he may already be able to pay this fully from his wages at the age of fifteen, or he may not be able to contribute to it at all until completing his education in his twenties. Now, despite the teenager's failure to be an adult as yet, the standards adults judge him by tend to be those of adulthood. The teenager has no choice but to reject this judgment since he is excluded from full membership in adult society in any number of ways. At the same time he also rejects being measured against the standards of childhood. Why?

Obviously, since the teenager is sociologically distinct from children and, in our culture, feels somehow superior, he does not want to be classed with them. But there is more to it than that, I would argue. It seems to me that what the teenager wants, the lever which he uses to break out of childhood, is more personal freedom. He demands freedom from parental control and domination and dependence. He cannot live by the standards of the sociological child because these would require him to knuckle under more than would be reasonable. My argument in fact is that what we demand of our children—that they be ideal, not mischievous—is too heavy a demand and is rejected by children as soon as they feel strong enough to assert themselves, i.e. at around the early teens. No longer able to stomach even the pretence of being an ideal child, the teenager somehow wishes to assert his individuality and capacity to make up his own mind.

What is the explanation of this heavy demand for ideal behaviour? Let us consider briefly the recent history of how children have been expected to behave. To begin with, the

Victorians, or perhaps the Victorian bourgeoisie, who certainly set the standard. The ideal child to the Victorian strikes us as odd because he resembles nothing so much as a perfect miniature copy of an adult. A child seems to have been expected, as soon as he was physically able, to speak, comport himself, think and even dress like an adult. John Stuart Mill, for example, had to teach his younger siblings while his elders were not teaching him. The ideal is idealized to the point of unconscious caricature in the American-invented ideal child, Little Lord Fauntleroy (but see White, 1970).

My contention is that the behaviour of Little Lord Fauntleroy is not a ridiculous caricature of Victorian ideals but a fair description of those ideals. I would also contend that Fauntleroy standards are still to a disturbing extent to be found lurking behind present-day criticisms of teenagers. If these critics were challenged to itemize what they would consider constituted good behaviour I think the disturbing similarity of their ideas to the Fauntleroy ideal would be clear. The 'well-behaved' teenager or child is a phantom with perfect manners, who speaks properly and only when spoken to, who defers to adults, who does nothing embarrassing or rebellious, and so on.

This view of how teenagers ought to behave strikes me as ridiculous and overdue for reform. Those Fauntleroy standards are almost pure adult: the value and worth of manners are not exactly obvious to children. Fauntleroy is permitted the odd childish trait, like expressing his emotions, but only within the framework of his otherwise adult behaviour. That we should judge our children and teenagers by such standards, that we should expect them to live up to such standards, that we should allow our 'strict' parents, probation officers and magistrates, to condemn deviations from such standards, is an anachronistic scandal. There is something deeply disturbing in the way deviations from Fauntleroy—behaving the way teenagers do, for example— are greeted with an hysterical outcry that the world is coming to an end. When we think about it we know better; but the outcry seems to be unthinking.

We have here, as I have said, another case of what seems to be the need for stability in our social lives; a need which no doubt has its psychological aspects. Deviations from the accepted standards are so shocking to some people that they feel personally threatened and that the world is crumbling. Here the problem is not one of no standards by which to operate, but the almost neurotic fear of those we have being undermined.

At first the Victorian situation might strike one as a nadir, but there are ways in which since then the situation has deteriorated. In particular the time which children are expected to remain sociological children has lengthened. Children in Victorian times were admitted into the adult world a lot earlier than they are now; this admission may have eased the strain on them a good deal. Bertrand Russell has related how this transition from child to adult sometimes took place with disconcerting speed, as when he found himself, a young lad, called on to be head of the household when Mr Gladstone dined there. Of course a price was to be paid for this early transition: the loss of childhood freedom. The working class child in particular would be sent out to work very early in his life and would rarely experience any of those things we think of as the pleasures of childhood.

Today the social pattern is very different. Today children spend the first four or five years of their lives simply playing; they then go to school until they are fifteen, or sometimes until they are eighteen or nineteen; and only then to a job or a university. Thus at least until they are fifteen our children are given no chance to participate in adult life. They must attend school where they are disciplined and controlled. At home they are usually economically completely dependent on their parents. Intellectually and emotionally they may be going through crises and what not, but they are still looked on as something inferior, and accorded few more privileges. In hide-bound working class areas there is sometimes a rule that when a child starts to work he more or less at once gets adults' privileges and treatment. But this is not very widespread. From my own experience and observation I would say that children begin energetically to chafe against this status of being socially or sociologically children as early as their thirteenth year.

Our social system, then, is structured so that normal school children reach physical puberty at least two years before they are legally allowed to leave school. At an age where in many cultures they would be heads of families and sociological adults they are still expected to conform to school-child standards, standards they are biologically and psychologically beyond. Up till school leaving, a certain amount of childishness on their part is tolerated, provided it is outside of school, although the ideal behaviour would still be Lord Fauntleroy. After school leaving, adults expect there to be a sharp transition, for the ideal *mores* of adolescence are much more adult than those of the child; Lord Fauntleroy ideals are stressed much more.

A further strain is caused by the fact that from puberty onwards the adolescent feels the urge to be like an adult in *some* ways—emotionally and sexually says Professor Carstairs—but he is not allowed the adult privileges he needs to do this; those ways in which he is expected to be adult are in comportment and responsibility, and when he does not behave in an acceptably adult fashion in these matters he is either attacked as 'rebellious', or sneered at as childish. The teenager is thus viciously squeezed between what he was and what he has not yet become.

The result of this pressure, or squeezing, together with teenage inclinations, may be seen in that there is a tendency for adolescents to consider themselves, or reconcile themselves to the fact of their virtually being, adults from the age of about fifteen or sixteen onwards. Similarly, a tendency may be detected for them to begin consciously to *imitate* selected adult *mores* from the age of thirteen onwards. Ours is an age when young men with styled haircuts may be anything from fifteen to twenty-five; when young girls, in their fashionable clothes and alluring make-up, could be anything from twelve to thirty. These are examples of teenagers *giving in* to the pressures on them to 'grow up'.

My interpretation of the rebelliousness of teenagers, then, is that while they want or are prepared to be adult in some ways (dress well, take an interest in the opposite sex) they still feel their differences from adults and will not bury them. They are not, for example, prepared to accept adults as their peers in all things. They may reject certain adult values (hard work, chastity, politeness, anti-violence [or violence], patriotism, and so on), at least for the time being. The usual view is that they put nothing in their place. My view is different. I think that they channel a great deal of ingenuity and creativity into inventing games, pastimes and new *mores* of social behaviour, dress, speech and culture, which serve the better to define themselves as a group. They create something, in these *mores,* which performs the useful social function of marking them off as a group from adult society until such time as they, as individuals, are prepared to enter it by accepting its values. Some of this is summed up more technically in Eisenstadt (1956, p. 46):

> Groupings of children or adolescents are common in every society, no matter what its structure. In all societies children are drawn together for various reasons, play together—often at being adults—and thus learn the various types and rules of co-operative behaviour and some universalistic norms which are of secondary importance in these societies. But it is only in universalistic societies that these groups become more articulated and develop a strong common identification . . .
>
> These groups develop, in part, as a defense against the expected future rôles, an attempt to maintain a pattern of relations differing from that expected in the future. But, on the other hand, orientations—latent or manifest—towards these future rôles already exist within these groups, as they exist in

most children's play groups in any society. These two attitudes—defense against future rôles and orientations towards them—are present in all these age groups and form some of their main components.

## Comparative observations

Now to exemplify all this a little further let me make some comparative observations. Many simpler societies provide better for the different biological and psychological stages of the growing human being than our own social structure does.

In the first place, the major physical stages of development are often paralleled, by and large, by a set of separate social stages in simpler or tribal societies. The major changes in the human body occur at about seven or eight; at puberty; and at the cessation of growth around twenty-one. In each of the stages between these changes, the growing person in many simpler societies has specific standards of behaviour, modes of speech and kinds of services to family and community which are expected of all persons in that stage, *and only of persons in that stage.* They have certain rights on and duties towards their family and the rest of society, rights and duties substantially different from those of persons in other stages. The various tasks connected with hunting, fishing, cooking, looking after the house and children, gardening, preparing for feasts and festivals, are so allocated that only people in certain stages may perform them, but that all must do their bit if they are to be completed. The tasks assigned to people in each stage generally progress in arduousness and responsibility towards the full-blown *mores* of adulthood. But there is little encouragement to veneration of this stage as a final end-in-itself. Children are not made to feel like deprived adults, longing only to grow up. The heavy social responsibilities and seriousness of adulthood are more often stressed; and besides, adulthood is not by any means the final stage, there are often several others beyond (father, grandfather, elder, etc.). Thus it is possible for an adjusted person to achieve satisfaction in any of the stages he happens to be in simply by striving to live up to the recognized standards of behaviour of the stage he is in. He is free from the restless longing for what is conceived of as the free-agent-status of adulthood which pervades our society. He realizes that he has more freedom at his present stage than he will have when he is older. No encouragement is given to the yearning for adulthood which secretly obsesses the young people of our society. Consequently, young people in such societies do not have a feeling of being oppressed, of being in an interregnum in which they are second-class adults. They can value their integral place in society as something special in itself. It is possible for both children and adolescents to enjoy a sense of direction—definite expectations of them—and a feeling of security.

In the second place, the fact that individuals undergo the transition from one physical stage to another at slightly different times is smoothed over in many tribal societies by marking off the corresponding social stages with clear, arbitrary lines. Newly born children are assigned to an age-set and they are not adults until that whole age-set is initiated. Difficulties arising from differences created by nature are thus smoothed over by social conventions. This is an instance of the simpler society being more conventional and our society being more naturalistic—for we employ semi-naturalistic criteria for adulthood. The rituals (*rites de passage*) which punctuate the life of the growing person in many simpler societies mark, more often that not, the transition of himself and his fellows from one social stage to another; a transition connected with, but not the same as, some biological or psychological change which has already, or is about to have, taken place.

Our society is quite different. Its principal institutions in childhood are the family and the school. But relations in the family are personal and individual (particularistic); relations in the school standardized and governed by abstract rules (universalistic). As Eisenstadt says (1956, p. 287):

> The modern family, despite—or perhaps because of—the great limitation of the scope of its activities, strongly emphasizes diffuse, particularistic collective values and relations. The family solidarity and emotional interdependence of its members are centred around these value orientations, which constitute the the main symbols of identification of the family group. In this respect, therefore, there is a basic difference between the structure of the family and the integrative principles of modern societies, which are orientated more towards universalistic, achievement and individualistic values. The basic structural discrepancy between the family and the occupational structure is a universal fact in modern societies, and is much more acute that in any primitive universalistic society.

The school, on the other hand, teaches universality, but does not provide goals or roles that are satisfactory. School roles are preparatory, not ends-in-themselves. School is segregated from the reality of adult life for which it is a preparation, hence artificial. Social maturity is postponed long beyond physical and sexual maturity. Eisenstadt sums it up:

Owing to the structural discrepancies between the family and the total social system, the development of hostility and competition between the generations is always possible. In these cases this hostility cannot always be easily kept within the bounds of communal solidarity, since this solidarity is weakened by the various structural differences (p. 289). . . . For this reason the child and adolescent always develops, although to various degrees, the predisposition to join in age groups in which the dignity of his current dispositions and values will be affirmed, within which a greater spontaneity of activities will be permitted, and which in some cases will also have a more direct relation to the symbols of identification of a total society, either the existing one or a new one to which he would like to develop (p. 166). . . . The rise of youth groups is due . . . to the relative inadequacy, from the point of view of the adolescent's needs, of the more official channel—the school (p. 289).

We demand that the growing person should remain at the social level of the school child whatever the biological or psychological realities, at least until the age of fifteen, and then suddenly become adult, in certain selected ways only, and remain pure Fauntleroy in others, without any intermediate stages. Both myths endorse Fauntleroy: the 'settling down' one allows Fauntleroy some scope in expressing his emotions; the 'bad lot' one sees the alternative to being adult and Fauntleroy as being juvenile delinquent, for the standard of what is good behaviour is set so high, so near Fauntleroy as not to be distinguishable from it, and deviations are greeted with the gravest of predictions. Here the comparative material demonstrates that the alternatives in our society: either, adult-cum-Fauntleroy, or delinquent, are not the only ones; possibly there are other ways of organizing society and other standards against which to see the behaviour of teenagers, standards which may be more admirable than Fauntleroy.

Against this pressure to be good little Fauntleroy children, or good little adults, teenagers are fighting a battle for recognition as an independent stage both different from, and intermediate between, childhood and adulthood. Teenagers, suffering disorientation from the absence of any acceptable *mores* and codes of behaviour being handed down by their adult seniors, have created these for themselves. No wonder adults either patronize or criticize and resent teenagers; for they have fought a battle for recognition, and won it! And if adults do not like the codes and *mores* of their progeny they have only themselves to blame for not providing better ones; all most adults who believe in the 'settling down' theory or the 'teenagers are a bad lot' theory give their children is complacent indifference and sermons about how they should behave in a more grown-up way on the one hand, or insults about how childish they are, on the other. There may be a psychological element in this resentment, but it is not relevant to my sociological purpose. Rather, I would like to stress that the adults—whichever theory they believe in—resent the teenagers for failing to be Fauntleroys—they never imagine that teenagers can be nice, 'well-behaved' people other than in Fauntleroy terms. Neither 'settle down' nor 'you are a bad lot' allows that there may be anything legitimate or normal in teenage behaviour. The pessimists are the worst of the two, however, since they hold that teenage rebellion is intimately connected with the increase in juvenile delinquency and this they take as a confirmation of the view that deviation from Fauntleroy is the beginning of the slippery slope. Alternatively, it could be argued that while in Victorian times there were two teenage stereotypes: Artful Dodgers and Fauntleroys (remember how quickly when Oliver Twist disappears with the books his benefactor's friend puts the worst interpretation on it), today we apply higher standards and expect there to be very few Dodgers, since there is little economic and social excuse for it. My contention amounts to arguing that teenage *mores* and teenage pop culture are not Fagin (who, as you remember corrupted Oliver).[3] However, the widespread view that the only alternative to the Fauntleroy-adult complex of standards is delinquency, undoubtedly yields an 'Oedipus effect',[4] since the teenagers accept the view and thereby tend to implement and reinforce it.

## What teenagers are trying to do

Teenagers, in general, I suggest, far from being the worthless, lazy, rebellious, criminal people they are often made out to be, have created by and for themselves valuable and viable social institutions which look as though they have solved a problem internal and endemic to all societies: how can an adolescent behave in a way that is between young and old? Rebellious teenagers are nothing new. If anything, the revolt of the younger generation against the next senior generation is as old as society. So strong is it that some tribal societies institutionalize hostile (or even avoidance) relations between parent-generation and children-generation and allow friendly or 'joking' relations only between the child-generation and the second succeeding or grandparent-generation. Why, then, should we be so interested in our present teenage rebellion? There are two reasons I can think of. One is that as more serious social problems, like hunger, old age, health, and so on, get taken care of, our interest swings round and focuses on issues not previously taken much notice of, although perhaps always with us. The second reason I would propose is this. If one can speak of any trend in these matters (and all this is frankly impressionistic, I offer it for what it is worth and for what can be made of it), there seems to have been a trend over the past few generations for parent-child relations to get progressively more permissive. Yet, if anything, the revolt of children against parents becomes more marked, if less violent (as I have hinted with my remark about the demise of the never-darken-my-door-again mentality). Why should there be as much or more revolt when the atmosphere is more permissive? Why, in fact, should the revolt more and more take the form of straight contrariness: teenagers are not just against adults, they want to be against adults diametrically, a you-say-black-I-say-white mentality? My answer is that the permissiveness has allowed teenagers to discover this gap in our social expectations which was concealed from them previously by the rigid infliction of adult dominance. There was a clear standard before, however unpleasant it may seem; that standard was 'non-adults must do as adults tell them without question, for children may be seen but not heard'. Now this standard is eroded and only the gap remains as to what standard shall be expected of teenagers. How is the challenge being met? Teenagers are creating, by and for themselves, in a striking affirmation of resourcefulness and creative capacity, a complete and acceptable set of rights and duties, of defined social standards suitable to their biological and psychological make-up. They have learnt from experience how to take care of certain matters which in many tribal societies are taken care of automatically.

But this teenage world tends to be ever more diametrically opposed to the adult world. This is because the adult world censures the teenagers' efforts. This puts the teenagers on the defensive and to turn the tables they get even more aggressively anti-adult.

In the teeth of the indifference, condescension, or even hostility of the rest of society, our teenagers have fallen back on their own resources. What they have produced may not be as negligible as those adults who resent it would have us believe. Consider the well-defined patterns of speech, dress, behaviour and even culture which distinguish teenagers nowadays; patterns which, it should be stressed, allow plenty of scope for individual variation. Also consider how original (i.e. to the rest of society, unorthodox) these patterns are. Adolescent speech is highly idiomatic and sometimes unintelligible to the uninitiated; adolescent dress succeeds in being both unlike adult dress and yet remarkably consistent over geographical and class distances; adolescent *mores* at work, at home, 'out' and courting are also different from those of the rest of society, and very similar within the group. These *mores* have a strength which allows their transmission to the constantly renewed membership of teenage society.

I am even prepared to maintain that the seemingly most worthless aspect of the teenage society (according to Wilson, 1964)—'pop culture'—reflects at least a certain amount of ill-digested education. Teenagers seem to be interested mainly in films, dancing and music; particularly the latter two. Significantly, they are less interested in television for which they often display contempt. Maybe because of its popularity with adults? . . . Let us ask ourselves just what it is that Tin Pan Alley churns out in such great quantities; it is verse set to music. It may not be *my* sort of verse and music, or yours; but it is *a* sort of verse and music.

To this it will no doubt be said that I am mistaking commercial products rammed down teenagers' throats for a genuine folk culture. My reply would be that it does not matter who invents pop music, it is teenagers who institutionalize it, who make it part of their *mores*.[5] They could easily reject it and once would have done so with the blessing of Tin Pan Alley—the establishment of the music industry hated rock-and-roll and was destroyed by it. I remember a striking television programme by Daniel Farson on pop music. A prominent popular music publisher was asked what he thought of teenage rock-music. He replied to the effect that it was a lot of rubbish. But why then was it popular? He said: 'they like it because the mums don't like it; the more the mums don't like it the more the kids like it. If the mums got to like it the kids'd drop it like a hot brick', or words to that effect. Accepting that the law of supply and demand has been modified by that useful applied science, advertising phychology, nevertheless, what is being demanded, supplied and bought in great quantities by a majority of young people is a sort of verse and music, and, in an important way, verse and music they have made their own. Those impatient to denigrate its level might reflect on the comparatively short time our economy has been able to allow both education and leisure time to the urbanized industrial masses. (We can ignore pre-industrial folk culture.)

It may be a hopeful sign that teenagers fill their leisure time creatively; it matters little that the efforts of that creativity are, as yet, to be found either entirely in social life or in rather mechanical pop music;[6] at least they are doing something creative. (Boredom, aimlessness, anxiety, violence would be far less creative alternatives—to which some, it is true, turn.) What all this creative energy might produce after a few hundred years of universal education of the present intensity, and of increasing time to utilize it, sustains some optimism.

## Conclusion

One conclusion which suggests itself to me is that any attempt to cope with teenage rebellion must take into account this fundamental fact of their situation: caught between adulthood and sociological childhood and finding both alternatives unsatisfactory. If we ride roughshod over this conflict we are unlikely to find ways to curb those excesses which really are harmful in teenage *mores*. My own view would be that while such matters as informal social behaviour can be stopped, they cannot be planned for. The most reasonable position would then be only to criticize and do something about stopping definitely harmful things like violence and hard drugs. And perhaps to attack the theory that the only alternative to adulthood or Fauntleroy is delinquency. We might leave the rest alone in the spirit that the teenagers are filling a gap in the system of expectations of our society, a gap which is better filled than not, and it would be very difficult and a bit repugnant to plan for its being filled (Young Pioneers?). Since the teenagers have solved a problem they did not create, they deserve rather more respect than our superficial myths about them betray.

# 4 The idea of social class[1]

There is nothing to prove the existence of a single predefined reality which can be christened class . . .

Aron (1957), p. 67

In the previous chapter my concern was to bring out how widely held beliefs play a role in explaining why people behave the way they do, and how the falsity of these widely held beliefs is crucial to understanding the behaviour engendering a social crisis. The false beliefs were called popular myths, and it was shown they become, in effect, part of the logic of the situation, both of the adults who believe them, and of the adolescents who have to cope with a world containing adults who believe them. It would not be difficult to envisage situations where the role of myths becomes more involved; where, for example, various segments of the society act on the basis of different and incompatible myths. Turning in this chapter from the topic of the separation of the generations to that of social stratification, I want to explore the further case of what happens when myths are so widely held that even sociologists accept them and act on them, just as the actors they are studying do, and which, for all that, remain no more than false beliefs.

The aim of this chapter is to explore, in a somewhat more technical case study than that in chapter 3, what might be called the problems of the naturalistic approach to society and social institutions. In the previous chapter the beliefs of adults about the nature of adolescents and adolescence were seen to have much to do with the friction between age groupings. This chapter looks at social stratification—a feature of social organization that has preoccupied sociologists. A simple naturalistic view will be set up to begin with and its difficulties progressively exposed. It will be argued that these difficulties are inherent to and insuperable within naturalism, which must thus be given up for a Hayekian convention-alism that is nevertheless (philosophically) realistic.

It would probably be impossible to over-emphasize the import-ance and interest of social class to sociologists. This interest of theirs seems to have some basis in its real importance. In nearly all societies, class pervades and influences the social organization. It is fascinating to explore its myriad manifestations in our society; the way it affects everything from our speech habits to our urban densities. And, of course, academics, being to some extent *déclassé* (and to some extent not), find the topic especially poignant. Perhaps as a result, the literature on the sociology of class is huge, and grows every quarter. Indeed the abundance and richness of the published material might suggest that the conceptual exploration on which this chapter embarks is hardly needed, since if there are any conceptual difficulties and confusions surrounding class they have hardly been impeding output. To answer this one could argue that the interpretation of this empirical work, the specification of what it 'means' and how it can be improved, may turn to a con-siderable extent on our having a clear conceptual understanding of class.

In this literature there are a number of rival schemes for defining the concept. This is my starting point: the fact that the concepts of class of Davis, Glass, Lipset and Bendix, Marshall, Ossowski, Rumney and Maier, Warner, and so on, differ from each other. But this chapter will not be yet another review and comparison of these rival schemes followed by a compromise forged out of them. Instead, an attempt will be made to go straight to the heart of the matter.

At the outset it may help to specify the points to be argued. The first thesis will be that the existing literature attempting conceptual clarification is vitiated by a confusion between the raw phenomena of social class and popular beliefs and theories interpreting these phenomena. Not only this, but the literature on social class is largely written in terms of these popular theories about social class which have been uncritically absorbed by sociologists. If these popular theories can be shown to be incoherent then their incorporation in the literature might go some way towards explain-ing the competing schemes, i.e. the incoherence, in the literature. That incoherent, i.e. false, popular theories are involved in what is being taken as raw data could explain difficulties in classifying that data. However, those who believe in these popular theories—and this includes most of us, as they are accepted even by sociologists of class—base certain of their social actions upon them.

Because someone has what his prospective employer considers a 'lower class' accent he may not get a job. The employer thinks there is a class system and that this chap, clearly being of a low class, would not get on with the other executive trainees—who are middle class, as is clear from their accents. Thus is re-inforced the idea that there is a class system and that one of its indicators is accent: accent indicates class, higher class leads to better jobs.

To penetrate this maze, in which the falsity of the popular theories is concealed by the fact that we all act upon them as though they were true (but not thereby making them true), I propose to subject them to close scrutiny and to see what follows if we take them to be false.

Put a little more traditionally, what I am investigating is what social class is,[2] or, better, how social classes are constituted. There seem to be three main candidates: an objective, or naturalistic, solution which says that social class is a system of readily identi-fiable groups within the society; a less objective or naturalistic solution which denies that the groups are readily identifiable, which says, that is, that the groups are there but are hard to pin down; and a third solution which denies that social class is any natural or objective groups at all. The main problem for partisans of the first solution is that, if classes are so readily identifiable, why is there such a large and incoherent literature on the nature of social class? The main problem for partisans of the second solution is to pinpoint those characteristics which will identify the groups. The main problem for partisans of the third solution is how to avoid seeming to deny the obvious, namely, the widely felt presence and (at least) semi-objective effects of the class system. I shall criticize the first two solutions and argue in favour of a version of the third, which could be called modified objectivism, or conventionalism, and which allows that the naturalistic solutions are understandable, but false, popular myths—popular myths which happen to be shared by sociologists.

This chapter, then, is about the relation between the concepts (or theories) of sociologists and the concepts (or theories) of ordinary people—the concepts (or theories) in terms of which ordinary people think and act. The background to the discussion is the general sociological idea that myths about society, especially popu-lar myths, or popular beliefs, or popular theories, about society—which are usually naturalistic—play varied and important roles in the workings of society. Functionalism recognizes this but tends on that account to endorse the myths, one way or another. My view is that the myths are by and large false and the sociologist, once he has exhibited their role, should criticize them and reveal their falsity if he is aware of it. With regard to social class, however, I am of the opinion that sociologists are themselves prisoners of the popular naturalistic myths and that this is a contributory cause of the wrangling and confused literature on social class.

This chapter will raise questions about social ontology (is class real?) which will not be directly confronted until chapter 6. But it may help if I indicate briefly at this point what my ideas on those questions are. Ontological conflict arises over whether social conventions are real. The view I hold is ontological pluralism: there are many different kinds of existent and real entities. Mountains exist, ideas exist, thoughts exist, social institutions and customs and traditions exist. It may be that there are degrees of reality connected with degrees of intersubjective testability. In this sense, mountains may be, in general, more real than social pressures, although one can easily imagine situations in which social pressures become the cardinal reality for an individual or group.

A confusion that must be avoided is the equation of nature and reality. Social conventions are not natural, but they are nevertheless real. Some conventions are more clearly recognized or acknowledged as conventions than social class. An example is money; and yet, in a funny way, money is taken to be a much firmer and clearer reality than class. Since the end of the gold standard, but even before that, money was a convention and seen to be a convention, yet there was a high degree of co-ordination between people's ideas about, for example, its value, even internationally. I suggest that this acceptance of the conventionality of money has allowed for a better co-ordination of our ideas about it than is possible with our ideas about class, which differ widely in their degree of naturalism as well as other things, and therefore are poorly co-ordinated and rather fuzzy.

To suggest some parallels. An example of a clear-cut yet very real convention would be the International Date Line. Everyone knows that it is not a natural line, yet it is easy to find and it is very real—crossing it is quite significant. Take, again, national boundaries like that between India and China. Since there is a myth[3] that nations are natural entities, it is widely believed that there must exist natural and just boundaries. Yet what is natural and just from the Indian side of the border is not natural and just from the Chinese side of the border. The situation is similar with class, which is like borders, and money, which is like the Date Line. The exchange value of money is much the same whether you have it or not and can easily and objectively be determined; the class boundaries and your position on them very often look different to you, to your neighbour and to your neighbour *qua* sociologist.

In short, then, many social institutions are conventions that seem to be natural because they are embodied in naturalistic myths. These conventions can be distinguished as having differing degrees of reality, depending on their fuzziness or intersubjective co-ordination. Those better co-ordinated are more real than those poorly co-ordinated. Money is well co-ordinated and therefore more real than class, which is poorly co-ordinated.

After an explanatory introduction to the common sense theory (pp. 95–7), I shall proceed: first to discuss the problem of defining social class (pp. 98–102); then to discuss the various attempts to describe class (pp. 102–6) and their relation to reality (pp. 106–18); then to propose that social class is an entity inferred from class phenomena or behaviour and that class behaviour is action based on theories (pp. 118–21); next to discuss how we have come by such incoherent theories (pp. 121–3), and what metaphysical problems make sociologists interested in class (pp. 123–6); finally I try to show (pp. 126–7) how my view succeeds, where class theories fail, in explaining the underlying problems better, and in accounting for the current myth that there has been an increase in social mobility.

### The common sense or Castle and Gate theory of class

The rich man in his castle,
The poor man at his gate,
God made them, high or lowly,
And order'd their estate.

Mrs C. F. Alexander,
*Hymns Ancient and Modern*

This quotation from a familiar Victorian hymn embodies a version of what I shall call the common sense or Castle and Gate theory of social class. The theory takes class to be a system of discrete groups of people, hierarchically arranged. Some such system of strata is a primary characteristic of nearly all societies. To the Victorians singing the hymn, social class, like the rest of the social order and its traditions, was God-given; it was just one of those facts of nature about which nothing could be done. Since that time the naturalistic tide has ebbed; people are no longer so prone to think of class as 'natural', 'inevitable' or 'right'. But they still do think there is some such system.

My reason for starting with the unsophisticated, widespread and popular Castle and Gate theory—as formulated in a hymn—is because science usually starts from some problematic theory, especially a common sense one. Especially in the social sciences we must start with common sense, because there is as yet nothing much in the way of more sophisticated problems and theories to start from. As will emerge in the course of the chapter, the attempts sociologists have made at sophisticated discussion of social class do not yield results that differ in any basic way from the fundamental common sense view I have outlined. As we shall also see, this popular theory turns out to be incoherent and inconsistent with known facts; hence highly problematic.

Why do most of us believe the society we live in has a social class system? It is no answer to the question to say, 'we believe society is divided into classes because so it is'. After all, not every idea we have is true and not everything that is true is known to us and believed by us. And we do not in general have ideas because we observed something and gave it a name—in this case 'social class'. How then did we come to mark off something called 'social class' and assign it to a special role in our society? We might try *The Oxford English Dictionary,* but it turns out not to be much help. It says the earlier usage was 'orders' of society (for example, 'lower orders') and that the modern sense comes partly from the constitution Servius Tullius is said to have given to Rome and partly from the modern sense of class as a group of particulars with common attributes.

But we need not go into the ancient history here of how we came to believe our society is ordered into social classes. We can simply begin with the fact that we have such a belief or theory about our society, and that the function of a theory is to explain. What facts does our common sense theory of social class come to explain?

It explains, first of all, why some people behave in a snobbish and offensive way towards others; why there are sharp differences of accent, education, income, style of life, etc., between people; and why there are discriminatory practices operating along the lines of these differences.

Besides explaining social differences between people, the common sense theory of social class explains the social organization, i.e. that there are not only differences between people but that these differences are means of organization into a system which we call society. If people are different, or at least do different things, in society, unless we are to have anarchy there must be some means of organizing them into a coherent system. Classifying them by their differences is one such means. Thus class differences are a means of social organization.[4] Only one further step is required for rendering this into a functional theory of class differences; simply to say that the function of class differences is to promote coherent social organization.

So social difference and social organization can be explained by reference to social class. It is my conjecture that this explanatory function of the Castle and Gate theory of class explains why we operate with this theory: it functions to explain aspects of our society.

My first thesis in this chapter will be that our common sense or Castle and Gate theory of a system of social classes does not explain those facts it is supposed to: it does not provide a satisfactory account of why existing social differences occur. Neither does it explain social organization or anything else. This is because it and all its weaker variants are either obviously false or extremely vague. The vast literature on the subject consists largely of attempts to reformulate the Castle and Gate theory so as to evade the difficulties—like vagueness, internal inconsistency, and failure to accord with very well-known facts. Successive definitions of social class have been offered which fail to cope with these problems of vagueness, inconsistency, or obvious counter-examples. In order to treat the literature as rationally as possible I shall try to show all this by showing how each of the variant theories can be obtained by weakening the Castle and Gate theory.

My second thesis will amount to this. It is a misdirection of effort to try to rectify the Castle and Gate theory of class. The classification of people into a system of readily and objectively identifiable social groups is false; it does not correspond to the facts about the people it classifies, but the classification itself, whether true or false, is itself an important social fact. Classes are neither 'natural', nor given, but entirely man-made. Members of a society classify themselves and each other into systems of social classes: since all classifications are conventional, it follows that the system of social classes we are alleged to possess is conventional and, I claim, is none other than a product of (though not the same as) the muddled common sense classification.

My third and last thesis is that it will be more profitable to study, explain and refute prevalent Castle and Gate ideas about classes than to make further attempts to modify them.

At this point the argument should move into an examination of the common sense theory and its derivatives, with respect to logical coherence, explanatory power, and accord with the facts. Unfortunately, before we can do this, a detour is called for. It is called for because the problem of the nature of social class, 'what is social class?', has often been taken to be the same as the problem of defining social class. What social class is, it is argued, all depends on what you mean by 'social class'. As we are discussing what social class is, we shall have to spend some time discussing the views of those who say this.

**Defining social class**

A long-standing discussion on the definition of social class fills the literature of sociology. Almost every text which touches on the subject of class advances a proposal as to how it should be defined, and rarely do two definitions coincide (except, of course, where one has been deliberately copied from another, perhaps an 'authority'). The problem, 'what is social class?', is vague; if it is a problem of definition it is the same as 'what does "social class" mean?' This problem, of defining the *words* 'social class', or finding the *meaning* of 'social class', is not serious; though the problem of how social classes are constituted is. It will not be hard to show this on general philosophical grounds. In addition, it can be shown by discussing the sociological literature, which will reveal an underlying concern with certain serious sociological problems, namely social differences and social organization.

What, we may ask, do people want a definition of the words 'social class' for? Obviously, they found that their ideas on the subject were not altogether clear, and hence they tried to gain clarity by the method of definition. Never for a moment did they question whether the Aristotelian theory that definitions help us to be clear is true. Indeed this theory is very convincing, as it rests on the view that we cannot know what we are talking about until we know what our words mean. Quite apart from the logical defects of this view, it is unnecessary: a sociologist might avoid this philosophical issue and plunge straight into sociology by asking the question: for what sociological purposes do you want to make your ideas clear? What is it about social class that makes you want to discuss it? In short: what is the sociological problem of social class? The answer, I would say, is that certain theories of society, especially Marx's, involved social class essentially and that it was these theories sociologists wanted to discuss. The definitions took so much discussion they almost never got around to the subject at hand (see below, pp. 123–6).

If asked why they wished to define social class, most sociologists would probably say something different: that they wished to do descriptive sociology, and a definition of class is an essential preliminary. Students of sociology, they might say, must be acquainted with the structure and characteristics of their society before they can progress to the theoretical and explanatory part of sociology. Class, they might say, is one of the most prominent characteristics of nearly all observed social structures—status hierarchies are to be seen in almost every society. This reply is all very well, but we may further ask why these preliminaries to descriptive sociology take so long. Generations of sociologists have been discussing the definition of social class, very few among these have ever got so far as the description of a class system. But if social class is a prominent feature of most social structures, it should not be *so* hard to circumscribe it.

Either explanation being accepted, that class must be defined in order to describe it, or in order to discuss certain theories which employ it, it is high time the preliminaries were over. If definition is a necessary preliminary and if we have yet to get a proper definition, then it is surprising that anything beyond preliminary work has been done. Yet it has. If we have a proper definition already, it is surprising there is so little agreement as to what it is. Yet there is. It would seem to me that we have yet to get the definition, but that it is hardly an essential preliminary since work goes on without it. Let us then return to the doctrine that definition is an essential preliminary, because we must be clear what we are talking about and the way to be clear is to use the method of definitions. The doctrine stems from Aristotle.

The logical difficulty alluded to above in Aristotle's doctrine is that in order to define one word you have to use other words, which, if those other words in their turn have to be defined, must lead to an infinite regress. The solution which Aristotelians offer to this problem is the so-called theory of ostensive definition: [5] some words can be defined without the use of other words simply by pointing at ostensible facts. We can say when pointing, *'that* is what I mean by a social class system'. This cuts off the regress. If social classes are such ostensible facts that we cannot do descriptive sociology without knowing the meaning of the words 'social class', we should be able to define 'social class' ostensively: if social class it not ostensible, since descriptive science begins with the ostensible, we can do, or at least start doing, descriptive sociology before defining social class. Either way definition is redundant, even from the traditional Aristotelian viewpoint. Yet the sociologist postpones his descriptive sociology until he has the definition. To explain this I think we have to bring in disagreement. Once the course of defining is embarked upon an awkward fact comes up: the definitions are not all the same. If there exists something like the facts, like objective social reality, we will want to eliminate all bar one of these differing definitions of what it is. Problem: how can we eliminate what is erroneous and be left with only what is true? Answer: by comparing these definitions with the ostensible facts. We can then, if we wish, raise the question of whether there is anything like common characteristics shared by these systems we have pointed to which might identify social class and be looked for in the definitions. In this way we might hope to get at the true core of the definitions of social class, the core which corresponds to the facts, the core which characterizes it and differentiates it from other kinds of social ordering. What this amounts to, however, is the admission that, though class *characteristics* are ostensible and thus belong to descriptive sociology, *classes* are not. Now, this being so, it follows again that even from the Aristotelian viewpoint descriptive sociology can precede definition of the word 'social class'.

To my line of attack it could be objected that vital questions are being begged. How, it could be asked, can we assume that Britain and the United States have a system of social class and ask what its ostensible characteristics are, before we know what class is? It is not much good when we are trying to isolate the characteristics of a thing just to assume, before we know what it is, that when we look at British and American society we will see it there. It is hard to get round this objection. The main reason it is hard to get round is because it is irrelevant. The main problem which the definition of social class is intended to solve is indeed the problem of whether social classes are ostensible or not. You do not have to bother defining the institutions of a General Election or the House of Commons before discussing them; they are ostensible. It is a little strange that the chief obstacle to a descriptive sociology of class, then, is that we are prevented from reporting our observations by not knowing what is observable!

To put it another way: to ask for a definition of class before undertaking study which will yield a theory of class is to put the cart before the horse. It is precisely because our ideas on class are vague that we feel the need for a theory of it and its workings. When we have developed such a theory it will have embedded in it such definition of class as is necessary for its purposes.

Another answer to the infinite regress criticism of the Aristotelian theory of definitions is the so-called theory of working definitions. Suppose we are trying to get at the true core buried in our differing definitions of the class system; we begin with a working definition which represents our intuition approximately; then we compare the definition with the facts and see if it is adequate; it is usually not very adequate; having found its inadequacy, we now know it has to be modified and in which way; and so on. In refining the definition the better to accord with the facts as we see them, we also come to learn more facts and to revise the way we see them. Thus, by beginning from simple intuitive working definitions, we learn and we refine them; we do not stand pat upon them.

This appealing theory seems very rational. Marshall, however, perhaps because he favoured the method of defining class ostensively, has argued strongly against this theory (1950, pp. 87–8):

THE IDEA OF SOCIAL CLASS

If we start with a word—class—we have already made important assumptions. We are assuming that, because the word is commonly and usefully employed, it must express a definable concept. We may proceed to review all the objects which it generally denotes and to identify the concept by observing their common characteristics. We may then exercise our ingenuity in composing a definition that covers all known varieties, and, in fact, behave exactly like an International Conference achieving unanimity through a formula. The process, when thus crudely described, appears obviously futile. But it is not easy to shake oneself entirely free from the tyranny of words.

Marshall's argument is that when you adopt the theory of working definitions you are making the unwarranted assumption that there is something to work towards. Unless you made this assumption—that there was something to work towards, or at least error to work away from—proceeding by working definitions would be futile. We can also see that the method of beginning with a working definition presupposes the faulty ostensive theory. When we have a working definition we have to be able to compare it to the facts, and the facts must thus be ostensible enough to be compared to the theory. And if they are ostensible, how have we become bogged down in definitional discussion?

Marshall's warning against 'the tyranny of words' is very valuable: just because our language contains the words 'social class' we are not free to assume that there is some clear and definite concept here which corresponds to part of the world and towards a definition of which we should strive. I would go a step further and suggest that we should avoid discussing concepts altogether because they do not have truth-values, only pragmatic values. We cannot really ask whether a concept is true, or corresponds to the world; we can only ask these questions of theories. It is more fruitful to discuss people's ideas or theories about the system of social class; there is no need for us to accept that because all statements of our ideas use the concept 'class', they have a rational or essential core which is true. It is characteristic of modern natural science that it has abandoned conceptual essentialism for conceptual nominalism.[6] Only in biology has essentialism borne fruit; and there, if we consider the animistic roots of essentialism, it is perhaps understandable, biology being one of the few fields where animism is acceptable. To indulge in a homily: we would do better in sociology to get on with discussing the problems and theories that are our concern and leave the words we use to take care of themselves; they will get their meaning from the context of our discussion. I proceed to the discussion.

## Models of the structure and recruitment of the class system

Sociological usage is to distinguish three types of stratification system: caste, estates and class—each less rigid than its predecessor. I follow British anthropologists in refusing to lump caste together with other stratification systems. Caste is an historically unique economico-religious complex to be found only in the subcontinent of India and the areas of its most immediate cultural influence. Estates are also left aside because the argument will employ *a priori* models of stratification systems not tied down to anything so specific as post-medieval Europe. To begin with, a simple model.

Imagine a society in which the following state of affairs obtains. There are three social classes, arranged in a complete hierarchy. There is no continuous shading over between the classes but a sharp break which marks the limit of each. The hierarchy of classes corresponds roughly to other hierarchies of accent, area of residence, style of dressing, education, family background, income, manners, source of income, and so on.[7] That is, people in the middle of the class hierarchy will also be in the middle of these other hierarchies, and people at the top will be at the top, etc. Most of these other hierarchies have no sharp breaks: there are borderline cases where we may be unsure whether, for example, a shade of accent is of the upper class or the middle class. This means these other *hierarchies of class characteristics* are no reliable guide to the discontinous class system such as the one we are constructing. Class membership is and has to be determined by some other clear-cut criteria (to be discussed later).

We should remember that any theory of class comes to solve certain problems and we should start by discussing whether it succeeds. The model we have outlined would certainly explain social differences. It says that everyone is assigned to a class in a simple, unambiguous way and that people in classes are possessed of certain characteristics which are also hierarchically ordered. Thus someone born into the upper of the three classes will have a distinctive accent, education, style of life, and so on. These are attributes or characteristics of a person's class position. The model also explains how social differences are means of social organization. Since the classes are ordered by some deeper or infra-principle than differences of characteristics, there is some logic in assuming the state of affairs to be such that those who are high in this ordering, according to the deeper principle, should also be high in all the other orderings. Thus, the model does solve the initial problems, but it raises the question of what is the deeper principle; what criteria determine how each class is filled? This is the question: how do people get assigned to their positions in society? By birth, by law, by general consensus, by conquest, by purchase, by default, etc. In regard to class, only one distinction is needed among these various ways: law or something else. Class is either a legal category or it is not. A *man* can assign people to class-positions only if his word is law (a man promoting his individual or family position, where some mobility is possible, is not determining the whole class system); the law, or some surrogate of the law, is the only *institution* which can do the job. So these two, men and institutions, can be collapsed into one: law. If people are not assigned to the class-position by law, let us say they are assigned otherwise, by 'Other Forces'. Other Forces can be social wholes, historical or social or economic forces, racial unconsciousness, 'natures', God, gods, etc.

Let us now work out the three-class model in terms of law and Other Forces, beginning with law.

On the law interpretation of the model a person has the characteristics of the upper class because he is a member of the upper class. He is not a member of the upper class because he has the characteristics; he can be a member of the upper class only if he is legally assigned there. This interpretation stands to reason, in a way: a man does not wear a cloth cap because he *is* a member of a class; rather, he has adopted (or been taught) a norm of behaviour because he *thinks* he is a member of a class to which he *thinks* such behaviour is typical and appropriate. A man does not have an aristocratic drawl because he is an aristocrat; but rather because whoever brought him up and gave him his accent *thought* it appropriate and typical to his class-position; and he has not subsequently seen fit to resist. (Such a move need not have been conscious, of course, especially since we speak of education.)

Certainly there are people who imitate the upper class: one of the charges constantly laid against upstarts and social climbers is that they adopt manners and modes of living not appropriate to their real class status. In making these charges we assume a 'real' class status; in other words, we assume that there are genuine aristocrats, bourgeoisie, workers, and therefore there can be fakes. The fakeness of fakes turns not simply on characteristics—a fake looks like a member: to find whether he is really a member we have to investigate whether he was recruited by bona fide means, or whether he only pretends to have been. In that it provides a clear-cut basis of recruitment, the law is important. It would not be hard to imagine recruitment by means which left no way of distinguishing real from fake.

Three principal means of recruiting people to classes have been enshrined in law from time to time; birth, religion, and race. Of course, such means of recruitment can work both positively and negatively: they can assign you to your place, or they can restrict your possibilities; they can be sufficient or merely necessary. If the law prescribes more than one criterion for belonging to a given class, the problem of how to classify those who possess less than all of them will lead us into an unduly complicated argument. So let us search for societies in which one criterion is a necessary and a sufficient means of recruitment. The law interpretation in this strong form would consist of cases where birth, or religion, or race was necessary and sufficient to determine class-position. My search for actual historical examples was unsuccessful. As to birth: birth into a position in a pre-existing hierarchy was *the* legal characterization of class membership in medieval Europe and hence it should be the strongest example, but is not in fact quite strong enough an example: birth was sufficient and almost but not quite necessary; other means of allocation existed, such as marriage, the church, etc. There was social mobility. As for religion: there is a prevalent myth that religion is in all societies as important as allegedly it was in medieval Europe—yet this is not so: many societies are known where the wrong religion was simply a disqualifying factor as regards recruitment to the higher class, or even to the system at all; usually religion is necessary but not sufficient. Although there have been cases where the religion of the top class has been a secret rite and only admission to it constituted upper-classness.

But let us return to medieval Europe. In it a Jew, like an infidel in Islam, found his religion determined his class possibilities (life chances?) to a large extent, but not entirely: it mainly put an upper bound on them, but even that not strictly. As to race: in contemporary South Africa, in Imperial Japan and, some say, from time to time in China, being or not being a member of the chosen race (non-whites, foreigners and barbarians respectively) was a major class assignment criterion, if not the only one. Semi-legal 'restricted' residence areas were known in the United States until recently. In South Africa, race is virtually, but not quite, necessary and sufficient to determine class in a two-class system. In the other cases, race was merely a necessary condition.

So much for the law interpretation of the model and (rather shaky) examples of it. What about the Other Forces interpretation? Plato and Aristotle put forward a theory that men's 'natures' assigned them to classes, and that they should come to rest in their 'natural' classes was 'just'; for their natures were given to them by the gods. Naïve Christians, not necessarily Victorian, have held that the social order, and especially the system of social stratification, are God-given and therefore God-endorsed. Their view, presented in more or less sophisticated forms, has been used often enough to attack attempts at social reform and social change. Again, some functionalist sociologists, like Kingsley Davis,[8] have argued that as people differ in what they can do, and as what they can do differs in its value to society, differentials of status are more or less inevitable, not to say valuable to them and to society. There is class in Russia as well as America, because Russia could not abolish the basic fact of different human capacities, and thus different contributions to social survival.

The Platonic and naïve Christian views are not worth discussing. Kingsley Davis's is more interesting but does not I think stand up to close scrutiny. Assuming that the higher classes are in fact filled with those whose value to the society is highest, who or what in America sees to it that socially worthless people do not infiltrate the upper class? How does the co-ordination come about between being especially valuable to the society and being a member of the upper class? In the Soviet Union it is the State machine which sees to it; what does it in America? Davis's answer I suppose would be along functionalist lines: had a person of low value and capacity to the society entered the high class he would get pushed down by competition. This would be a functional theory of Davis's explanation of class. On Davis's theory, if class assignment were once legalized, then frozen, the classes should lose their relative statuses once they no longer have survival value. But what of the British aristocracy and the Boston four hundred? Their survival value is questionable; their social status unquestionable. Davis's theory certainly cannot explain the prestigiousness of being able to trace one's family link to before William the Conqueror in England, or back to the Pilgrim fathers in the United States. Besides, there are people of high value to these societies, like *nouveau riche* and inventors, whose class standing is rarely commensurately high. On Davis's theory, great thinkers should belong to the upper classes whereas never were they so middle class as in twentieth-century America.

So much for some less interesting and important cases of Other Forces handling recruitment. Now what about the forces of history? The only theory I know of, worth discussing here, is Marx's of the capitalist society of the nineteenth century, if such a society has ever existed as he pictured it. Marx did not say that class membership was then legally definable, if anything he would have said that stratification is much more fundamental than law. He suggested that in the inevitable progress of history a society emerged in which some people owned the means of production and other people were their employees. He argued that the logic of their objective situation *vis-à-vis* the means of production (the source of all real power), forced them into separate classes. He argued that the situation was such that the classes would be forced further apart until the employees could abide it no more and they would revolt against the owners. Thus it was not being born into a class which gave you its characteristics, but the objective situation which you faced as a born owner or worker which compelled you to act in certain ways.

Having worked out interpretations of the model where class membership is determined by law and where it is determined by the forces of history, we can now discuss the extent to which either interpretation of the model corresponds to the patterns of structure and recruitment in present-day Britain and America. The answer will be that they definitely do not.

## Comparison of the models with reality

To begin with, there is obviously no discrete class hierarchy in either country along anything like medieval or 'estate' lines. The hierarchy, if hierarchy there is, is dense: between any two points in it there will be an intermediate one. Moreover, none of the three examples I gave of legally controlled recruitment (birth, religion, race) fits the three separate classes' model because they give rise to ample undecidable cases. In other words, at best, the hierarchy we live in has no sharp breaks and ample ambiguous and undecided cases, so that the lines cutting between upper, middle, and lower class are more arbitrary than the lines cutting between red, orange, and yellow on the spectrum. I shall now merely show that both legal and Other Forces' interpretations of the model give rise to borderline cases and ambiguities; that this undermines the model completely I shall show later in the section.

A legally instituted system of birth or race qualifications for class membership gives ample opportunities for borderline cases: where does a birth system allow us to place illegitimate sons of the youngest sons of peers; where does a race system allow us to place octoroons? Even with religion there is room for borderline cases; there exist in all religions areas of doctrine and practice which are not fully mapped out and laid down, and sometimes the variations people make in these areas will move dangerously close to the beliefs of the religiously unacceptable. Any good book on sects and heresies will point up the multitude of possible variations here.[9] Perhaps where the law provides or endorses a decision-procedure on class status,[10] something resembling a discrete system is possible, but religious differences are rarely a factor operating over the whole of any system; rarely, if ever, have they marked the differences between all classes. Jews have entered the English aristocracy; and Coptic Christians had a very high class position in Egypt.

Perhaps, then, none of the legal determinants of class is as clear-cut as we should like them to be for our three discrete classes' model. Where borderline cases are possible and they are arbitrarily decided, then the issue is confused because it means at least two factors are now deciding how classes shall be recruited: the law and the arbitrary deciding authority cannot be operating on the same principle (or the arbitrary authority would be redundant). South African law segregates people by *race;* Racial Classification Boards segregate people on *their judgment of race.*

Incidentally, it is the logical aspect of the situation, not its being legally determined, which raises the uncomfortable, ambiguous, and borderline cases. This can be shown by reference to the Other Forces' rather than the legal interpretation of the model. Borderline cases and ambiguous cases arise whether 'nature', God, or social necessity does the assigning. The Marxist account sits equally uncomfortably on the three-class model because, in addition, it speaks mainly of only two classes (the working class and the capitalist class): Marx's analysis was mistaken already for the nineteenth century. Now Marx could easily have postulated three classes: for, obviously, he had noticed the existence of the middle classes; but he probably disposed of them *because* he thought they were borderline. He disposed of them, incidentally, by saying that they are a disappearing residual group (cf. Walton, 1970). (This turned out to be in flagrant contrast to the facts.)

Purely for internal reasons, then, this three discrete classes' model—whether legal or not—is far from being as obvious and straightforward a scheme as it at first seemed. It would be difficult, if not impossible, to find anything in the world even roughly resembling it.

To sum up. A class system with three distinct classes with sharp breaks between them, and its membership unambiguously recruited by a single factor, is neither a true picture of our society nor a particularly unambiguous model. I would argue, however, that this model is extremely important: it is the fundamental model behind the Castle and Gate theory of social class.[11]

Continuing the attempt to get a true theory of our class system that will also solve the problems it should, namely those of explaining social differences and social organization, we remember that our first model solved the problems but turned out not to resemble the facts and to be ambiguous. Let us modify its components as systematically as possible to bring it more into line with the facts.

107

We shall continue to operate throughout with the idea that there are three classes. But we shall drop at once the idea that they are unambiguously discrete. For the moment, we shall retain the idea that there is one single criterion which determines a person's class. We then raise the question whether it is the case in Britain today that a person's position in the class system is monotonously dependent on: birth, or race, or religion? The answer is no. Well, perhaps it is dependent on one of the other attributes: wealth, or accent, or education, or style of life, occupation, etc.? No to the first four, but what about occupation? In his article on social class and ideology, MacRae (1961) points out that in every society jobs are ranked in the same prestige order. Cannot we say that recruitment to the class system more or less corresponds to position in this job ranking? Assume for a moment it does. We can then make a destructive dichotomy. The question arises whether people (1) are in those jobs because of their class-position, or (2) have their class-position on account of those jobs? (1) seems unsatisfactory. Jobs may help us to recognize putative members of a class, but they do not discriminate true from false members. Not all professors are middle class, not all millionaire executives are upper class. If (2), since there is so much prestige attached to certain jobs there is bound to be competition for them. What is the criterion for deciding between these competing claims? Ability to meet this criterion will determine job and hence class. Who is 'fit' for what job will depend upon how the social structure works, and what the criterion encourages. Suppose the favour of the powerful is the way to get jobs—this will encourage hierarchy and choke off access to the powerful. So (1) will arise again. It remains unsatisfactory.

Our next modification is to consider the case where no single determinant of class is necessary, but one of two or more characteristics may be sufficient. If being born into the upper class is not your good fortune, you may still become a member of the upper class by being both wealthy and well-educated. This case could be ignored where there were sharp breaks between the classes, because once the determinants are multiplied, borderline cases are inevitable and the discrete model would break down in most situations (we exclude the situation of a perfect correspondence between all the characteristics, so that, for example, education, wealth, and high birth always go together). But having discarded the idea that classes are discrete, we must consider this new case where two or more characteristics are sufficient. Before going to any detailed analysis, we should notice that dropping the idea of discreteness raises the vexed question of recognition. Previously we have talked blithely of who is and who is not a member of a class, leaving the problem of how we *know* which class a person belongs to to one side. But now recognition becomes central, and we can no longer do that.

The problem of recognition is not merely a technicality, but a serious problem. The Castle and Gate theory we began with was certainly objective: castles and gates are clear enough, and so are the inhabitants of castles and the leaners on gates. The problem of recognition arises because the intersubjective testability of the theories we are discussing begins to be watered down. Let us, then, begin with the strongest form of recognition. We can know when a person is a member of a class because we can see that he is, we can observe he is. In other words, social classes are readily identifiable groups of people which can be observed. But if social class was so ostensible this enquiry would never have begun. Yet I do not think the eminent names involved here should be let off without a mention: Durkheim asserts that social institutions are observable and Radcliffe-Brown holds that even social structure can be observed.[12] As neither presents any arguments in favour of his views it is difficult to discuss them; it is even difficult to under-stand them: imagining trying to do something as simple as observing the present-day class of swans in London reveals at once the difficulties involved in the claim that direct observation is pos-sible. Inasmuch as we cannot observe a class of particulars which is objectively easily circumscribed like swans, surely we cannot see how there can be talk of observing social classes. So we must conclude that seeing the class of swans in present-day London means, for Durkheim at least, recognizing an object as a swan (classifying it) when encountering it in present-day London. To come back to social classes, although we cannot point to the upper *classes* any more than to classes of swans, we can point to *people* and say 'that man is typically lower class' or 'there goes a typical aristocrat', just as we can point at a bird and say 'here is a swan'. Although the classes cannot be observed, the individual member-ships to the classes can be. How is it that we can make such state-ments; how do we recognize people as members of this or that class? Presumably by their *class characteristics*: an English aristocrat will wear tweeds, speak with a drawl, pop in and out of St James's clubs, have a town house in a good district like Knights-bridge or Chelsea, have a place in the country, and so on. The theory, then, is that by examining people's characteristics we get an indication of their class-position. We are still assuming that they have the characteristics because of their class-position and not vice versa. Birth, or relation to the means of production, are hardly observable (descent and ownership are abstractions); but all the hierarchies subsidiary to birth, race, and religion, such as wealth

109

and education, are observable (wads of cash and diplomas are not abstractions).[13]

So now we come back to our question: can we say membership in the upper class is determined either by birth, or by wealth plus education? Assume that birth is sufficient; *and* that neither wealth nor education is sufficient, but the two together are sufficient. How is it, then, that a person becomes a member of the upper class when he has wealth and education: is he there on account of the money and education, or has he them because of his class membership? If we assume that the man who has money and education is *thereby* a member of the upper class, then we have a completely new theory: *anyone manifesting the characteristics of a class is a member of that class*: one cannot be a fake by manifesting characteristics of a class to which one does not belong: there is no 'belonging' to anything any more, only possessing the characteristics. Since we have assumed that one characteristic—be it birth, or wealth and education, or any other characteristic—suffices for class membership, one cannot be a fake, unless of course, one forges a birth certificate or a bank account. The theory is that upper class membership is the same as either wealth and education or birth (or both); these are no longer (forgeable) membership cards, but (objectively) true membership lists. At once the question arises: who or what determines that people with such and such characteristics, and not other characteristics, are members of such and such a class? After all, land-owning is a class characteristic both in Britain and in the USA, but it is characteristic of different classes in each country. The question, again, is not just technical; it is the problem of the degree of objectivity, which has now become most poignant; who is the person who recognizes, who provides the criteria for class membership—who draws up the membership list?

The situation here is odd. Normally when a theory is watered down it gets less and less open to criticism. Here we find a case where weakening the original objective theory does not do this. We started with a simple three-class model and a single criterion of class and weakened the theory to allow that any one of a set of characteristics suffices as a criterion. This stresses the arbitrariness of the class system described by the theory, as we have just seen. Thus, weakening the theory leads to the morass of subjectivism. But the theory is open to even more severe criticism on account of its being weaker.

As I have claimed before, no single characteristic is sufficient; thinking of counter-examples is too easy. Assuming that more than one characteristic is sufficient leads to interesting counter-examples. Imagine Mr B., who has a sharp cockney accent *and* a million pounds; or imagine upper class party-giver Mrs M., who has none of the attributes except style of life and intimacy of contact, yet is counted (let us ignore the fact that 'is counted' is here problematic) a member of the upper class. If the characteristics are not in accord in indicating one class-position, how do we know which to take note of? Further, both these counter-examples would provide counter-examples to the theory that one must needs possess all the attributes associated with a class before one can be counted as a member of that class.

Thus, the weakened theory has to be discarded. Two openings for weakening the theory further seem to crop up here. One is to assume that the characteristics are a *probable* determinant of class; the other is to say that they can be weighted and added into an *index* of class-position.

The first move introduces probability: instead of allowing us to infer high class from, for example, high income, it only allows us to infer *probable* high class from high income. My argument against the efficacy of this modification is as follows.

Question: what are we inferring from what? Is it probable that high class people have high income, or is it probable that someone with high income is of a high class? The one says that there is class and we can infer about income from it; the other says that there is income and we can infer class from it. We are back at the question of whether class membership determines characteristics or characteristics determine class membership. Now: if class probably determines income, how are classes recruited? If income determines class, then income is more objective than class and we explain social differences and organization by income —class is redundant. Thus we come again to the problem of recruitment.

If we are told, 'high income leads to high social class', we know where we are; this solves our problem of what determines as well as of what recruits: one is recruited to the upper class by making or having money. But if we are told, 'high income probably leads to high class', the problem is left open. 'High income probably leads to high class' entails 'high income more often than not leads to high class membership'.[14] Yes, but what about those left-over cases where it does not; how are *they* determined? Not by high income! So, the question arises again: how are high class members recruited? Here again the watering down raises more problems than it solves.

Probability is resorted to in order that counter-examples can be kept at a safe distance. There are counter-examples to the theory that high income determines high class. To say high income probably indicates high class accepts the counter-example but

111

renders it innocuous. But only at the price of giving up income as a determinant. Yet it is determinants, not indicators, probable or otherwise, that we are interested in. What then are the determinants of the system which is probably indicated by wealth? Why might rich people be upper class?

A number of answers are possible: (*a*) rich people are the most socially useful—the social function of the person determines his class; (*b*) rich people are cleverer at being socially useful—the capability of the member to exercise his function determines; (*c*) the will of God—who likes or has smiled on rich people; (*d*) the historical destiny of society—which assigns that role to rich people. All these have been discussed above. Only one possibility now remains: that class and its characteristics are still the same thing, but in a subtler way, namely as weighted probabilities of characteristics, the so-called index of class-position. This introduces the problem of how to weigh the various factors so that we can have an index of class-position. The thesis is that we can sum a person's characteristics, after they have been duly weighted, according to their relative importance as rankings in the society, and this sum will be an index of class. If we normalize the range so that everything lies between 1 and 100 we can then ask people how many classes they think we have, and where they lie, and fix ranges over which we shall call people: for example, lower class 1–30, middle class 35–70, 30–35 intermediate, and so on. This is a very appealing method of discovering class membership, which completely leaves aside the question of how that membership is determined or recognized (usually adherents of this theory are also adherents of the recognition theory, as I shall argue below), and allows for borderline cases. First, however, we should take the theory in its strongest form, where it would be said that this indexing is simply a sharpening of the things we intuitively take into account when trying to guess a person's class. The question is, what determines a person's class? Answer: mutual recognition along the lines of our indices. So the characteristics have become the determinants at last. I shall deal with the index part of the theory first; the recognition component comes later.

Weighting has been introduced, we remember, to cope with counter-examples to a simpler model. But it does not do the job. The claim that 100 per cent in some hierarchies (income, birth) was necessary and sufficient to give 100 per cent in the class hierarchy could be refuted by the fact that there are people in the upper class who have neither money nor birth (Mrs M.). The claim that no one factor is sufficient to raise one to the top class can be refuted by the fact that some people are upper class and yet have *nothing but* their money or their birth. With these two counter-examples the attempt to construct a theory with indices is demolished.

We have exhausted by now all the possibilities of rescuing the theory that there exists a single class hierarchy which we have been assuming all along in our model, even after having rejected the thesis that classes are discrete. Sociologists, like everyone else, include in their ideas of the class system an implicit, and sometimes an explicit (cf. Marshall, 1950, p. 90), notion of hierarchy;[15] the class system is conceived of as being hierarchically ordered. From common sense theories upwards we all seem agreed that the notions of ranking, of 'upper' and 'lower' etc., are central to what we mean by a system of social class. The question here is: to what extent is this system ordered? Is, especially, the ordering complete; that is to say, is any class superior or inferior to every other class?[16]

I suggest we begin with the theory that the social classes themselves are hierarchically ordered, though the set of individuals within each class is not necessarily hierarchically ordered. This amounts to saying that the set of classes is ordered such that for every two distinct classes one is lower than the other (no class is equally high as any except itself). The very last model contains the hierarchical ordering of all individuals. It is essential to this model that each person has his index number exactly determinable —at least in principle. Assuming that an individual has the index number 36–37 will lead to the impossibility of dividing people into hierarchical classes, in view of the existence of borderline cases. Let me explain.

If a person is, for class purposes, a Euclidean point, then there is no problem. A point has no part, no area if you like, and cannot therefore have the index number '36–37', which is a range. But as people are not really points, we would have constantly to round their index numbers. Accepting this, consider for a moment someone who lay near the borderline; his position would be clear. What about someone on the borderline? For the sake of simplicity, we could say all people on the border belong to the class below. But this creates a new borderline between the class below and the class above, so how shall we classify those that lie on that? If we go on including those on the border into the class below, everyone eventually ends up in the class below. There will only be one class.

Now we can go one step back to the case where the classes are ordered hierarchically but the individuals are not. We cannot go back to a model where both the individuals and the classes are partially ordered, because this would amount to a confession that there was no class system—only some scattered hierarchies. And we have already disposed of attempts to construct a strict hierarchy of all individuals. This ordering we are now considering seems reasonable enough, even if it does leave us with two comparatively minor difficulties; minor, that is relative to the problem solved— that of ordering. The one difficulty is the problem of ordering within classes, which, since it is partial, means that some people may be undecidable cases; the other is the problem where to draw, on the partially ordered set of all individuals, the borderlines between classes.

As to the first problem: to say we have difficulty assigning a person to his place is not to say that he does not have a place; as to the second, 'It may be difficult to determine the class membership of a particular individual or even marginal groups. This does not deny the reality of classes' (Rumney and Maier, 1953, p. 141).

However, although separately considered, each of these two difficulties is quite minor and need not affect the success of our ordering; together they demolish the whole idea that there is a hierarchy of classes. The reason is as follows. Take the undecidable cases. Are they near the border or not? Since it is not clear whether $x$ is lower than $y$, and we know $y$ is just above the border of the class, we do not know whether $x$ is in the class or not. If there are $x$s in the border area then we cannot be sure where to draw the line, so the border becomes ambiguous. Now if the border is ambiguous how do we know it is there? To this it could be replied that we cannot draw a line on the spectrum between red and orange, or yellow and green, but that does not belie the fact of these colours being different. Unfortunately, what it does belie is the self-sufficiency of colour-talk. Whenever precision is required about electro-magnetic waves, colour-talk will not do; and to explain colour appearances, colour-talk is totally inadequate. For with the spectrum there is a deeper level involved which explains surface colour appearances and is precise—wave-length. That we see colours, and that we see the colours we do in the way we do, can be shown to be dependent on wave-length, conditions, and eye-response. It is easy to get confused about 'obvious' colour differences. If a colour is ambiguous we can go under the surface to the physical reality. Is there any similar court in which we can appeal cases of ambiguous social class membership? We have reviewed many in this chapter. The only objective one we have left is God. If we appeal to the God of Mrs Alexander, with his castles and gates, we may get a clear answer. But what if God has become sophisticated since then? What if, for example, he is a God who has read the physicist Heisenberg? In simple terms, Heisenberg says that there are no dots but only minimum distances, under which the reality (the facts) is ambiguous. There is no question of clearing up the ambiguity here; God has ordained that, to questions about certain parts of the universe, only ambiguous answers can be true. That God has been ambiguous about classes is precisely my position.

The fact is that there is no border between red and orange, yellow and green—these orderings are arbitrary impositions on the spectrum of wave-length; they are not identical from culture to culture or person to person; colour-blind people and certain animals see them quite differently. If we are to use the spectrum to defend class models we can but make the model realistic, and then it would be no good. It would dash our hopes of a model of points, and borderlines, whether or not doubtful cases were near the border, unless we could find a theory of the underlying reality which would allow us to sort people into groups and order the groups. But any underlying reality must be such that it genuinely enables us to recognize class membership.

The classifications in a model where people are partially ordered and classes are hierarchically ordered, like all those elsewhere, are arbitrary. They simply amount to drawing lines at arbitrarily chosen points in the continuous spectrum of social differences and distances. Faced with these arguments, sociologists are inclined to fall back on the theory of *converging hierarchies*. This idea is not as sophisticated as it looks. It starts from the undisputed fact that there exist genuine hierarchies in the social world, for example, of income, educational achievement, and so on. The theory says that the system of social class is a hierarchical system which emerges from the convergence of these other hierarchies: 'These form not one hierarchy but a pyramid of sub-hierarchies' (MacRae, 1961, p. 67). One way to interpret this theory is to see it as a geometrical expression of the index theory. It is more rigid, of course, unless the lines traversing the pyramid horizontally veer a great deal. The index theory we have already discussed. The idea of convergence of the hierarchies was obviously introduced to accord with the idea that the top class of people have everything (the 'ruling *élite*', as MacRae calls them). But, as we previously argued, sometimes they have not. Indeed it is widely agreed that sometimes a person may possess only one attribute—say very high birth—and yet be upper class.

Another way of interpreting the pyramid theory is this. Every hierarchy in society has a top; can we not say that each top person belongs to a level above, which in turn converges on a top? At the head of a trade union of workers there are officials who stand in the white-collar groups. At the head of the white-collar groups are people who stand high in industry and in 'society'. This we can say describes the structure of the class system. It is recruited in multiple ways. Such a model explains social differences and social

115

organization. The only question is whether it is a system of social class.

Counter-examples may be ignored as exceptions to be treated by pedants only. But both the index idea and the pyramid idea encounter a general and serious objection: in what way do they correspond to the facts? Do people operate with indices or think of social positions as a pyramid? I submit that they do not, that these ideas are arbitrary constructions refined beyond anything which we generally think about class. However they do it, people just recognize the class-position of other people without such complex ideas. And this brings us to the problem of recognition in its sharpest form since, if class exists and is a pyramid or a set of pyramids, only a few dozen sociologists recognize class.

The problem of how to recognize members of a class is solved by the theory of acceptance. Those people can be recognized as upper class who are accepted as upper class. Accepted by whom or what? Not by any institutional authority, of course, because we have abandoned the idea that there is a sole objective determinant of class. *Burke's Peerage* or the *Social Register* are hardly reliable guides to such an ineffable as class; no more than is Mr Michael Barrett-Brown's list of interlocking directorates. The reference groups of these works—peers of the realm, and the economically powerful—contain persons whose class-position cannot just be read off. There does not seem to be anything like an unproblematic group of people in each class to whom reference can be made. How then does the acceptance theory deal with this? The answer is provided by Lipset and Bendix in the following quotation (1959, p. 275).

> Social classes are usually defined as strata of society composed
> of individuals who accept each other as status equals, and
> are hence qualified for intimate association. Men may change
> their occupational status by changing their job, but they
> can improve their social class-position only by being admitted
> to relationships of intimacy with those who already possess
> a higher rank.

The first thing to ask is how they can talk of 'those who already possess a higher rank'. It is because there is no reference group that their definition was phrased in terms of *individual* recognition of status equality. Their definition says that social classes are classes of status equals and that classes of status equals are classes of people each of whom *recognizes* the others as status equals. The idea of mutual recognition is subjective, since we are given no objective way to recognize status equality. Moreover, status equals, by this definition, means mutually-recognized-status-equality.

Mutual recognition may mean no more than that people consider themselves members of the same class. This says social classes are any collection of individuals who consider themselves to belong to the same class. This is a confession that there is no objective class system, no 'higher rank', especially as we have no way of finding out which statuses are higher and which lower.

The theory of acceptance, then, is too strong. We can now try to solve the problem of recognition with the theory or recognition. Am I a member of the upper class because I think I am?[17] No. If I am not, what is the difference between myself and someone who thinks he is and is? He is. How do we know? Because others agree that he is; they recognize him. This is the least objective theory of social class I know, and something of a last resort. The theory is that there is no objectively determined system, only a set of self-perpetuating groups (or quasi-groups) whose estimates of themselves correspond largely with others' estimates of them. This mutual and agreed ranking of each other is barely systematizable. But recognition as a member of a class functions both as recognition and allocation; indeed recognition does allocate. This is the theory of class I myself hold. Whether this can be called a system of social class, rather than simply some shifting groups, is doubtful. But the theory is more often held with a corollary that these groups have more power, money, privilege, and leisure time, than others; no member need possess all of these, but the class as a whole possess substantially more than do the other classes.

Now two possibilities arise here: either every member of the class possesses at least one of these things; or some do not. In general, social wholes do not possess things like leisure, only people do: every characteristic possessed by a class must be possessed by at least one of its members. Therefore, what the classes are said to have must belong to at least one of the members. This either determines his membership or it does not. A destructive dichotomy is again possible. If it does then we seem to be back with the problems we discussed earlier. If it does not then we do not know what does and the possession of these characteristics is unimportant or non-essential.

I call the recognition theory the weakest for good reason. A continuous hierarchy of class-positions, however they are determined, provided it *is* hierarchically ordered, definitely solves the problems of social differences and social organization. Indeed, it is a sophisticated solution since it does not pretend that social differences are sharp, but rather pictures them as shading over into one another. As the model is weakened and made more subjective and the ordering becomes less objective (acceptance and recognition) and less ordered ('impressionistic typology', see p. 118 its explanatory power lessens too. Social differences which are something semi-objective at least cannot really be explained when the co-ordination between different people's different acceptances and recognitions is left open. Where it is explained (as in my theory of social myths co-ordinating behaviour) the problems can still be solved. The weakest theory I have come across was formulated by Professor Sprott: 'At present one can only rely on impressionistic typology.'[18] We can call it the *I give up* theory.[19]

## How to look at social class

My suggestion for getting to the heart of social class is, roughly, that we all have theories about how social classes are constituted and—muddled and mutually conflicting as they are—we use these to interpret people's actions in such a way that they explain certain obvious features of society, like social differences and snobbery. The explanation can assume either that there is a class system or that the people acting, and the people explaining (these groups overlap almost completely) the actions, themselves believe there is a class system and they act on the basis of this belief. But either assumption is questionable, for reasons adduced in the previous section. Not only are the assumptions vague (or incoherent when weakened), they do not explain the social differences, etc.

This expositionally involved and curious, but basically rather simple view can perhaps be understood if we remember the following fact. The ambit of social studies embraces, strangely enough, the fact that the theories people hold about the world (for example, that men can't fly) influence the world of facts (that men build aeroplanes). Many of our theories about the world are specifically about the social world; are, that is, theories, hypotheses, guesses or expectations about social relations and about the structure of society. Among these theories about the social world are those concerning the system of social classes we are thought to have. Believing there is a class system, people act in accord with how they imagine it to be. From this follows the important insight that the muddles sociologists have got themselves into in the discussion of class are not solely the result of their confusion, but rather of their trying to eliminate confusion which is ineliminable, since it is built into the society. The reality *is* confused because people are acting on the basis of muddled popular sociological theories (for example, that there are social classes of such and such a structure); were these muddled theories to be eliminated and hence people cease to act on them, the class system might be eliminated as well (and it might not: inertia, unintended consequences, unconscious habits might sustain it).

If we visualize the confused class system as debris—the rubbish strewn across the path to knowledge—then we can put the position thus. Sociologists want an 'orderly framework of concepts' (Bendix and Berger, 1959, p. 92) for their investigations. They believe that when they clear away the debris of confusion a clear essence of the concept 'social class' will stand revealed. Marshall counters this by saying that when the debris is cleared there may be revealed the fact that there is no essence. Common to both their positions is the idea that we must clear the debris before we can find out about the essence. My suggestion is that the debris is the essence. Why should an essence be clear and simple; why not confused and difficult? The belief that it is clear is an idolatry of common sense or of the concepts of common language.[20] My position is that what sustains the reality of the system of social class is that real people believe in it and act on these beliefs. If anything, I put class in an Hegelian third world of concepts, neither physical nor mental; in the realm of objective mind, of ideas realizing themselves in the world (see chapter 6). In this way I dissolve the problem created by the fact that no description of the class system seems adequate or even consistent.

Besides this theory of class we need a theory of social distances, in order to explain the sense of separatedness in society. The most interesting discussion of this I know is by MacRae who says that people have to cross a social distance to contact each other.[21] He points out that social space is not isotropic, because Sam Weller goes a longer distance to reach Mr Pickwick than Mr Pickwick goes to reach Sam. He might also have pointed out that there are cases where the lower have direct access to the higher but not vice versa. The story of the emperor's clothes is such a case.

But this story illustrates something important about social distance. We are separated, true; the main problem with social distance then becomes how to overcome it, how to get contact. Especially where the separation is greatest, say between leader and led, king and people, politician and critic, it is vital for both that there be channels or bridges which cut across the social distance, which reduce it almost to nothing. Henry V wandered among his troops to find out how they felt; medieval kings like Lear kept a court jester to act as critic and advisor; many ruling cliques have elaborate intelligence networks simply to bridge the social distance; all the trappings of democracy can be seen as attempts to institutionalize means of communication and criticism between politicians and public.

Having means of channelling information up and down is one way of overcoming social distance. Since people are separated, the crossing of social distance becomes the main problem, since com-

119

munication is essential. There is another means by which it can be overcome and that is by social mobility. The existence of social distances and the need for them to be overcome explain the importance of social mobility. In all stratified societies there is mobility, or channels of information, or both. Generally, we would expect that where a society is flourishing the two would vary inversely with each other, for if you have considerable mobility channels will not be required, and where channels are flourishing it may be because there is no mobility. Some societies have inadequate provision for particular situations, that is why Henry V found it necessary to go among his troops. Mobility can be more or less institutionalized; in medieval Europe, joining the Church, doing well in war, or getting yourself or a relative married to someone who counted socially, were standard means of mobility. Our society is in a situation where mobility is hardly institutionalizable because there is no class system clear cut enough to allow it, and because social distances are anyway ambiguous. While it is true, as MacRae says, that the route from officer to batman is direct, while the route from batman to officer is devious, that is only the situation in the army. Should both men meet in civilian clothes in a pub, or when they have both become MPs, there would be no question but that they would be an equal social distance from one another. Everyone knows of the problems created by sergeants and schoolmasters shouting at Dukes and bowing to them and their family. Society is a multiplicity of organizations, contexts, and distances, which cannot nowadays be over-simplified into a cut-and-dried model of the common sense social class type.

My view, that people have *theories* of class, and that they act *as if* these theories were true, adequately explains the 'class' phenomena. So I am not denying the reality of those snobberies and discriminatory practices which operate in our society.[22] That people believe in, and act on, their theories of class adequately accounts for these things. One might put the point this way: the concept of social class, like most sociological concepts, is dispositional.[23] It describes people's disposition to believe and act in certain typical ways; as a belief held in common and acted upon it is a social myth or tradition; a social class is a quasi-group of people whose links are that they *think* they have similar interests, and who share common *beliefs* about the system of social class, their own position in that system, and similar dispositions as to the behaviour appropriate to their position in that system.

Snobberies, discrimination, and class consciousness then are still among our worst social diseases, and they are made to seem doubly vicious by my view that the hierarchy of classes they are thought to be anchored in is chimerical. Surely it would be a great achievement if sociologists could refute, and by propaganda destroy, the false theories underlying these pernicious attitudes— as a first step towards discrediting the latter.

## Origins of our popular theories

How is it that present social myths about class came to be held? Normally, questions about the origin of our theories would be the concern of the historian of sociology (who should include in his province the origin of widespread social myths) or of social historians. Since, however, I hold the theories to be myths, some case for my explaining them can be made. If I can show that these myths look like sensible theories it would count as an argument for my case, because it would explain why they are held—but not why they are held uncritically. Of course, this particular question of origin, like all others, is a vexed one and I do not claim to be able to give a complete answer to it. But I have one or two suggestions to make on the subject.

There was, it seems to me, at least one time in English history when a state of affairs obtained which to some extent resembles the state of affairs pictured in the basic common sense theory of the social class system. I am referring to the feudal system of the Middle Ages. Its main characteristic for our purposes is that there was supposed to be no continuity between the classes. Officially there was a sharp break between each class. There was a *legally defined* hierarchy of social classes which were characterized by certain non-conflicting indicators—although it is easy enough to argue that the reality belied the theory and no effective system of breaks operated even then: borderline cases can, as we have seen, be produced. My conjecture is that, *although any basis this system may have had in law has long since disappeared,* our Castle-and-Gate-type theories by and large still describe it. Or, at least, our theories depict a structure closer to that state of affairs then than they are to the actual state of affairs now. In particular, although if we have any system at all now it is clearly a continuous and not a discrete one, we still think in our theories in terms of sharp breaks, lately characterized by intimacy of association. But even that is something of a continuity: a peer will more readily talk to a lawyer than to a factory worker, although he is unlikely to be particularly intimate with either.

Apparently society changes faster than our ideas about society; our theories of social class are anachronistic. For example, Ginsberg (1934, pp. 174–9) in the early thirties still found it necessary to take up space to argue the chestnut that there are no inheritable differences of intelligence or capacity between people of different social

121

classes. This is a graphic illustration of the staying power of those myths of blood and descent which have been so influential for so long. It is not impossible that a fairly accurate description of the legal, that is the ideal, state of affairs was current in the Middle Ages. The description was falsified by the rise of a new class during the break-up of the feudal system. One is tempted to explain the retention of these falsified theories as a reaction to the strain induced by social change.[24] The break-up of the feudal system, followed by the enclosures, the political revolutions of the seventeenth century, and the trade and the industrial expansion of the eighteenth century, must have disrupted many lives and created feelings of insecurity (see Barbu, 1960, pp. 151–2). Need the comfort brought by theories which sustain an 'optical illusion' of stability be further gone into? To put it another way, current theories about the structure of society are anachronistic because of what looks like a built-in resistance to change of ideas; a resistance the function of which is clearly to lessen the effect of social change itself.

Should this somewhat elaborate explanation prove hard to swallow, there remains the possibility that the theories were retained because no one had noticed that they had been falsified. Ample illustration of this kind of thing is to be found in the history of science (see Agassi, 1963a, passim). Still more can be said. The medieval system was certainly, in theory, clear cut and easy to understand. The facts now bear tempting resemblances to those then and the system they conceal is very complicated and confused.[25] Naturally prone to try to understand society rationally (how else?), people would tend to resist ideas which claim the reality is confused. Something we might call 'popular essentialism' might also be at work. To be an aristocrat one would have to be aristocratic. Without a clear-cut notion of aristocracy this would be difficult. Thus, harking back to a time when these matters were clear makes sense.

No doubt some will find it hard to believe that medieval beliefs about class were true. Indeed, my own mode of argument could be turned against me: if *our* ideas of class are anachronistic, what is to say that those of the Middle Ages were not too? In fact, I am not claiming that the description abroad in the Middle Ages was entirely accurate. Yet there was, after all, a fairly clearly (that is, legally) defined system operating in pretty unambiguous ways, especially compared to the so-called 'class system' we have today. Medieval society was a smaller-scale and less complex society than ours, easier to grasp, harder to get wrong ideas about. Authority and hierarchy were understood and accepted. Progress, change and individualism were not abroad to distort received views. There was far less self-conscious reflection on how society was. These are the arguments that lead me to claim that medieval beliefs about class bore a closer relationship to the facts of the case as they were then, than current beliefs about class bear to the facts as they are now. The facts then were fairly simple and known; and it was important to know them; the facts now are very complex and partly unknown; and it is not so important for most purposes to know them. Ignorance of them is not likely to bring you into conflict with the law; in the Middle Ages it would. So, although our ideas of class have undergone *some* change, I believe they still reflect a post-renaissance rather than a post-industrial revolution society.

All this is, I admit, pretty sketchy; a major study has yet to be written on how these theories arose,[26] were fostered, and transmitted from generation to generation with such remarkable verisimilitude. It would also be interesting to know how far they have actually escaped the distortion normally attendant upon oral tradition.

## The metaphysics of social class

Various metaphysical problems seem to me to lie behind the sociological discussions of social class. One of the most difficult, the ontological, I have only touched on. This is concerned with in what respects the reality of societies, institutions, actions, events and social myths, can be said to resemble the reality of the things and facts of the physical world. Most people are agreed that social entities do not have a 'table-and-chair', furniture of the universe, sort of existence, although Durkheim and Radcliffe-Brown stubbornly maintained that they did (see pp. 106–18 above). Certainly they have some characteristics in common with tables and chairs. You can run into them. You can run into the law or the Inland Revenue and if you 'kick' them they often 'kick back' in a way that hurts. On the other hand, they are not in all cases locatable in buildings: some have no location, such as war, scientific knowledge or religion; others happen to have location, but more or less accidentally. We do associate them with buildings sometimes, and even look for them there, for example, the House of Commons and the London School of Economics. However, as World War II showed, both of these institutions can be divorced from their buildings and still flourish.[27] Here the metaphysics are of a purely philosophical interest, I imagine; and I prefer not to enter into their subtleties in this chapter. A sub-problem of ontology is raised by the holistic theory of class. This theory, which I did not discuss in any detail, says that the class characteristics are possessed by the class as a whole and that the members participate in them. I reduced this theory to another with the principle: every characteristic possessed by a class must be possessed by at least one of its members. How about if we deny that principle? We then face the problem of a social whole with characteristics like money, education, etc., independent of its members. Now, in general, holism is a confusion arising out of the fact that social institutions are something more than the individuals who comprise them; the problem holism comes to solve is why people do not act as they wish. Its answer is that wholes constrain them. The individualistic answer to that is that institutions are social causes only insofar as they are part of a person's situation, such that he must take them into account. But anyway, my problem is not why people accept and act within a framework of a social class system, although they would like to get rid of it (see Agassi, 1960, note 18 and text), but why they continue to believe in it despite the evidence. My individualistic theory says that the situation of the individual is such that class beliefs have become a reinforced prejudice of the type discussed by Bacon.[28] We can hardly see beyond them because, by our belief in them and an acute Oedipus effect,[29] they verify themselves. Only by setting about them critically has it been possible to by-pass them.

A basic problem which has to be looked at closely is why sociologists are interested in social class at all. The answer that it is a prominent part of the societies they are describing is too naïve; we all know nowadays that what seems important or interesting is a function of our preconceptions, our theoretical preconceptions. One proposed explanation of sociologists' interest in social class was that they were interested in the power distribution in society and that social class was relevant to that (Blau, 1964). That statement was hardly fundamental enough though. What theory gave rise to the interest in power distribution? My suggestion would be Marx's theory, which contradicted the prima facie theory that political power was the real power and suggested instead the primacy of the power distributed in the economic infra-structure.[30] Ever since Marx, sociologists have been discussing the Marxian and prima facie theories of power in society without really confessing that both are false. Dissatisfied with this explanation, I sought another, somewhat more fundamental still. Why should sociologists be interested in power and theories of power at all (I exclude the naïve answer, 'because they are interested in all aspects of society', for the same reason as I stated above)? And my answer brought me to metaphysics: since the Enlightenment we have all believed in the unity and equality of man. Since anthropologists investigated race we have strengthened those beliefs. Yet there remain divisions and differences between men: power structures, intellectual levels, degrees of privilege, and so on. Problem: are these to be explained by the falsity of the doctrine of the equality of man, or by other things? I think the whole theory of social classes is one elaborate attempt to cope with an aspect of this latter question (cf. Nisbet, 1968, p. 110).

As support for this I adduce the fact that sociologists very often find themselves arguing against those who do not believe in the existence of social class.[31] Who are these people? The authors never say, but I think they mean the kind of person who, when asked what class he is in, replies that he does not believe in classes. This is partly an ontological assertion, and partly a moral refusal to accept or have any truck with class. Such convictions are clearly inspired by a strong faith in the unity of mankind and a refusal to acknowledge things which seem to run contrary to it. There may also be an element of idealism: belief that ours is a classless or at least highly mobile society.

Another metaphysical root for sociologists' interest in social class is the long tradition of positivism in the science. Comte, because he coined the word, is generally and mistakenly regarded as the founder of sociology. He was just as much the founder of positivism. Durkheim and Radcliffe-Brown, as Evans-Pritchard rightly points out,[32] were also positivistically inclined, to say the least. One characteristic positivist doctrine is that the aim of science is to discover laws with which to predict. It is thought that a person's class membership permits of a certain amount of prediction of his behaviour. A working class person will vote this way, dress that way, etc. (Theories of social class are thus attempts to find out how many ideal types are needed to explain society.) Apart from the obvious criticisms that can be made against any specific attempt to predict, the whole aim can be explained. It is quite true that natural science has laws and predictions derived from them, but they are not ends-in-themselves: they are subordinate to the fundamental aim of explanation. Theories of social class are, similarly, for explanation, not prediction. A man does not wear a cap because he is a member of a class but because he thinks he is and he thinks that is the norm and he has decided to follow it. But this means we cannot predict from class membership, only from imagined class membership, and that is hardly a scientific basis for anything.

(This suggests a general point about the problem of predicting in the social sciences. In one way we can predict very well: our whole system of reciprocal expectations, rights and duties, incorporates predictions. In another way we cannot. If people act on the basis of how they see their situation, it may in many cases be true that we can only reconstruct how they see the situation after we have seen how they act. Moreover, how a person sees his situation will not be fixed until the last minute, as it were, since events of only a moment ago may restructure his appreciation of his situation and hence lead to his acting differently. It is because of such insuperable difficulties that we are forced, in the social sciences, to use ideal-typical, or simplified approximation methods if we are to make any headway at all.)

Marx said that people are equal but their relationship to the productive process separates them—his theory of social class reduced it to economic class. My argument has been that people are divided from themselves: their theories or beliefs, their myths, are what so tragically separate them. And these theories, because they are acted on, themselves create and sustain the imagined divisions.

## Conclusion

Finally let me show how viewing the class hierarchy as simply an interpretation of action based on a false theory throws light on another interesting problem. Although ordinary people feel that these days there is great social mobility in Great Britain, I have heard sociologists say they were unable to find any evidence for it;[33] they can find evidence only for a decrease in social distance. This chapter has shown there is no objective and clearly demarcated system of social classes; but has accepted that there are social differences, and everyone would agree that social differences are decreasing. People's feeling of increased social mobility then, I would argue, is a sort of 'optical illusion' brought about by their belief in false theories which distort their ability to interpret accurately decreasing social differences.

To sum up. Hayek has already shown that social phenomena (money; class) are primarily ideas (1949, chap. III). They are not *only* ideas, for two reasons. First, they are public; second, therefore action is based on them. We sometimes confuse the actions or parts of them (coin, cheques; snobbery, discrimination) with the fact. The terms simply indicate people's disposition to act. So, although these things are mind-dependent (no minds, no things: as with secondary qualities, minds are here necessary conditions), they are not mental figments or illusions but in some sense or other *real*. I stress that classes are, like money, part of our theories of society, although they are not only theories. I suggest that our differing ideas of class are imperfectly co-ordinated, while our ideas of money are in most respects highly co-ordinated. I further suggest that the preoccupation with class in Britain stems from the poor co-ordination between people's ideas of class—the many diverse ideas people have of class and their efforts to sort them out—whereas in America there are relatively few ideas of class and thus a greater degree of co-ordination and therefore a more placid attitude to the subject. People who know where they are will be less agitated than people who do not.

'The' class system does not exist at all; it is a myth, an ordering of social experience introduced by ordinary people and taken over by sociologists. Basically, the phenomena of social difference which we label 'class phenomena' are phenomenally complex and not reducible to our naïve common sense models of social class.[34] One interesting and fruitful way of seeing the alleged social class system, which has not been previously tried and which I have striven to present here, is to consider it as a problem within the sociology of knowledge. That is, I hold that people's theories, hypotheses, conjectures, beliefs, call them what you will, about social class are part of *their hypothetical knowledge of their society*. And it is not surprising that this knowledge, like their knowledge of science, but less justifiably because, after all, they have a privileged access into the behaviour of people in society which they do not have into the behaviour of particles in an atom, is vague, confused and even mistaken. People do not belong to a social class system—*we put them into one; the* constitution of the system of social class does not exist; all that exists is our differing and poorly co-ordinated theories of how the social class system is constituted. This suggests that perhaps one major task of sociology has been neglected, namely: the refutation of a vast mass of popular myths,[35] followed by attempts to devise educational checks which will impede the uncritical transmission of such erroneous theories, simply by showing how little they correspond to the facts.

Having shown how empirical and conceptual difficulties about class can be resolved by resort to the sociology of knowledge, the question of social knowledge in general, of the reality of society in general, needs to be explored. To this end we shall now make an excursus into a revised and improved version of the sociology of knowledge, which avoids all the crudities of Mannheim, and draws its strength instead from the views of Scheler and Schutz.

# part three

# Concepts and society

# 5 The sociology of knowledge reconsidered

Definitions of reality have self-fulfilling potency. Theories can be realized in history, even theories that were highly abstruse when they were first conceived by their inventors. Karl Marx brooding in the British Museum library has become the proverbial example of this historical possibility. Consequently, social change must always be understood as standing in a dialectical relationship to the history of ideas. Both idealistic and materialistic understandings of the relationship overlook this dialectic and thus distort history.

Berger and Luckmann (1966), p. 118

The argument developed in the foregoing chapters suggests that the world studied by sociology, so far from being a 'given' within which man lives, is, rather, a man-made construct. This might suggest that sociology is irremediably plunged into subjectivism or even solipsism. But this is not so. The constructed social world is not personal or private (except in psychotics, and it may be questioned even with them); it is shared—as indeed it must be if the co-ordination essential for co-operative living in society is to be maintained. How does this constructed, intersubjective world come to be? How is it sustained? Such answers as I have found in the literature are classed as 'the sociology of knowledge'.

By 'the sociology of knowledge' I understand that part of sociology which discusses the doctrine that we do not acquire our knowledge, opinions and beliefs in a vacuum, but in a social and political atmosphere; that what we take to be true, and especially what we take to be obviously true, is conditioned by these social and political surroundings, and especially by our social and political *interests*. That he is being exploited will be taken for granted by a worker, but will be denied by his employer. That he is doing disinterested scientific research will be clear to a scientist; that he is serving the interests of the military-industrial complex will not occur to him. The worker and his employer, the scientist and his accuser, are operating from different sets of basic assumptions; assumptions so basic they may not be aware of having made any assumptions at all. Assumptions so different, moreover, that no discussion or compromise between them seems possible. Such systems of assumptions are called a 'total ideology'. This total ideology governs not just the particular ideas a person may have, but the entire way in which reality is seen, as it were; what reality is defined to be. People's total ideology varies systematically with their social and political circumstances for, fundamentally, what they believe will be things that serve their personal or class interests.[1] The only exceptions to all this are the ideas of free-floating intellectuals who, armed with the insights of the sociology of knowledge, can see through the total ideologies, without being imprisoned in one of their own. Ostensibly. And it is indeed true in some degree; for though they must be caught in the web of an ideology of 'detachment', which is often a pseudo-detachment and hot under the collar, there is a sufficient degree of truth in it to ensure that their assessments are worth a considerable amount in their own right. They are able to manage this because they are a class emancipated from the pressures of social and political circumstances, able disinterestedly to seek the truth.

Popper criticizes the doctrine of the sociology of knowledge in *The Open Society and Its Enemies* (1945). He begins by arguing that the sociology of knowledge is an Hegelian development of Kant's categories. These are no longer the unchanging presuppositions of all knowledge, but are a constantly developing part of man's social heritage and vary from nation to nation, race to race, even class to class. The doctrine of the intellectual unity of mankind is thus radically rejected and replaced by relativism. Men are now imprisoned in their self-serving total ideologies and unable to engage in rational debate. The intellectual pessimism of the sociology of knowledge is only ameliorated by the powers attributed to the intellectual. Yet this attribution has dangerous élitist consequences: a class is declared to exist which is free from the prejudices of everyone else, which is privileged to be clear-minded and thus able to see the truth, correctly to identify virtue. We all know how people have seen fit to behave once convinced they, and they alone, have exclusive access to truth and virtue.

Playfully applying 'socio-analysis' to the sociology of knowledge itself, Popper next shows how it is self-serving for intellectuals to peddle such an idea. Making the intellectual the exception to the doctrine of total ideologies, to whose ideas socio-analysis should not be applied, is inconsistent. The arguments for making an exception of the intellectuals are unconvincing.

Popper's most important argument is that the sociology of knowledge pays no attention to what its name would suggest it should deal with, namely: the social character of science. Science is a paradigm of knowledge; scientific activity is a social activity; *ergo* the sociology of science will be a paradigm of the sociology of knowledge, or at least the sociology of the nearest thing to knowledge that we possess. The failure of the sociologists of knowledge to go into this betrays their fatal misunderstanding of what constitutes science. The idea that science can or should be free from presuppositions is self-contradictory (Popper, 1945, ii, p. 230). Science does not consist in a mind (or consciousness) directly perceiving the true or the real. Science consists in a body of theories and procedures which are the outcome of a friendly-hostile co-operative endeavour among scientists to propose solutions to problems and subject them to the check of free criticism. This process is maximized by organizing it within a framework of institutions: rules of debate, emphasis on the appeal to inter-subjective arguments from experience.

Thus the sociology of knowledge makes no impression on the truth-value of our putative knowledge. True, science begins from presuppositions, but the objective force of the problem, and the institutional force of scientific procedures, compel us bit by bit to subject these to severe criticism. It is precisely because science has more sharply focused its problems and more carefully organized and orchestrated discussion of them (in laboratories, journals, conferences, seminars, etc.) that it has the best claim to represent mankind's knowledge.

## The roots of the sociology of knowledge

At the time Popper was writing, he may have feared that the doctrine of the sociology of knowledge was gaining ground amongst social scientists. We are now informed in two recent books (Berger and Luckmann, 1966, p. 4; and Holzner, 1968, p. 17) that on the contrary the sociology of knowledge (in German *Wissensoziologie*) has been widely ignored by sociologists.

It has been expounded and criticized here and there,[2] but used very little except by Mannheim (1936, 1952, 1953, 1956) and Stark (1958). How is this surprising neglect to be explained? Berger and Luckmann offer an explanation of the neglect that is almost as surprising as the neglect itself. Their explanation is that sociologists have ignored the sociology of knowledge because it was invented by a philosopher—Max Scheler—to solve a philosophical problem.

Scheler intended to overcome 'the difficulties raised by relativism so that the real philosophical task could proceed'. The real philosophical task is 'the establishment of a philosophical anthropology that would transcend the relativity of specific historically and socially located viewpoints' (1966, p. 7). One is tempted to ask why Scheler did not revert to Kant, who already had a non-relativist philosophical anthropology. Berger and Luckmann do not succeed in making their point clear. Why Scheler wanted to overcome relativism in a new way, and what sort of relativism he wanted to overcome, need to be discussed before we can understand his attempts to overcome relativism.

We might seek help elsewhere. A field in which relativism is both widespread and well worked out is anthropology. Trying to trace the source of the urge towards relativism, I have argued at some length (1964a) that it arises from the clash between our belief in the unity of mankind, and the facts—disclosed to us by anthropology—of human diversity. We are trying to reconcile, among other things, our knowledge and values—which include respect for other cultures—with the different knowledge and values found in other cultures. Forced to choose between our culture's universal and absolute claims, which exclude the discrepant claims of other cultures, whether these be universal or particular, anthropologists frequently opt for the other cultures and downgrade our knowledge and value claims from universality and absoluteness to particularity and relativity. (This is done less in the name of science than in the name of decency. To criticize is thus to invite the charge of opposing decent treatment.)[3]

There seems no reason not to generalize this source of relativism —the clash between the manifest diversity of mankind and our yearning for its unity—to areas other than anthropology. Philosophers, too, are perturbed by the tension between the search for universal truth, common to all men and all cultures and hopefully yielding truths acceptable to all cultures, and the manifest diversity of human views on the search and the results, and the inegalitarian necessity of appraising them. We can now return to Scheler and see that he was pulled both ways on these issues. Aron (1964) tells us he was in revolt against the claims of civilization to be superior. He was an egalitarian (men are equal) which led to relativism when it was applied to cultures (cultures are equal and hence the truths of one, while not necessarily true in another, cannot on that account suffer invidious comparison). Berger and Luckmann tell us that he was seeking a philosophical anthropology which 'would transcend the relativity of specific historically and socially located viewpoints'—in other words an absolutely true doctrine not known to all and hence hardly egalitarian. Scheler had thus to choose either egalitarian-relativism or inegalitarian-absolutism.[4] Surprisingly, and quite unlike the anthropologists, he seems to have chosen to give up egalitarian-relativism—but only minimally. He minimizes his concession by distinguishing the date and circumstances of the appearance of an idea, from its content. Relativism is true only of appearances not of content, i.e. the explanation of when an idea appears may be relative to social or historical factors, but the content of an idea cannot be explained as being relative to these factors. Accidents of birth may cause inequality between families of ideas (or cultures), and may be studied sociologically. Not so the truth or falsity of their content. So, *Wissensoziologie* discusses the birth certificates of ideas, not their legitimacy.

We may now understand Scheler a little, but it remains difficult to see how all this is supposed to explain the neglect of the sociology of knowledge by sociologists. It also does not explain why the sociology of knowledge has been similarly ignored by contemporary analytical philosophers, a point Berger and Luckmann fail to make. This may have been because of separation of disciplines, as Berger and Luckmann's explanation would seem to hint, but there may be a much more straightforward explanation: neither sociologists nor contemporary philosophers are much attracted to Scheler's solution. When on the horns of this particular dilemma they both give up inegalitarian-absolutism and embrace relativism wholeheartedly, maintaining that no other view is compatible with belief in the equality and dignity of the brotherhood of mankind. More than this, relativism is widely hailed as a shattering discovery setting severe outer limits on what sociology, anthropology and philosophy can aspire to.[5]

There is some irony in all this. Kant's epistemology is entirely compatible with the unity of mankind; indeed emphatically asserts it. Hegel's relativism undermines it in a fundamental way.[6] Yet the influence of Marx and of the sociology of knowledge has led to a paradoxical situation. On the one hand we have Scheler striving to regain the unity of mankind through a new philosophical anthropology which will supersede relativism; on the other, social scientists repudiating the attempt to overcome relativism in the name of the unity of mankind!

Of course, a few sociologists, anthropologists and philosophers are not relativists, and we have the additional task of explaining why *they* ignore the sociology of knowledge. Berger and Luckmann do not raise this problem, yet they do provide a solution to it. In the form that it has come down to us, i.e. Mannheim's version, the sociology of knowledge has been vulgarized in a crucial way, not in order to overcome relativism, but to serve as a strange and inconsistent hybrid between relativism and absolutism. Whereas Scheler argued that socio-economic conditions could determine the *arrival* of an idea at a particular time and place, but *not* the content of that idea, Mannheim claimed that socio-economic conditions determine content as well as arrival. He thus used the sociology of knowledge to expose the distortions and 'false consciousness' of total ideologies. Only the freely poised intelligentsia, he allowed, could escape this relativism of ideologies and see them for what they were, limited and partial.

The trouble with Mannheim's sociology of knowledge is that it became, in his hands, a self-validating technique, or, as Berger and Luckmann put it (p. 12), Mannheim's readiness to

> include epistemological questions concerning the validity of sociological knowledge in the sociology of knowledge is somewhat like trying to push a bus in which one is riding.

In their critique of Mannheim, Berger and Luckmann entirely fail to mention that, as long ago as 1945 in *The Open Society and Its Enemies* (or even 1944, when *The Poverty of Historicism* was published in *Economica*), Popper, as we have seen, had executed a more extensive critique than theirs. Popper's criticism goes much further than Berger and Luckmann's, especially in his charge discussed above that the sociology of knowledge completely fails to 'understand precisely its main subject, the *social aspects of knowledge,* or rather, of scientific method' (Popper, 1945, ii, p. 217). Whether Popper's critique had any influence in bringing about the situation of neglect of the sociology of knowledge, which Berger and Luckmann complain about, is difficult to tell. Popper's work is widely diffused and read, but rarely referred to. Moreover, believers in the sociology of knowledge could easily dismiss Popper's criticism. Being unattached intellectuals, at least ostensibly, i.e. free of imprisoning ideologies, it would be easy for them to ignore Popper's criticism as the hopeless distortions of bourgeois ideology. However, there were attempts to study the sociology of science, stemming as much perhaps from Merton's pre-war beginnings (reprinted in Merton, 1957, chap. XV) as from anything. Unfortunately, much of what has been done thus far is done in such a way as to be vulnerable to the same criticism as launched against Mannheim: to discover a theory of discovery is to push the bus you are riding in.[7] Historians of science, as opposed to sociologists of science, *are* becoming sociologically aware, and they do take notice of works like Agassi's (1963*a*), Feyerabend's (1965) and Kuhn's (1962). This suggests that there is yet hope that Popper's programme for a real sociology of knowledge will be carried through.

So much for the vulgar version of the sociology of knowledge, which restricts to an élite the possibilities of gaining objective knowledge. Berger and Luckmann choose to remedy the poor response to the sociology of knowledge not by eliminating Mannheim's vulgarisms but by a move in a totally different direction. They argue that the sociology of knowledge should not concern itself with exposing the hidden truths behind ideologies, but take as its province anything that generally passes for knowledge among the population at large. Thus common sense folk knowledge, out-of-date and garbled science, truisms, maxims, and so on, become the subject of the sociology of knowledge. At first sight this seems laudable enough, since their programme presumably includes science. Regrettably, however, this is not so; the history of ideas is not stressed and science is excluded altogether because both are esoteric. A sociology of knowledge concerned with what generally passes for knowledge in the society, then, will principally comprise the common man's common sense view of the world, and, perhaps, the accumulated folk-wisdom he uses to cope with it.

One could argue against this suggestion of Berger and Luckmann's that we take common-or-garden knowledge as an object of study, as follows. Today's common sense knowledge is yesterday's superseded science. If today we have any knowledge at all it can only be found among the current theories of science.

The argument I have made here relies heavily on the classical distinction between certain knowledge (current science) and mere delusive opinion (anything else). It would make Berger and Luckmann's proposal to encompass everyday *beliefs* within a *sociology* of *knowledge* a contradiction in terms.

But let us set this basic objection aside for the moment and see what their programme yields. All human beings who survive for any length of time do so because they can call on a stock of beliefs; we could call it their practical knowledge: factual, theoretical and even metaphysical (Berger and Luckmann call religion, metaphysics, any overarching set of justifying beliefs, 'symbolic universes'). Somehow, and to some degree, people everywhere organize their experience, order their expectations, and plan their actions. We can call all this 'knowledge'—or 'folk knowledge'. In its detail, a lot of this folk knowledge may be demonstrably false, but, like much superseded science, it may still have its practical uses. Berger and Luckmann do not fall into the trap of pragmatism (whatever works is, *ipso facto,* knowledge) or into the jaws of the pushing-your-own-bus criticism; their interest is to explain how and to what extent this stock of folk knowledge is articulated and sustained in the society, how and to what extent it is transmitted from one generation to the next, how and to what extent it is internalized by individuals, and how and to what extent it develops and changes. Let me proceed by means of a summary of their argument. (The titles on pp. 98, 102 and 106 are taken from Berger and Luckmann's titles.)

## The foundations of knowledge in everyday life

Berger and Luckmann's thesis about everyday life is that it is worth study because it is the 'paramount' reality, reality *'par excellence'* (p. 21). No example of 'lesser' realities is given, although it is said that different objects present themselves to consciousness as constituents of different spheres of reality. Reference is made to dreams, memories, neuroses. It looks as though we can conclude from the assertion of the paramountcy of the reality of everyday life that Berger and Luckmann's problem is whether the 'multiple realities' or 'spheres of reality' which we can move between (as between dreams and waking) can be ranked. Their criteria for ranking everyday life number one (most real) are that it imposes itself 'in the most massive, urgent and intense manner' (p. 21) on consciousness. (Whether imposition on consciousness is an adequate criterion of reality and what the alternative desiderata of an adequate criterion are, are not discussed. A sceptic might wonder what this criterion would do to the realities discovered by science, which hardly impose themselves on consciousness at all.) The reality of everyday life presents itself to us already objectified, independent of us. For example, the temporal structure of everyday life—that it takes place in time—is even called 'coercive' by Berger and Luckmann: we get older and have no choice about it; we cannot avoid referring to time when we want to re-enter or fix everyday reality.[8] The reality of this everyday world is here and now, near and far, intersubjectively shared, unproblematic for the most part.

How is this world of everyday life objectified? By means of language, according to Berger and Luckmann. Language provides us with the necessary objectifications, and also posits the order of shared meaning within which these make sense. That language enables us to name and describe and discuss this world and its objects in a way that makes sense to us and to others, confers on that world the status of objective reality.

> Language marks the coordinates of my life in society and fills that life with meaningful objects (p. 21).

Within this shared world of meaning are localized provinces of restricted or special acts meaningful only to subgroups—for example, dreams, private games, plays—entry into which induces a radical change in the tension of consciousness (jargon for the sense of reality), and so these realities cannot easily be handled by everyday language. Language is inescapably grounded in the shared meanings of everyday life and so distorts these far from everyday provinces of meaning. While such sub-universes of meaning (group perspectives, etc.) will be related to the concrete social interests of the group,

> this does *not* mean . . . that the various perspectives . . . are nothing but mechanical reflections of the social interests (p. 80).

What is it to objectify something? Can it be done only by language? Throwing a knife at someone, according to Berger and Luckmann, objectifies them and expresses intentions towards them. Signs (language) explicitly perform this function; knives do not. Language is rooted in the everyday and is coercive, it typifies and anonymizes experience. Language can objectify a great many experiences into the here and now, whole worlds in fact. It can also transcend the reality of everyday life altogether (mathematics, metaphysics, physics?). But such transcendent ideas come back to be part of everyday life and affect it—we live in a world of signs and symbols everyday. Most of our knowledge is not transcendent but pragmatic. In addition to knowing what we know, we have a sense of relevance—who to tell what. We also know that there is more knowledge than we know individually, so we have to know our way around its social structure: who to ask, where to go to find out.

So much for how everyday life is objectified by language and how language is rooted in everyday life, but allows us to pass beyond it. Everyday life surrounds us and fills our consciousness; it is both objectively and subjectively real. The rest of Berger and Luckmann's volume explores each of these facets separately.

## Society as objective reality

Having asked what does the objectifying, and what it is to objectify something, we can now ask how exactly does society become an objective reality for us? Berger and Luckmann give an answer that is intentionally both ontogenetic and phylogenetic. Face-to-face relations with other people are possible because of our capacity for expectation and anticipation; but expectation and anticipation involve degrees of typing or typification of people and their actions. The more remote the social relationships the greater the degree of typification involved. Institutions arise whenever there is 'reciprocal typification of habitualized actions by types of actors' (p. 51).

> The institutional world is objectivated human activity, and so is every single institution (p. 57) . . . *Society is a human product. Society is an objective reality. Man is a social product* (p. 58).

Unlike animals, which live in closed worlds as far as their relations to their environment go, man lives in an open world, and even produces himself (p. 47).

Once they have existed over time, institutions become something over and above their component individuals: an objective, external, coercive fact (p. 55). The existence of an institution as such is a primary social control. So a humanly produced system of conventions like language strikes a child as an intractable given. How can this objective social world be explained and legitimated (and sanctioned) to the new generation? This is the problem of socialization. People are born diverse, but they come to share universes of meaning, consistency, and logic. They understand what they and others do because of these shared meanings, a common stock of knowledge, which is the basis of an understanding of the social order, as well as of the production of social reality.

> Institutions are embodied in individual experience by means of roles. By playing these roles, the individual participates in a social world. By internalizing these roles, the same world becomes subjectively real to him (p. 69).

Yet an institutional order cannot adequately be understood as a system, but only at the level of meaning, of legitimation (p. 183).

> Society exists only as individuals are conscious of it . . . individual consciousness is socially determined (p. 73).

Nevertheless, social facts are things, i.e. human products, not subjective phantoms. So real do they become that socialization could be said to reify them. The problem then becomes how to de-reify them if we are not to be bemused and coerced.

Legitimation is the process of giving new or second-order meaning to disparate institutional processes. It is both social and individual; the social order and the individual's life must be rendered meaningful. There are levels of legitimating explanations. (1) Who is a cousin, who is so *named*? This is a request for *rules of usage.* (2) How is a cousin *treated*? This is a request for *pragmatic rules of how to behave,* not just how to speak. (3) Why treat cousins so? This is a request for specific *theories* about cousinship. (4) Still more general questions must be answered by reference to *symbolic universes* which legitimate all spheres of life and experience and all aspects of the social order. The function of the symbolic universe is nomic—to order, to control, especially to control threatening or marginal experiences like dreams, madness, death. Otherwise we are helpless and terror-stricken in the face of them.

Specific procedures of universe-maintenance become necessary when the symbolic universe has become a *problem*. As long as this is not the case, the symbolic universe is self-maintaining, that is, self-legitimating by the sheer facticity of its objective existence in the society in question (pp. 97–8).

The oldest symbolic universes, historically, are the mythological ones; next came, in order, theological, philosophical and scientific ones. The latter three are specialized and élitist in character, the former is easy to understand but secretive. Especially at the mythological stage there is an incipient tendency to heresy, and to experience culture shock, hence alternative universes abound. Power will usually settle (define) such disputes as arise.

This . . . need not mean that such definitions will remain less convincing than those accepted 'voluntarily'—power in society includes the power to determine decisive socialization processes and, therefore, the power to *produce* reality (p. 111).

If some group of persons is singled out for exclusion by the symbolic universe, then it becomes an ideology. In modern society symbolic universes coexist in pluralism. A unique class of men grow up—intellectuals—who, unlike 'men of knowledge', i.e. priests or scientists, are experts whose expertise is not wanted by the society. Whether their reaction to this is to withdraw from society, or become actively involved as revolutionaries, it is notable that they need others to objectivate their reality and they strive to make it socially meaningful through social processes.[9]

## Society as subjective reality

Externalization, objectivation, and internalization of social reality are simultaneous during socialization. Primary socialization is that which takes place in childhood, secondary socialization is any subsequent induction into new sectors of reality.

The self is a reflected entity, reflecting the attitudes first taken by significant others towards it; the individual becomes what he is addressed as by his significant others (p. 121).

Secondary socialization is the acquisition of role-specific knowledge. The new social reality has to be superimposed on the primary reality which is possibly inconsistent with it. Secondary realities are less subjectively inevitable, less charged, more easily bracketed. Secondary realities (i.e. our jobs) are not threatened in their reality by death or dreams, but trivialized thereby. Routine encounters with non-significant others, such as commuters and writers in the *New York Times,* put aside these metaphysical terrors and act as a chorus in confirming identity.

Subjective reality is thus always dependent upon specific plausibility structures, that is, the specific social base and social processes required for its maintenance (p. 143).

Perfectly successful and unsuccessful socialization is unknown. Only because of this imperfection is legitimation and explanation necessary. Psychology serves to legitimate the identity-maintenance and identity-repair procedures established in the society, providing the theoretical link between identity and the world as these are socially defined and subjectively appropriated. Changes in psychology can arise either from identity crises (i.e. social changes) or theoretical changes.

Berger and Luckmann contend that their view of nature and of society is neither psychologistic, nor sociologistic, but dialectic. Class (society) can affect life expectancy (the physical); sex and food (physical) can be canalized into impotence or nausea reactions by socialization (see Roth, 1969, pp. 90–4): 'man produces reality and thereby produces himself' (p. 168).

**Commentary**

So much for the main drift of Berger and Luckmann's argument. Leaving aside the distraction of their terminology—which horribly compounds sociological barbarisms with the making of neologisms and non-words so characteristic of phenomenologists—Berger and Luckmann succeed in giving an account of the constructed social world that bears interestingly on a number of other problems. One of these is that of reconciling the views of Weber and Durkheim on the nature of the social, the one stressing its meaning to the actors, the other its objectivity, and even lack of meaning or opacity to some of the actors some of the time. In doing this they are addressing the fundamental problem of holism (society is over and above the sum of its parts) versus individualism (society is a collocation of individuals and their interactions). Nothing they say seems to conflict with non-psychologistic individualism (only individuals have aims) as outlined by Popper (1945) and Agassi (1960). They flesh out what it is to say that a social order is somewhat more than the sum of its individual parts. This is well explained in the following.

An institutional world . . . is experienced as an objective reality. It has a history that ante-dates an individual's birth and is not accessible to his biographical recollection. It was there before he was born, and it will be there after his death. This history itself, as the tradition of the existing institutions, has the character of objectivity. The individual's biography is apprehended as an episode located within the objective history of the society. The institutions, as historical and objective facticities, confront the individual as undeniable facts. The institutions are *there,* external to him, persistent in their reality, whether he likes it or not. He cannot wish them away. They resist his attempts to change or evade them. They have coercive power over him, both in themselves, by the sheer force of their facticity, and through the control mechanisms that are usually attached to the most important of them. The objective reality of institutions is not diminished if the individual does not understand their purpose or their mode of operation. He may experience large sectors of the social world as incomprehensible, perhaps oppressive in their opaqueness, but real nonetheless. Since institutions exist as external reality, the individual cannot understand them by introspection. He must 'go out' and learn about them, just as he must learn about nature. This remains true even though the social world, as a humanly produced reality, is potentially understandable in a way not possible in the case of the natural world (p. 57).

Another problem they confront is why it is that man goes in for explanations of his social organization. Here we get their queer idea of us all living comfortably only because we have been able to 'bracket' our basic terror in the face of death. We create symbolic universes like myth, theology, philosophy and science to order and control experiences which threaten to force us to confront these matters nakedly. This may be where the existentialist temperament runs up against Anglo-Saxon sanguiness, for it seems to me that we organize our thoughts into systems of ideas for quite good reasons having nothing to do with death. Order is control, chaos is helplessness. We resist helplessness not so much because of dread of death, but because of a thrust to survive and thrive. Our drive to survive does not require dread in the background; it can be contrasted with lassitude, fatalism, take what's coming.

By and large I find their account useful and illuminating and their influence will show in the next chapter. Before that, I want to enter two reservations, one about their treatment of scientific knowledge, which seems to me to show traces of unreconstructed vulgar sociology of knowledge; the other the problem of why the objectivity or even intractability of our self-made social world is important.

Popper has argued (1945) that the best approximation we have to knowledge is scientific knowledge. Science is located by Berger and Luckmann as the latest phase or development in the chain of legitimating, nomic, symbolic universes which are themselves self-legitimating and self-maintaining unless problematic. The reality dealt with by science, for Berger and Luckmann, is an overarching one which backgrounds the everyday reality of everyday life which they are exploring. They do not make clear that yesterday's advanced science filters down to the public and becomes today's natural way of seeing the world (despite their remark on p. 20 that common sense is impregnated with pre-scientific and quasi-scientific interpretations). There is, to use their favourite word, a dialectical interplay between the worlds of the scientific intellectual *avant-garde* and of the man-in-the-street *arrière-garde*. Scientists move between the two worlds, and it is often the contrast between them that sets them off on new problems (such as, why is the night sky dark?). Rare is the case of the psychotic scientist who mixed up his two worlds and began wearing snow shoes because he was afraid of falling into the interstices between the molecules!

Apart from the obvious objections which could be raised to the evolutionist tinge in the sequence: mythology, theology, philosophy, science,[10] there are other serious objections. In particular, there is such a yawning gap between the former two and the latter two that it is difficult to see how Berger and Luckmann can put them together in the way they do without sensing the incongruity. The very idea that science or philosophy is *a* symbolic universe, or even *a* way of looking at the world is a gross oversimplification.[11] Philosophy and science can also be seen as the opposite of legitimating symbolic universes. They are rather *methods* of critically challenging and scrutinizing those symbolic universes that are on offer. Philosophy uses the Socratic method—and science adds to this the empirical method—to evaluate symbolic universes, and these methods do not themselves incorporate or favour any particular symbolic universe.[12] Moreover, historically, neither science nor philosophy share a core in the way much mythology and theology do. The theories of myth and theology are specific metaphysics suffering only minor variations from one part of the world to another. The theories that have been from time to time entertained in philosophy and in science include a great many types of metaphysical notions, including crypto-mythological and crypto-theological ones. Mythology and theology are in that sense parochial: they do not examine themselves, and they do not give critical attention to other doctrines. Philosophy and science, so far from being legitimating symbolic universes on a par with mythology and theology, are non-parochial *frameworks* within which symbolic universes are appraised and brought into organized conflict, in the hope of approaching nearer to the truth.

Finally, I want to turn to the problem of how human social conventions (inventions) come to take on an almost overwhelming givenness or intractable reality. What Berger and Luckmann do not explain about this, their central problem, is why it is important. The answer, it seems to me, is that none of us wants society to brainwash its members into a state where they accept the social world as it is: given, unalterable. We do not want this because we know that the social world we have created (or had created for us) is far from perfect, far from our ideals, deeply vulnerable to all kinds of criticism, and that, however hard we work to improve it, this will always be true. Also that it needs to be worked on even to stay as good as it is. (For example, we need a new budget every year because each year the problems are a bit different.) Thus there is a twist in all this socializing, objectifying, legitimizing: it must not go too far. As Berger and Luckmann explain, were it accomplished perfectly there could be no problem. Happily it is not, and that leaves us free to confront our shortcomings.

At this point Berger and Luckmann's suggestion that we must de-reify social reality comes to mind. My understanding is that they say this to allow room for criticism and reform. This will hardly do. Our contemporaries in campus revolts try to de-reify by making calls to resist illegitimate authority, etc. This might seem like trying to cope with problems by casting spells. Other reformers and radicals appear to believe that bits of society, like buildings, can be pulled down piece by piece and replaced by something bright, shiny and clean. This is very naïve. All institutions are coercive; all actions and all institutions have undesirable unintended consequences. Moreover, institutions cannot be wiped out like chalk marks on a blackboard: often enough they leave their footprints. Institutions are collections of statuses, associated role-sets, and the actors within these build up many reciprocal social relations, both face-to-face and abstract. This network may have been created by creating the institution; it cannot be so easily dismantled. Effective and useful social relations have ways of establishing and maintaining themselves. Just as individuals revert to type, so do social relations built up between classmates long after they have left school, or couples long after their divorce (cf. the film *The Odd Couple*). Perhaps, the answer may go, not enough has been de-reified if objectionable things continue. Let us renew our efforts to wipe the canvas clean. No. People have to organize their social lives somehow; to imagine that it is possible so to shatter every piece of the social nework that they will have to undertake this task from scratch, along prescribed lines, is a sinister fantasy of omnipotence, based on poor understanding of social life. If Berger and Luckmann's argument gives credence and comfort to such fantasy it is open to criticism.[13]

The study of social reality is important because, I am arguing, we want to change that reality. To change it you have to believe it is there. This involves a form of naïve realism. The social world, like the natural world, is much as it seems. It is not a house of cards that will collapse if we blow on it. However, how the world seems is not clearly separable from the way we evaluate it, the dispositions we attribute to it and to ourselves, and so on. Somehow or other we acquire standards against which we measure the society we make and that makes us. Furthermore, such evaluation is intimately linked to what our critical and scientific researches reveal to us about how things work and what really goes on. What is, is affected by what we think should be: at the same time, our demands for what should be have to take into account what is.[14]

# 6 Concepts and society

PETER: . . . Children know such a lot now. Soon they don't believe
in fairies, and every time a child says, 'I don't believe in fairies'
there is a fairy somewhere that falls down dead. (*He skips
about heartlessly.*)

*Peter Pan*[1]

## Society and the third world

The institutions and other social entities which make up society
are not, perhaps, altogether like Peter Pan's fairies. They do not
depend quite as heavily as fairies do on our belief in them. 'Belief
in' something or other is an ambiguous expression. 'I believe in
you', can mean either, 'I have faith in you as a person', or it can
mean, 'I believe that you exist' (Simmel, 1959*a*, p. 30). Clearly,
the latter is weaker: I cannot have faith in you as a person unless
I believe you exist. Institutions, as I have tried to argue at the end
of the previous chapter, do not as a rule obediently fall down when
we wish them to. When they refuse to budge in this way they might
be described as independent of our belief in their existence, as
'mind-independent'. Nevertheless, to an extent, and in some ways,
they are also mind-dependent: they sometimes wobble when we
cease to believe in their existence, and at other times fail to stand
up, although we will them to.

To take an example from the previous discussion: money. When
people cease to believe in the stability of their money, or, in
general in the economy when 'confidence' is lost, the situation is
already serious. One can end up needing a wheelbarrow to carry
the price of a loaf of bread and still not get it; one can end up like
Roosevelt having to close the banks to shore up the tottering structure of credit. Sometimes one finds the phenomenon of 'confidence'
discussed under the rubric of 'credibility'. It is notorious that a

147

politician whose words repeatedly belie his actions creates a 'credibility gap'—his words lose authority; similarly, if people believe a specific law will not be enforced and on that account is sufficiently generally flouted, it becomes unenforceable; if a sufficient number of people share such attitudes towards all laws and authority, there is little question but that the whole system breaks down. One needs only to remember that Russia, even with three-quarters of a million hastily assembled policemen, found it very difficult to get the Czech people to believe in its authority. It succeeded, after considerable delay, only by classically executing the policy of divide and rule.

Would a complex of beliefs, laws and practices like racialism (or racism) similarly collapse were it not sustained by people's belief? Belief in racialism is usually taken to mean that people have faith in the rightness of racialist ideas or institutions[2] or practices. I mean it in the somewhat weaker sense explained before of 'belief in the existence of'. To have faith in ideas of racial discrimination you have to believe racial discrimination is possible, to believe racial discrimination is possible you have to believe races *exist*, and that there are observable differences between them that allow us to discriminate the one from the other, and thus to practice discrimination.

(This is not to ignore the fact of unconscious or institutional racial discrimination, which could hardly depend on conscious existential beliefs; but those accused of this kind of discrimination would most likely *deny* any belief in the rightness of racial discrimination.)

During his term of office President Lyndon B. Johnson, as I recall, once carefully explained that laws could be passed and enforced, speeches made, largesse and opportunities made available, but that without a fundamental and widespread change of heart the problem of racial discrimination would not be finally solved. Suppose the laws and the change of heart did come about, suppose people on a large scale stopped believing in race, would then everything in the garden be lovely? Personal, commercial, and political behaviour might experience sudden changes, certainly. However, sociology teaches us that such practices and institutions as we dub 'racialist' are not quite as compliant to our thoughts as Peter Pan's fairies. Unlike fairies, monsters do not always go away when you cease to believe in them.

We might try to explain this by pointing out that racialist institutions and racialist role-performances clearly must serve *some* functional purpose, must be *a* means of social (and individual) organization. People use their racialist behaviour in role-performances, which in turn reinforce their identity. To the extent that people use racialist notions to organize themselves, their social relations, and their society, to that extent will racialism constitute a set of vested interests which will resist re-organisation. Indeed, the nature of their commitment to the *status quo* will make such people interpret attempts to change their ideas—directly or via their children—as threats to the stability of their society, and even of themselves. Yet we know too that despite all this, societies do make attempts to suppress racialism. What then happens to the factors previously organized around misconceptions about race; how will they now be organized? Answers to this problem are not hard to construct; we have simply to think it through. Such problems are challenges to our ingenuity, to our mental powers. Just as racialist attitudes are vulnerable to a change of mind on a large scale, so are the institutional aspects of racialism compliant with our mental efforts.

(First will come an acute sensitivity to language. By abjuring racialist language an attempt will be made to give the appearance of overcoming racialism. This sham being exposed, and institutional reform persisted with, there will be a long campaign of retreat, in which the entire spectrum of mechanisms available for delay will be employed: personal, social, legal and even extra-legal. By the time all this has been done there will already be a new generation almost formed. Their parents will already be a write-off and will disappear into the background grumbling. Clearly, I am drawing on the progress of desegregation in the southern United States since 1954, but the movement to abolish slavery, and the processes of de-Nazification in Germany, strike me as closely parallel. This meagre knowledge of such processes will not satisfy those who want to know how to make instant transformations in society, who want to purify it immediately. The sad truth is that this is impossible; people cling to their ideas and attitudes not only when these are thought to be erroneous, but even repugnant by their fellows. The truth does not have the power it was once thought to have of inducing a blinding revelation when the person in error is confronted with it. Change may take a generation or more, unless means of coping with the fears wrapped up in the vested interests are given alternative outlets. This slowness is as it should be. The truth is hard to come by, and each man has the right to quest for it himself; he also has every reason to resist being bullied. A deeper argument also tells against instant purification. One consequence of successful reform is that the society's sights are raised; what were minor irritations now seem like major problems.[3] This is also one reason why Utopianism is infantile: the process of social improvement, like that of self-improvement, is coextensive with the life of the improved.)

The word 'race' in the previous discussion is a variable and an example for all social entities that are conceptualized as part of the system of belief of substantial numbers of the members of the society. But this, after all, incorporates more entities than appears at first sight. Other examples are social class, caste, and even slavery; money, cheques, and even credit. Some members of the society may go so far as to internalize much more grand social phenomena like democracy and capitalism, or even an abstraction like their country, choosing to regard any criticism of these as a personal and social threat, to be denounced as a personal and even moral affront. It is felt intuitively that someone who threatens the root of your being, your identity and its conceptual maintenance apparatus, is morally repugnant; a destroyer. It is difficult to explain why this reaction is so odd and so widespread. After all, our upbringing and hence attachments of this kind are mere accidents of birth. But, then, so are we: we are who we are. If someone offers criticism and suggestion for reform of some aspect of our social organization, we do not appraise it calmly in the light of inputs versus pay-offs, as we would with a machine. We feel that we ourselves are questioned. This is Berger and Luckmann's (and Goffman's, 1961, pp. 319–20) analysis of how identity is defined and maintained by objectifying institutions and social relations, which then reflect and create the self; or by identifying one's person with one's institutional role and positions.

If an insufficient number of people cease to believe in the reality of class, or racialism, or capitalism, then those few who start acting as though it did not exist will soon suffer a rude awakening. Humiliation, ridicule, ruin, or gaol can easily result. There is little doubt that the law works because, by and large, people comply with it: their actions confirm and maintain the objective reality of its authority. Sudden loss of this supporting belief would undermine its authority. This is why a minority which tries to do it is made to suffer severe consequences. Indeed, when a minority which pretends that an institution does not exist is left unpunished, it thereby goes a long way towards abolishing it in fact. The reverse tactic is intriguing: a minority acts and talks as if there were an entity—an example from current fashion would be The Revolution—and one sees at times the peculiar phenomenon of others coming to perceive it too.[4] A sufficiently strong challenge to the legitimacy of an institution, even when made by a minority, can sometimes reveal a hitherto concealed loss of moral authority and inability to respond to determined challenge. Loss of moral authority might seem like a case of belief in the sense of faith in, rather than belief in the existence of. It could be argued, though that loss of moral authority stems from loss of belief in the reality or attainability of the goals to which the institution is dedicated. It is as though Orwell's Ministry of Peace was shattered by the realization that it was conducting war. A current example is the many liberal academics who seem to have reached the conclusion that their institutions (all institutions: Good morning!) are to some extent repressive, that faculty are no better than their students, do not know more, have not really anything to teach such intelligent and concerned young people. This prevents them from defending themselves or their institutions from attack, for they do not recognize the distinction between brainless anti-intellectualism and reasoned disagreement over the aims and means of intellectual institutions.[5]

We can assemble, then, several ways in which the ideas people hold about the society they live in can call forth response or lack of it. Laws which are universally ignored usually cannot be enforced. On occasion a community may agree to abide by a defunct law until it is officially cancelled in the legislature. One way or another, widespread *disbelief* can alter reality; however, *individual* attempts to will away a social reality can result in forcible reminders of that reality. But where there is uncertainty in the institutions and a strong challenge, *minorities* can sometimes work their will in surprising ways. One could cite racialism in Britain. When West Indian immigration began, the official consensus was that race did not exist and could create no problems. Slowly, the vociferous assertions of those who claimed that it did exist and did create problems won first a hearing, and then confirmation, when there were race riots in Notting Hill Gate. At first, rioters were severely punished as if thereby the *status quo* could be maintained. It could not. And so, slowly, with much overlay of hypocrisy and doubletalk, more or less overtly racialist immigration legislation was passed, and increasingly prejudiced behaviour by immigration officials was tolerated.

These examples give rise to certain questions about social entities like institutions and groups, and the relationship between these entities and the mental conceptions of them that we possess. My aim here is to try to solve these problems by working out the consequences of some very important recent work by Popper. In his 'Epistemology Without a Knowing Subject' (1967) and 'On the Theory of the Objective Mind' (1968), he expounds the view that

the world consists of at least three ontological categories; or, as I shall say, there are three worlds: the first is the physical world or the world of physical states; the second is the mental world or the world of mental states; and the third is the world of intelligibles, or of *ideas in the objective sense*; it is the world of possible objects of thought. ('Objective Mind', p. 26.)

He notes that the first two worlds can interact and so can the last two; but the first and the third can interact only through the mediation of the second.

Here, in a nutshell, is a philosophical idea which clarifies and resolves the difficulties we have had with the notion of the situation (chapter 1), with the contrast between understanding and explaining (chapter 2), with the relationship between social reality and our ideas or conceptions of social reality (chapters 3 and 4), and with the sociology of knowledge and socialization (chapter 5). Hitherto, argument has raged between those social scientists who insisted on the reality and observability of the social, even of social structure (Durkheim, 1897; Radcliffe-Brown, 1952, p. 192), and others who saw the social scientist describing structures and entities 'which exist only as logical constructions in his own mind' (Leach, 1954, p. 5). The one group is in the tradition of Durkheim drawing attention to the solid facticity of the social; the other is noting that real people in the real social world do not include social structure in their inventory of the furniture of that universe—that social science involves much rational reconstruction (but then so does much social living; see chapter 1, ref. 15). Like Hayek (1952), Popper treats social entities as real for some intents and purposes; as given and unchangeable; but not for all. They are the results of human action, but rarely of human design, functioning above all (in Agassi's phrase) as conventional means of co-ordination.

Popper does not work out all the implications of his ideas on the third world. Is it, for example, enough for an idea to be thought up for it to be in the third world? Hardly, for that would collapse the second and third worlds into each other. What then marks the transition from thought to third world entity? An idea is a mental state until, perhaps, it is *communicated* in a language or on paper. If the Wittgensteinians are right that Wittgenstein has produced an argument to show that there can be no private languages, that languages cannot be confined to the second world, then the articulation of an idea in a language in a crucial manner objectifies that idea, thrusts it into the public domain, the third world. But marks on paper, it might be said, are public because they are physical states of the physical or first world. This will not do. Marks on paper are physical states, they evoke mental states, and the mediator which does the evoking is their third world content. The unanswerable question is, what is the dependence between the three aspects of an entity such as the American Constitution . . . ?

On this dependence our decisions, for instance, as to whether false ideas, rejected ideas, as-yet-unthought ideas, forgotten ideas, and defunct institutions are in the third world. If the answer is 'yes', then it looks as though ideas and institutions are not like Barrie's fairies. On the contrary, they *are,* because, like dead fairies, they are real in the same way that dead people are real: they existed once, but no longer. Ideas in the third world can die; so they can be born too. What is their status before birth and after death? Our questions concerning the objectivity of an institution as a third world entity turn on questions of the reality of third world entities as such. A troublesome matter in the discussion of the objectivity of institutions is, as with ideas, the pre-natal and post-mortem status of an institution. We could use some help on the question of how third world entities are born and die.[6] (Or do they, like corporations, never die?)[7]

Leaving aside these difficulties, what I shall here try to explore is the meaning or import of Popper's claim when applied to society; the claim that society, social structure, institutions, traditions, groups, and so on, are all objective entities *of the third world*. (The most dramatic unstated consequence of Popper's idea is that *persons, we ourselves, are creatures of the third world.* Where else could we be situated and be successful mediators, manipulators of the other two worlds?) Both the actors and social scientists try to give third world descriptions (statements—preferably true) of these third world entities and their relationships one to another. These attempts constitute activity in the second world of thought and belief, and in the first world of physical actions and behaviour. (Such second world cogitation may have been brought about by a third world conflict, such as whether there is a logical inconsistency in a mathematical system, or, a clash between the way the social world is and the way our third world values tell us it should be.) Whether or not an event in the physical world is a socially significant *action* is a question of interpretation at the level of the second world, but which is an attempt to capture a truth of the third world.

Under this conception, the social world bears a striking resemblance to Barrie's fairies in that its entities are mind-dependent, but they are not mind-originated. The social world is *not* a dream I am having which disappears when I wake up, any more than a true idea I have discovered and published ceases to be true just because I have ceased to believe in it. Unlike a true idea, however, the status of which is not threatened even by universal disbelief, social entities can be jeopardized by universal disbelief—a widespread disinclination to treat them seriously. This view would also supersede a phenomenalist view which held that social entities are constructed out of some universally available raw data. Apart from the idealist underlay in most versions of phenomenalism, Popper's third world allows that our ideas of social entities (abstracted from people's behaviour and many other sources of information) correspond to real entities in a manner not unlike the way in which our ideas of physical objects (abstracted from various direct perceptual data and a lot of projected interpretation and selection) correspond to real objects.

A brief philosophical digression may be in order here. A dream is mind-originated and mind-dependent: wake up and it is gone. Barrie's fairies are mind-dependent but not mind-originated. Social institutions are also not mind-originated, and less mind-dependent in the sense that, as we have seen, our collective disbelief may kill them, yet our individual belief may fail to sustain them, and our most strenuous collective or individual attempts to wish them away may fail.

Both the problem of reality and Popper's three worlds may seem far removed from the realities of social problems. But I aim to show that on one's concept of the nature of the social a great deal turns, including: attitudes to social action, reform, mobility, and change; intellectual grasp of social processes; and perhaps even psychological matters like feelings of insecurity and social strain. We all have a view of the social, whether well or poorly articulated, whether carefully worked out or deeply buried as unscrutinized assumption. Because it is inescapable and so important it demands to be raised as an explicit issue.

My strategy shall be first to explore the dimensions of the problem and the divisions that have arisen over it (pp. 154–9); then I shall explore and develop the thesis (pp. 159–64); and conclude by discussing the problem of depth (pp. 165–72).

## Holism and individualism again

The temptation to state the problem under discussion as, 'what is the nature of society, of the reality of the social?', is very strong. Put in this way, the problem will be readily grasped by conventionally trained philosophers and sociologists; this should, perhaps, be sufficient to recommend it. Yet the temptation must be resisted, I believe, for the problem as so stated becomes a pseudo-problem. It is a pseudo-problem in the general category of essentialism. This word, coined by Husserl and used by Popper,[8] connotes the error of posing 'what is?' questions: 'what really is . . . ?', 'what is the nature of . . . ?', 'what is the essence of . . . ?', etc. These are questions which sound deep and seem to demand deep answers—indeed, the deepest: penetration to the essence or most basic fundamentals of things. Unfortunately, it is all too easy to twist them into the most superficial, namely verbal or definitional: that a word denotes something that has an essence, and the job of definitions is to capture essences. This view stands opposed to that which regards words as conventional names for putative entities that for various purposes have been individuated. Since all definitions are arbitrary conventions, problems of how to define such and such are easily resolved.

'What is the nature of the reality of the social?', then, begs an utterly worthless kind of answer, or an answer beyond our present reach. No verbal formula would solve the genuine problem I have in the back of my mind, but I think the problem may well be within our reach. Closer to what I want to convey would be, 'How is it that some parts of society (for example the law) are much easier to change than others (for example tradition)? How is it that in a tradition like language, progress towards standardization (of pronunciation, spelling, for example) is slow, despite strong propaganda, while growth and change (new phrases and words) are bewilderingly rapid, though entirely unaided (even resisted) and spontaneous? Why is it that a tradition like that of rational critical discussion has constantly to be defended against suppressive attack, whereas a tradition like racism persists in the face of concerted efforts to destroy it? Why does it make sense for an individual to pit himself against apparently overwhelming social forces, but not to pit himself against a brick wall?' My thesis is that the answer has something to do with the role of thought in action, of concepts in society, the metaphysics of the social world.

The most extended philosophical discussion of issues resembling these among contemporary social scientists has appeared in the work of G. H. Mead (1934), his followers Berger and Luckmann (1966), Holzner (1968), and in papers by Agassi (1960), and Gellner (1962). I have devoted the previous chapter to the first four, and will here only briefly look at the latter two.

The principal candidates for serious ontological status in society have been people and groups. Extreme ontological monists have ascribed reality to people and denied it to groups (individualism); others have ascribed it to groups and denied it to individuals (holism). In each case the apparent tangibility of the putative entity denied reality has been explained as an outcome or derivative of the entity endorsed. Agassi's paper 'Methodological Individualism' is an extraordinary compressed discussion of this conflict between holism and individualism in the social sciences, which exists at the level of methodology as well as that of metaphysics. (Many metaphysical existence claims can be turned into methodological injunctions to continue searching until all explanations are satisfactory, i.e. utilize only the entities endorsed by the metaphysics.)[9] Agassi traces connections between these philosophical conflicts and the political conflict between collectivists and individualists.

A methodological holist holds that social entities like groups, institutions, classes, societies, have to be studied as a whole. This, he says, is because they combine and organize discrete individuals in such a way that new macro-entities emerge, possessing macro or emergent properties distinct from those possessed by the component individuals. Moreover, this macro-social level is the level at which sociological problems are posed, and explanations, laws, and theories, found. A methodological holist wants to stress that society is a 'whole' which is more than the sum of its parts; that social factors affect the aims of individuals; and that social factors influence and constrain individuals' behaviour when in pursuit of these aims.

An ontological holist is one who holds that groups combine and organize individuals into a new entity, a super-individual, from participation in which the individual gets his sole reality. It might seem, then, that all ontological holists are methodological holists and vice versa. This is not so. Structural-functional anthropology in its more extreme Durkheimian wing could be regarded as ontologically holist, yet anthropological fieldwork is methodologically individualist. Similarly, a methodological holist like Marx might be described as an ontological individualist in some of his moods.

An ontological individualist wants to argue that the only real entities in the social world are individual persons;[10] that social structure and social organization would be patterns of interrelatedness between persons and not stand over and above persons. Institutions would be unreal abstractions: when it comes down to it, you are not arrested by the police but by a policeman; you do not do things for the sake of your family but for the sake of your wife and/or your daughters and/or your sons, etc. Persons are usually construed as individual entities in social space. The ontological individualist will not have social space, so persons can only exist in each other's psychological space. That is why Agassi identifies ontological individualism with psychologism: the doctrine that psychological factors, laws, and theories are the ultimate constituents of explanations of social behaviour. Ontological individualism only clashes with ontological holism if they are formulated so as to be mutually exclusive.

A methodological individualist, on the other hand, while stressing that society and social entities are made up of individual people, their actions and relationships; that only individuals have aims and interests; that individual actions are to be explained as attempts to realize aims, given the circumstances; and that the circumstances are changeable as a result of individuals' actions; need not deny the equal reality of social circumstances.

With the aid of an ingenious analytical table, Agassi is able to show that the principal doctrines of holism and individualism are not always incompatible. Only when the holist adopts the doctrine that wholes must have aims does the clash begin, for this makes the individualist appear to be denying aims, and thus existence, to wholes. Agassi insists that only individuals, not wholes, or groups, have aims. Apparent aim-directed behaviour in wholes can be explained as agglomerations of individuals acting to gain their individual aims. To the holists Agassi is prepared to concede that a social whole is more than the sum of its individual parts.[11] He refuses, however, to concede Gellner's earlier charge (1956) that methodological individualism reduces sociology to biography *en grande série*. Methodological individualism is not a reductionism that would eliminate all but individuals from sociological explanation. That this is a gross misinterpretation has already been suggested by Watkins (1957). True, were aims to be made the criterion of social reality, Agassi's view would confer reality only on individuals; doubtless Agassi would regard such a criterion of reality as idiosyncratic. Both wholes and individuals are real for Agassi; the one moulds and constrains, the other aims and initiates.

In his paper 'Concepts and Society' (1962) Gellner discusses the claims to ontological priority of neither people nor groups, but turns instead to the question of ideas: are *they* part of the furniture of the social universe? Current doctrines like functionalism find this a problem. Those who accept Agassi's methodological pluralism, but not his methodological individualism, will find functionalism a most attractive way out. Various versions have currency, all of which explain patterns of behaviour by showing their relationship to other patterns and institutions and how they function to sustain each other and the society as a whole, or, at least, its stability. Among the difficulties that face functionalism is the explanation of concepts and beliefs. These are institutions among others, but they may be diverse and even obscure. How can functions be ascribed to obscure and diverse concepts and beliefs? The difficulty is that functionalism involves interpretation, for example, that ostensibly divisive Nuer feuding promotes cohesion because it unites disparate groups together when they take sides along prescribed kinship lines. But an obscure utterance—for example, the Nuer's 'twins are birds' (Evans-Pritchard, 1956; Firth, 1966)—or an ambiguous, diversely used concept—for example, 'alienation' (Feuer, 1962 and 1969a)—is not so readily susceptible to the dialectical twist. Against those who argue *a priori* that, since everything must have a function, so must concepts and beliefs, so if they are obscure or even absurd and hence difficult to interpret then interpret them symbolically. Gellner wants to turn the tables and say that perhaps their very obscurity, divergent use, and ambiguity are their chief function.

Gellner comes at the problem through the problem of how to translate literally obscure or absurd concepts of one language into concepts in one's own language. The usual answer is to search for interpretation, by taking into account the context in which they are used. But where does one draw the line? Does one go on incorporating context until a translatable meaning is found, even if that involves unconscious or symbolic interpretation (the context making nonsense of literal interpretation)? No, says Gellner, this is taking a charitable attitude to other people's assertions too far. Part of the true translation of the concepts may preserve their vagueness, obscurity, or absurdity, because these attributes may be essential to their functioning as they do. Thus does Gellner very strongly endorse the reality of ideas, not only true ideas, and possibly true ideas; not only beliefs descriptive of what people do, or ought to do, or might do; but even of the meaningless and of the absurd. Whatever functions is real.

Neither Agassi's endorsement of an ontological pluralism that includes wholes and individuals, nor Gellner's argument for the reality and effectiveness of even absurd ideas, constitutes more than a peripheral attack on our problem. In another work of Heraclitean tinge, Gellner (1965) produces a new candidate for the ontological inventory. Besides groups, people, and ideas, he brings up social processes, and especially the massive social process known as 'the transition to industrialization'. Indeed, Gellner wants to argue that The Transition is the central social, political, historical, and philosophical reality of the present day. He thinks that wherever it occurs it has such impact on society, history, values, *and thought,* that to ignore it is to be fundamentally out of touch with reality. While I find his argument about the centrality of industrialization convincing, I would not care to reify it in quite the way I fancy he does (probably without intending to). The process of *transition,* it seems to me, is an abstraction we construct, but not a reality as such. One reason might be this. The Transition is not a concept which enters into our grasp of the logic of our situation. True, the social sciences reveal hidden realities to us and perhaps The Transition is one of these. It may thus allow us to systematize and explain things. But it will remain for some time an abstraction of science and will have to be spelled out into more concrete components when the logic of the situation of those involved in it and affected by it is studied. Perhaps such components as the desire for a higher material standard of living, for industrial employment, for surplus wealth, leisure and welfare. Indeed, perhaps The Transition is meant only as a shorthand for such items as these. If so, then I have no criticism to offer. But The Transition as such has not yet, so far as I know, entered into the reality I am concerned to explore, that which is constructed without benefit of the social sciences, that which can be conceptualized as part of everyday experience.

This reservation would probably not perturb Gellner. His is a work of philosophy, although some contemporary philosophical technicians attempting to review it have been unable to grasp that this is so. In calling The Transition the cardinal reality of our time, for thought *and* action, Gellner wants to alter our whole way of looking at the world. The traditional name for this enterprise of changing an outlook is 'metaphysics'. Although the present chapter is concerned with metaphysics, it is not quite on the grand scale of Gellner's. Gellner is concerned with each item of social life as an aspect of The Transition, whereas I am concerned only with the changeability of social entities as a problematic aspect of their objectivity.

## Mapping the social world

When we choose and act we are constrained on the one hand by hard reality: our physical surroundings and bodily limitations; on the other hand by soft reality: our putative knowledge, our morals, fears, neuroses, imagination, etc. Between hard and soft, constraining us, canalizing all we do—the frame of reference, so to speak—is the social world made up of other people, institutions, groups, friendships, relatives, etc. These are neither hard nor soft, but a bit of both. How are we to characterize this simultaneous intangibility (our five senses give us no direct access to, say, the institution of marriage or to the social structure in which it is embedded), and manifest effectiveness of social entities (so effective that the debate over the paramountcy of nature or nurture seems endless)? On the one hand, social entities are, like mental states, intangible; like friendliness and goodwill they may come out of nothing and fade into nothing. On the other hand, they are like physical states, they react strongly to our probes: when, as an exercise, one *acts* as though a brick wall is not there, one may suffer severe consequences, and the same is true of many social institutions, from table manners to taxes.

The problem, 'how real are social entities?', is usually, and quite naturally, studied within the matrix of a general theory of reality. Philosophers have usually contrasted the real world with the (delusive) world of appearance. Naïve realists deny this contrast (albeit implicitly, of course), holding that the world is naturally just as it seems. Phenomenalists hold that the world is constructed by us out of the phenomena which impinge on our senses. Idealists fantasize that the world is a mental projection (either by us [psycho-

159

CONCEPTS AND SOCIETY

logical idealism or solipsism], or by the Absolute [sociological idealism]); materialists fantasize that mentality is an aspect of the material brain. All of these positions, and their variations, can be found knocking around among the casual remarks gathered together in textbooks of the social sciences, under titles like 'the nature of society'. Strangely enough, when the matrix is applied to social entities a short circuit takes place, since the viability of social entities turns to such an extent on what people take them to be. This means that all monisms when applied to social entities are self-refuting, because they have repercussions and hence feedback in worlds other than that permitted by the monism. Mentalist monism says that society is mental, it can be explained as being what people think it is. Yet laws, traffic lights, etc., are out there, not just in the mind. They are out there precisely because of thought, but thought is not all they are. That they are out there and that we know it, shows that co-ordination is possible between persons, and the co-ordinating thing is not of the mental order (see ref. 10). So, beliefs affect action and action beliefs, and no purely mentalist or psychologistic account of society is adequate. This brief argument is embarrassingly sweeping and one should give seriously entertained doctrines more of a hearing. Mentalist monism about social entities (society is in the mind) is really not much more serious than solipsism (of which it is a variant), so let us instead look in more detail at a materialist monism, perhaps the most prevalent position in the philosophy of the social sciences today, namely, the positivist-phenomenalist doctrine of behaviourism. This serves to assuage the frustration felt by sociologists and psychologists when forced to state their problems using notions like 'mind', 'thought' and 'social institution'. Are not these entities at the very best inferred rather than directly perceived? How can vague, subjective notions of this kind undergird 'hard science'? Why not stop inferring and work only with raw observations?

A special complication, however, appears when behaviourism is applied to the social. To a very considerable extent social entities depend on what people think they are, upon ideas. To what extent and in what way? Well, Hayek (1952) distinguishes two levels here, some 'ideas . . . are *constitutive* of the phenomena we want to explain . . . a condition of the existence of "wholes" . . . which will exist irrespective of the concepts which people have formed about these wholes' (p. 36–7). Contemporary philosophers might call these ideas inferred rules (to use Kleene's idiom) as opposed to explicit rules. The existence of the institution is constituted by these rules, but perception of it is not. Perception takes us to the other levels: to the ideas people have *about* the social entities that surround them. But this is another matter again. Since social entities

160

are not directly perceived, but rather 'inferred', our actions taken in regard of them are already predicated on inference.

So the behaviourist, by forswearing inferences, can neither identify social entities, nor understand why people act, because inference has been intrinsically involved in both. Thus, if we mistakenly infer from a news broadcast that a race riot has started and we roam the streets attacking those of the race to which we do not belong, then the net effect is not greatly different from what it would have been had the news broadcast been accurate in the first place. The explanation of the race riot, however, would be somewhat different —it would be an unintended consequence of the news broadcast. We could sum this up in the slogan: society is what society does.

The behaviourist has an answer to this. Skinner says, society is what people do, where 'do' includes 'say'. This does not bridge the gap from saying 'There is riot in the street' to rioting in the street. Yet riot sometimes makes people report riot and vice versa.

People living in a society have to find their way around it, both to accomplish what they want and to avoid what they do not want. We might say that to do this they construct in their minds a conceptual map of the society and its features, of their own location among them, of the possible paths which will lead them to their goals, and of the hazards along each path.[12] The maps are in a way softer than geographic maps—like dream maps they create the terrain they are mapping. Yet in a way this is a harder reality: geographical maps are never real but sometimes reflect real terrains, yet social maps *are* terrains to be studied and mapped by other people. The difficulty that the view I am outlining immediately faces is that everyone will be seen as having his own map, a product of his personal interpretation and selective perception, and drawn to his personal projection. Are we, then, confronted with a chaos of subjective maps and no way of getting at the reality that is supposed to be being mapped? Two means are at hand to avoid this consequence: (1) the fact that individuals' maps are to some extent—but not fully—co-ordinated with each other; (2) the fact that on occasion—even if not always—individuals can test for the truth or falsity of their maps. (1) is the possibility of description and communication. The fact that people can describe, discuss, and argue about the features of their social world, and then act in concord, constitutes an on-going process of intersubjectively testing the co-ordination of these maps. (2) Even without explicit co-ordination with others, people can act, observe the outcome, and learn. This process is only a special case of the co-ordination and interaction described in (1), because in the social world all action is interaction. We can reasonably argue, then, that the possibility exists that our maps bear some relation of verisimilitude to that of which they are supposed to be maps. The fact that that which the maps try to map is in a continual state of change, makes the process of checking and revising our maps of paramount importance. (Indeed, one might even try to relate the rise of these self-conscious and explicit attempts to map society and its workings, which we call the social sciences, to the increasingly diverse, abstract, massive and complicated nature of the social world.)[13] It is a process we begin as soon as we attempt to grasp and come to terms with the world as infants. We acquire our initial maps during primary socialization within the nuclear family, but the process does not stop there—or, if it does, sociopathy may result. As we attempt to come to terms with social realities outside the nuclear family, in school and job (secondary socialization), our perspective on the social world constantly shifts. We are always having to redraw out internal maps as we go along. Some people do this less than others. If a map has hitherto been a perfectly satisfactory guide, one will not easily jettison it. Yet we value schooling and travel because, among other things, they broaden the mind—to wit, alter our perspective on things, and especially on the social world.

The mental map of the social world, I say, is largely about other people's mental maps. The mental map is also one on which it locates itself and, inasmuch as one does identify with one's mental map, it locates one's self; in this way it contributes to one's identification of self and thus one's internalized sense of reality. Consequently, the failure of actions guided by the map can seem threatening and ego-bruising. This can lead, not to learning, but to the attempt to coerce society to bring it into line with one's map. Freud argued that children and certain neurotics suffer when they attempt to work their will on the disobedient world. The dictator leading the army, or the exultant revolutionary, are both fantasizing that the world is theirs to command. Fear of ego-bruising can also result in over-eagerness to learn and adapt, resulting in severe loss of identity and individuality. Armies and other total institutions sometimes deliberately make use of this reaction in order to remould people to their purposes (see Goffman, 1961, especially 'The Moral Career of the Mental Patient').

The social sciences would appear to be in the awkward position of trying to stand outside the point of view of any one individual and drawing maps of society which only show features on which there is some general agreement, where people's maps overlap. But this will not suffice. The social sciences also attempt to reveal 'hidden' realities behind the appearances, to show counter-intuitive connections, to point out phenomena like poverty in rich countries which hardly anybody seemed to have noticed, or to show feud as a cohesive force between tribes. Assuming some of these things are discoveries by individual social scientists, the maps they will be proffering will initially be as idiosyncratic as those of any individual. Yet, somehow, superior scientific status is being claimed for them, and with the short circuiting result that they are soon mapped by many others and thus enter the public domain.

Here we are coming up against another weakness of the map metaphor. It is somewhat instrumentalist: maps are usually drawn to serve a purpose, to be useful. Doubtless this is why we try to acquire knowledge: because it will be useful in the struggle to survive. The sciences, however go beyond this, and seek to judge our ideas by whether they are true or false (Simmel, 1959*b*, p. 310). Clearly, grossly false maps will not be useful. Nevertheless, we can navigate around cities with sketch maps, which are for many purposes misleading, and some people may get through life with the equivalent of sketch maps of the social world. In the social sciences too, we aspire to truth even beyond its manifest utility. But just as no map is useful for all purposes, no social map can correctly represent the whole truth about the social world. The set of all possible useful maps of either the social or the physical world is infinite. And so the search for the perfect map is a dream, an essentialist wild goose chase.

Essentialism leads to an arbitrary and uncritical metaphysics. The dream that there is a perfect map is epistemic essentialism. Dreaming after it is acceptable; believing you have it is not. One's principal objection to epistemic essentialism is that there are no criteria for knowing that we have the essence. In the absence of criteria, the logical thing to do is declare all claims on the essence tentative. This will avoid the danger of arbitrary and uncritical metaphysics. This danger may explain why Popper, who is far from an essentialist, so strongly endorses the value of keeping practical aims uppermost in the social sciences. Having a practical check on our mapping operations, our search for the perfect map, is better than having no check at all, especially when the thing we are trying to map in the social sciences is so elusive. This elusiveness of social reality is at the heart of what is being argued in this chapter: the conceptual nature of social reality: the location of social reality in the third world, a world the features of which are constantly changing as they interact with physical states through the mediation of mental states. However, it needs to be said that not all societies and social entities in this third world are equally difficult to map. Some are smaller and changing less than others. One of the big differences between the societies that are as a rule studied by anthropologists, and those taken as the province of the sociologists, is the greater difficulty of constructing accurate maps of the latter. One of the beauties of small-scale, largely face-to-face societies, is the close co-ordination of the component individuals' social worlds or maps. Kinship network, political system, co-operative agriculture, rights and duties, role performance, all are closely defined and co-ordinated by constant exchange and intercourse. This may be what gives these societies their strength and endurance, until their world-map is shaken by contact with another and cognitively more powerful one.

Interaction between ideas and mental states is stronger in our large-scale and abstract society; where only very small subgroups are aware of each other and what is going on; where total communication and therefore total co-ordination of maps of society is impossible; indeed, much of the dynamic of the society arises from clashes and tensions between these discrepant maps. There are two levels of lack of co-ordination: there is lack of co-ordination between the maps of different people, and there is lack of co-ordination between people's maps and the world as it is. Yet the so-called 'world as it is' is a product of people acting on the basis of their maps, discrepant or not.

The shortcircuiting of their interaction is, indeed, particularly strong in the case of discrepancies just because people try to sort out the discrepancies on both levels. They try to co-ordinate their maps of what it is like out there by communicating about them, discussing them, refuting, refining, and replacing them. They also try to bring their maps into line with the way the world is. Every action is a probe into the social environment, and from the feedback is gained certain information relevant to the map. But we go further than this. We overtly try to persuade other people to bring their maps into line with ours. (This may not be the most efficient way to approximate the reality mapped; but in view of ego-involvement it is perfectly understandable.) The other people may be quite content with their understanding, but we may take it on ourselves to rouse them from that state with new revelations and map projections which they are encouraged to adopt. This persuasion may be gentle, or it may be violent, done in a critical spirit, or done in the heretic-exterminating frenzy of the religious fanatic. We also may take similar attitudes towards the world out there. We may gently probe it and try to refine our ideas about it; we may also assault it violently in order to try to force it to come into line with our ideas of how it should be, even if it isn't.[14]

So much for what is going on, for the changeability yet objectivity of social entities, for the separateness of social entities from mental and/or physical states, and for the interplay of the three, especially in modern abstract society. This may be the place to express an evaluation in two paragraphs. This constant struggle, this pushing and pulling between competitive maps, this attempt by people to persuade others that things are not quite the way they think, their direct attempts to see that things do not remain the way they are, provide much of the motive force for change in a modern, large, pluralistic society. As Berger and Luckmann rightly stress, it is the failure of perfect socialization that makes this possible. If children were perfectly socialized so that they all internalized the same accurate map of their (closed?) society and its workings, then their adopting a critical attitude, either to change or to learning about society, would be very difficult to conceive. Happily, no society socializes its young perfectly, and the bigger and more complex the society the less is this feasible anyway. So that there is no problem in the fact that large modern societies have wide discrepancies between the maps of their members, rather is that the secret of their success.

It should however be admitted that pluralism of this kind imposes a great deal of strain on the individual. The adaptive purpose of human knowledge seems to have a lot to do with expectation, and hence control of, or at least defence against, the environment. Constantly disappointed expectations, repeated failures of defence, can produce anxiety and poor function of the organism. While a plural society is not necessarily one that is threatening directly, its diversity, unpredictability, and liability to change, can produce strained reaction in many people. Their survival may not be threatened but they sometimes act as though it is. This dysfunctional tension is only the other side of the coin of the creative tension engendered in a similar way.

We have argued, then, that the social is an independent realm between the hard physical world and the soft mental world. Indeed, as we shall see below, it is the crucial mediator between the two. This realm, reality, world, whatever we choose to call it, is very diverse and complex and people in society are constantly striving by trial and error to come to terms with it; to map it; to co-ordinate their maps of it. Living in an unmanageably large and changing society permits neither perfect mapping, nor perfect co-ordination of maps. This means that the members of the society are constantly learning about it; both the society and its members are in a constant process of self-discovery and of self-making.

### Objectivity, depth and criticism

Various objections, clearly, could be levelled against the view here developed. Positivists, behaviourists, functionalists, phenomenologists, doubtless could all attack its radical deviations from their respective points of view. Of more direct concern would be attempts to discover inadequacies or inconsistencies within this view itself.

**165**

One claim in particular seems vulnerable to such attack: that viewing social entities as like theoretical constructs in the third world explains the increasing depth and progress of social studies. Depth in that we grope after new 'hidden realities'; progress in that we refine our gropings by argument, including empirical evidence. There are various ways in which the critic can deny that the introduction of the third world of concepts legitimizes and explains depth and progress in the social sciences. Let me phase his argument into four thrusts and parries, which I will try to summarize now. (1) The idea of third world maps is vague and wishy-washy, hardly a promising tool for hard-headed scientific probing of the world. The answer to this is that by criticism we try to increase the verisimilitude of our maps (and, hence, decrease their vagueness and wishy-washiness) and we have a basic control on them because they must, like all scientific models, at least conform to our metaphysics. (2) It could be claimed that my own metaphysical view on the reality of maps does not admit depth because maps are simultaneously the entities to be explained and the explanations of the entities. This means I am stuck in a circle in one plane. Answer: maps are not always their own true or satisfactory explanation, and by exposing and discarding false ones, and replacing them, we may hope to increase verisimilitude and depth. (3) What can be used to expose and improve maps in this way? Maps are self-verifying for the reason given in (2) and so cannot be gone beyond. Answer: not always in a plural, abstract society where there are competing maps and people compare notes, and so on. (4) Such depth and progress of ideas as is attained is worthless if not dangerous because it is confined to an 'enlightened' élite. Again the answer is: not necessarily in a diverse and abstract society in which people strive to compare notes about discrepancies of ideas, including the conventions of being critical, and so on. Now let us look at these parries and thrusts in more detail.

(1) How is objectively deep and progressive social science possible if the world the science is investigating is a kind of shifting sand of overlapping mental maps? This is a difficult objection to cope with; clearly we have not yet had any really spectacular successes in the social sciences. We are thus arguing about possibilities. Perhaps the fluidity or lack of 'givenness' of the social world could be used to explain the difficulty of getting the social sciences going. A second point to be made is that science always proceeds by building models and theories, which necessarily over-simplify complicated situations. All science is over-simplification, and the enterprise consists primarily in making strenuous efforts to reduce the degree of it. This is why we explain in the social sciences by means of the device of the logic of the situation of the typical

individual. One of the things we have to typify is his mental map of the society he imagines he confronts. It is important at this point to bring out that the social world he confronts and the social world he thinks he confronts are rarely one and the same. To argue otherwise would be a form of idealism, if not of solipsism, which is wholly out of spirit with my main thesis. All along, I have stressed that while society is mind-dependent it is not a mental fiction, or a malleable clay on which we can work our will.

This latter characteristic, this hardness or intransigence of the social world—which may be, as I have suggested, a product of the overlapping of the maps of others—is perhaps what makes the social sciences possible. That thought is translated into action, and that action and reaction reverberate through chains of groups and institutions, not to mention individuals, gives us something tangible to get a purchase on.

In a way, my reply to this first charge of vagueness has been proceeding backwards. Before anything else I should have counter-attacked the assumption that science is the study of *things;* science is in fact the attempt to solve *problems.* Things are disclosed to us by the theories we produce to solve the problems. If the social world is sufficiently objective for us to be able to formulate communicable problems, problems which mean something to other people not imprisoned within our viewpoint, then it would seem logical enough to claim that similarly communicable solutions can and should be sought, can and should be implemented. The study of these problems and solutions, and the struggle to correct and improve both problems and solutions, is the activity we know as empirical science. Its objectivity, as I have explained elsewhere, is not a property of the particular relations thought to obtain between the statements made in the science and the thing-world of which they are thought to be descriptive. Those sorts of relations are covered by the various notions surrounding the idea of truth. Rather is objectivity, as Popper has emphasized, a third world property; it resides in the social relationships which constitute scientific activity, and especially the relationship of communication. If the problem and solution can be shared with other scientists, can be criticized, improved, rejected by other scientists, then the social set-up exists for objectivity to be possible.[15] If objective enquiry is possible, then objective increases in depth may be possible.

(2) Is this idea reconcilable with the society of map-makers pictured earlier in this chapter? Are not people's mental maps of their society no more than folk wisdom, couched in the characteristic mental limitations of pre-scientific ideas and therefore bearing very little resemblance to the main features of society as detached social scientists would analyse it? Can there be a detached analysis? Are

these folk maps not necessarily used, even by social scientists? Does not that mean that social science must remain with the concepts—deep or not—as they are found? This issue, of the relation between the concepts used by ordinary men in the course of ordering their social activities, and the analytic concepts it pleases social scientists to use in the course of explaining what ordinary men are doing, is one that has aroused much discussion.[16] Peter Winch has specifically attacked a passage in *The Poverty of Historicism* (Popper, 1957 *a*) on these grounds. Popper writes (p. 135) that

> in the social sciences it is even more obvious than in the natural sciences that we cannot see and observe our objects before we have thought about them. For most of the objects of social science, if not all of them, are abstract objects; they are theoretical constructions. (Even 'the war' or 'the army' are abstract concepts, strange as this may sound to some. What is concrete are the many who are killed; or the men and women in uniform, etc.) These objects, these theoretical constructions used to interpret our experience, are the result of constructing certain models (especially of institutions), in order to explain certain experiences . . .

In criticism of this passage Winch writes (1958, p. 127–8):

> the ways of thinking embodied in institutions govern the way members of the societies studied by the social scientists behave. The idea of war . . . was not simply invented by people who wanted to *explain* what happens when societies come into armed conflict. It is an idea which provides the criteria of what is appropriate in the behaviour of members of the conflicting societies. Because my country is at war there are certain things which I must and certain things which I must not do. My behaviour is governed, one could say, by my concept of myself as a member of a belligerent country. The concept of war belongs *essentially* to my behaviour. But the concept of gravity does not belong essentially to the behaviour of a falling apple in the same way: it belongs rather to the physicist's explanation of the apple's behaviour.

Winch's contention seems to be that because ordinary social concepts inhabit and govern our actions in a way that physical concepts do not, they are not disposable explanatory tools, so the social sciences must be less conceptually free than the natural sciences.

Winch's argument puzzles me, because I do not see that it contradicts what Popper has said at all. To begin the task of

explaining this it is necessary to stress a distinction already introduced (p. 160 above), due to Hayek and recently reiterated in
another form by MacIntyre (1967). This is to distinguish those
concepts, rules, and ideas which *constitute* the phenomena we want
to explain, from those concepts, rules, and ideas which we marshal
to do our *explaining*. There may well be an overlap between these
two categories, but the differences remain considerable. The rules
people follow need not necessarily be the rules they professedly
follow. As Hayek says (1952, p. 37):

> The beliefs and opinions which lead a number of people
> regularly to repeat certain acts, e.g. to produce, sell, or buy
> certain commodities, are entirely different from the ideas they
> may have formed about the whole of 'society', or the
> 'economic system', to which they belong and which the aggregate
> of their actions constitutes.

Habitual actions may indeed follow rules and yet may be given no
thought at all. War, however, is a rather complex case. If I open
my blackout curtains at night and the ARP Warden enquires
rhetorically, 'Lights out; don't you know there's a war on?', what
will my response be? It may be indignation if the idea of war, or
that there is a war, or that this is the way war is, is new to me.
If I call back, 'Sorry', and put out the light, Winch could say that
my behaviour is governed by my concept of myself as a member
of a belligerent country. 'War' functions as a dispositional: because
we conceive of ourselves at war, we are disposed to behave in
certain ways and not in others. In another area of war, the obedience
of well-trained infantrymen to the orders of their commanders
obeys rules, but is not at all governed by their concept of themselves as members of a belligerent community, or by any concept
of theirs at all.

So, some actions are informed by our concepts of what war is,
and the associated rules of appropriate behaviour (Winch); some
actions are not (Hayek, MacIntyre); and sometimes social scientists
may introduce concepts and distinctions which are not available
to the actors at all (Popper, Hayek, MacIntyre). We shall have to
probe deeper if we are to get at what Winch objects to. He seems
to think that what a social scientist does is to ask why you are
doing such and such and, upon being told that there is a war on
and such and such behaviour is appropriate to war, is satisfied.
This somehow allows that the reasons an actor may give for his
behaviour are the last word. (A motto for a modest social science:
neither the first word nor the last word be.) Such questions would
not arise without a background of problems needing explanation;

169

such reasons could not possibly be acceptable solutions to those problems.

Someone of the Winchian inclination could argue as follows: Ordinary people do not use categories like 'role-set' and 'socio-economic status grouping' in constructing their mental maps of the meaningful universe, and their use therefore leads to a false and scientistic objectivity. Gellner, in the paper already referred to, rebutted this argument by pointing out that indigenous concepts may simply not be adequate to the task of conceptualizing what is going on and that if translation from one language or set of concepts to another has any point, then there can be no objection in principle to developing analytic categories which are not indigenous.

My own reply would incorporate two further points. The first is that whether or not a war is going on is not a question to be decided by asking the participants. They are not at war because they think they are, even if they also behave appropriately. Similarly they are not *not* in a market because they don't know it or understand it. Their point of view is not privileged. Whether or not a war is going on in a certain place depends on various arbitrary legal, political and even *post hoc* historical criteria. Contemporary America is a vivid case in point where the application of indigenous notions like 'war', 'revolution', 'uprising', 'legitimate resistance', etc., are heavily in dispute. Students think they are conducting a struggle to revolutionize society; Feuer explains how they are merely replaying the eternal conflict of generations. Black militants describe the police and the National Guard as imperialist occupying forces; Presidents and Governors describe them as peace officers. This sort of non-communication is one among many reasons why social scientists have developed some descriptive models which do not rely wholly on the vocabulary of the actors. From Marx and his 'exploitation', 'surplus value', 'class consciousness' and 'class struggles', through to the plethora of categories of modern sociology, such vocabularies have served to explain, to go deeper than, conventional categories.

This connects up with my second point which concerns the overlap between mental maps and the actions and reactions of the individuals possessed of the maps. The categories of the social sciences are needed precisely to describe and discuss: the relations between the maps of different people; the patterns of map distribution in the population; the relation of map overlaps to patterns of action; and so on. A map is like a universe of discourse: in order to describe and evaluate a universe of discourse one has to step outside of the universe of discourse.

(3) Do the maps allow appraisal and even supersession? The

argument that people's behaviour stems from their dispositions, which in turn stem from their concepts, suggests that people's maps are self-verifying—that they implement their maps, they live out their concepts. This is because of imperfect socialization (or brainwashing) which has left us with a diverse society in which no one map is true for any length of time, if at all, and so is, must be, constantly being revised and superseded. In societies more homogenous than ours maps are not superseded so readily. Evans-Pritchard is able to list twenty-two ways in which Azande sustain their magic map in the face of failure (1937, p. 475–8). The struggle for depth is not an easy one.

(4) This raises a final objection, perhaps broader in scope and implication. Does not the argument for the depth of social science maps, as opposed to folk maps, put the social scientists in a privileged position, with god-like insight into what really happens, which is concealed from the little human ants scuttling around inside their limited mental maps? Is it not dangerous and corrupt for any human being or group to arrogate to themselves such an all-seeing capacity? Is not this precisely the objection raised against Mannheim's sociology of knowledge (chapter 5)? This sort of attitude might be appropriate for ethologists studying baboons, but it is quite another thing for human beings to take it to each other.

This criticism, I confess, perturbs me. True, we do this sort of thing: censors and judges, for example, make a profession of it. We even do it to ourselves as we reflect on our doings of yesterday, or last week, or last year, and feel a bit like a god in doing so. But to say that it is done is not to say that it deserves to be institutionalized as a practice in new areas. Especially is this to be feared when social scientists are notoriously of a radical and opinionated cast of mind, prone to react with frustration when their beautiful revelations and schemes are not treated with due respect, to preach that it is man who has to be moulded to fit the new social order, rather than vice versa.

How, then, to cope? First perhaps by saying that the difference of depth between the maps of ordinary chaps and the maps of sociological chaps is not yet very great. Social scientists are constructing maps which include the maps of other chaps as part of the landscape. But their maps also overlap, to a considerable extent, with those of ordinary people who co-inhabit the society with them. (Social scientists cannot, happily escape being men, however hard they sometimes try.) Furthermore, the social scientist makes his information public and thus offers his maps to whoever cares to master them. Still further, the social scientist, by exposing his maps to public gaze, in a sense exposes them to criticism, test, and improvement. Thus he does not arrogate to himself a privileged position denied to others. He is no worse than a doctor, who also can regard human foibles as something to observe with amused tolerance. A doctor knows that funny behaviour and beliefs are a delusion of illness; he may even know of very widespread misperceptions—or think he does. Where danger lurks for both him and the social scientist is when he concludes that not everyone is really capable of, or up to, possessing the kind of enlightenment he has. It follows that, for others' sake, the enlightened élite should be in charge.

This is a dangerous doctrine. It is best controverted not specifically from the social sciences, or even from political principle, but from the canons of good scientific method. *Hubris*, pride, the view that we and we alone know, is an attitude incompatible with critical and objective scientific enquiry. If the only thing we learn from history is that no one ever learns from history, then the only thing we know for sure in science is that we never do know for sure. Only those who know for sure will try to work their will on the world, however much it resists; and those who know for sure have no place in the ranks of scientists. So my final answer to this criticism is: no doctrine is without consequences, no consequences are other than a mixture of potential good and potential evil. Our view of things cannot be altered or constrained by the possible temptations such knowledge may place in front of some people. Ye shall know the truth and the truth shall set ye free. Yet some may use it to try to enslave you again. The latter idea cannot, without self-contradiction, be used to constrain the former. If, in fear of enslavement, we curb the pursuit of truth, we in that act introduce enslavement. To be set free involves taking risks and decisions, involves having intellectual, political and moral courage. But then so does living in the society—any society—we are trying to understand.

# Appendix

## The methodological individualism debate

One of the liveliest debates to have graced the philosophy of social sciences has taken place over the issue of methodological individualism. Spread out over most of the nineteen-fifties, and taking in several journals, the debate and its component articles and discussions have become classical, anthologized a great deal. Since the ideas developed in this book stem from a sophisticated methodological individualist position, it may be of interest to review the debate as a background to my own contribution. Since the debate was so vigorous and concentrated, I shall try to set it out as a dialogue.

Hayek (1952, originally 1942, pp. 37–9): 'It is a mistake to which careless expressions by social scientists often give countenance, to believe that their aim is to *explain* conscious action. This, if it can be done at all, is a different task, the task of psychology. For the social sciences the types of conscious action are data and all they have to do with regard to these data is to arrange them in such orderly fashion that they can be effectively used for their task. The problems which they try to answer arise only in so far as the conscious action of many men produce undesigned results, in so far as regularities are observed which are not the result of anybody's design. If social phenomena showed no order except in so far as they were consciously designed, there would indeed be no room for theoretical sciences of society and there would be, as is often argued, only problems of psychology. It is only in so far as some sort of order arises as a result of individual action but without being designed by any individual that a problem is raised which demands a theoretical explanation. But although people dominated by the scientistic prejudice are often inclined to deny the existence

173

of any such order (and thereby the existence of any object for theoretical sciences of society), few if any would be prepared to do so consistently: that at least language shows a definite order which is not the result of any conscious design can scarcely be questioned . . . the ideas which the popular mind has formed about such collectives as "society" or the "economic system", "capitalism" or "imperialism", and other such collective entities . . . the social scientist must regard as no more than provisional theories, popular abstractions, and . . . must not mistake for facts. That he consistently refrains from treating these pseudo-entities as "facts", and that he systematically starts from the concepts which guide individuals in their actions and not from the results of their theorizing about their actions, is the characteristic feature of that methodological individualism which is closely connected with the subjectivism of the social sciences.'

Popper (1945, 1957*a*, p. 136): 'the task of social theory is to construct and analyse our sociological models carefully in descriptive or nominalist terms, that is to say, *in terms of individuals,* of their attitudes, expectations, relations, etc.—a postulate which may be called "methodological individualism" . . .'; (1945, 1962, ii, p. 91): 'Psychologism is, I believe, correct only in so far as it insists upon what may be called "methodological individualism" as opposed to "methodological collectivism"; it rightly insists that the "behaviour" and the "actions" of collectives, such as states or social groups, must be reduced to the behaviour and to the actions of human individuals.'

Watkins (1952, 1953, pp. 723–43): 'An understanding of a complex social situation is always derived from a knowledge of the dispositions, beliefs, and relationships of individuals. Its overt characteristics may be *established* empirically, but they are only *explained* by being shown to be the resultants of individual activities . . . An explanation may be in terms of the *typical* dispositions of more or less anonymous individuals, or in terms of the peculiar dispositions of specific individuals . . . Hence holistic ideal types, which would abstract essential traits from a social whole while ignoring individuals, are impossible: they always turn into individualistic ideal types. Individualistic ideal types of explanatory power are constructed by first discerning the form of typical, socially significant, dispositions, and then by demonstrating how, in various typical situations, these lead to certain principles of social behaviour.'

Brodbeck (1954): To explain people's actions we need to know more than they do. An election can be explained in terms of individuals or in terms of macroscopic laws about the fate of parties in power for a given time, the relation to world crises, prosperity, etc. The latter are good, enlightening, simpler to formulate, and more testable. Sometimes methodological individualism is appropriate, methodological holism at others.

Watkins (1955): Individualism uses anonymous individuals, not specific individuals in its explanations. 'If "The Great Depression caused the defeat of the Labour Government in 1931" is short-hand for something like "Most electors blamed the Government for the unemployment and poverty and voted anti-Labour", then it is permissible; but if it were really meant to suggest that the behaviour of voters is controlled by an economic cycle, then it is . . . impermissible' (p. 60). It is important not to confuse methodological individualism with detailed individual explanation, or to confuse methodological holism with anonymous or in principle explanation.

Mandelbaum (1955): Understanding actions of human beings as members of society involves reference to social facts which are not reducible to a conjunction of statements concerning the actions of individuals. While testing may require specification in individual terms, in such specification other social facts will have to be referred to.

Goldstein (1956): Classificatory kinship terminology says nothing about the particular persons involved and yet is not holistic. Watkins's 'anonymous individual' concepts answer ignores the cultural conditioning of those dispositions.

Watkins (1958): Such dispositions can in turn be explained: if Huguenot prosperity is explained by their disposition to re-invest, this in turn can be explained by Calvinism's encouragement of thriftiness and/or the fewer alternative outlets for those not allowed to buy landed estates or political office. Similarly, kinship relations are created by people's beliefs about and hence attitudes towards each other. Their stability and distinctness derive from certain rules, and rules of this sort express widespread dispositions. Primogeniture is the acquiescence of widows, children and the authorities in inheritance of a man's property by his eldest son.

Gellner (1956): 'Individuals do have holistic concepts and act in terms of them', such as General De Gaulle's *idea* of France. 'The fact that holistic terms are ineliminable from the thought of participants may well be a clue to their ineliminability from that of observers.' 'For, in one sense, social environments *are* the *Gestalten* projected by individuals onto reality, provided they act in terms of them and provided reality is compatible with them and contains some devices for reinforcing them, such as rituals or other symbols, e.g. public buildings, totems, etc.' (p. 494 in Gardiner, 1959).

'The real oddity of the reductionist case is that it seems to preclude *a priori* the possibility of human dispositions being the dependent variable in an historic explanation—when in fact this

175

is what they often or always are—and secondly to preclude the possibility of causes, in the sense of initial conditions, being a complex fact which is not [describable]* in terms of the characteristics of its constituent parts alone—which again seems often to be the case.' 'As a matter of causal fact, our dispositions are not independent of the social context in which they occur; but they are not even independent logically, for they cannot be described without reference to their social context.'

'Certain tribes I know have what anthropologists call a segmentary patrilineal structure, which moreover maintains itself very well over time. I could "explain" this by saying that the tribesmen have, all or most of them, dispositions whose effect is to maintain the system. But, of course, not only have they never given the matter much thought, but it also might very well be impossible to isolate anything in the characters and conduct on the individual tribesmen which *explains* how they come to maintain the system' (pp. 495, 501–2).

Watkins (1957): 'methodological individualism certainly does not prohibit attempts to explain the formation of psychological characteristics; it only requires that such explanations should be in turn *individualistic*, explaining the formation as a result of a series of conscious or unconscious responses by an individual to his changing situation.' An individualistic explanation of the stability of a kinship system might proceed as follows. 'The very fact that the tribesmen *have never given the matter much thought*, the fact that they accept their inherited system uncritically, may constitute an important part of its stability. The explanation might go on to pinpoint certain rules—that is firm and widespread dispositions—about marriage, inheritance, etc., which help to regularize the tribesmen's behaviour towards their kinsmen. How they come to share these common dispositions could also be explained individualistically in the same sort of way that I can explain why my young children are already developing a typically English attitude towards policemen.' (pp. 607, 608n in Krimerman).

Gellner (1959a): 'The impact of rules and how tribesmen come to accept them can indeed be explained individualistically—to that extent I agree—meaning by this that a description of what is happening to individuals is always involved; but not without reference to the social background as a factor, and to that extent I disagree, at least with what I take methodological individualism to be saying.' (p. 515).

Mandelbaum (1957): 'it is assumed that all so-called "methodological holists" view a social system as an organic whole, the

* Misprinted as 'desirable' in all three printed versions. Correction verified with Professor Gellner.

component parts of which are individual human beings. This is not necessarily the case. Some who reject methodological individualism would regard the component parts of a social system as being the institutions which comprise that system.' *'in some cases* a knowledge of the initial conditions under which individuals act, and a knowledge of the laws of individual behaviour, is not adequate to explain the outcome of their actions: for this one must also employ abstractive-functional generalizations concerning societal facts.' (pp. 643, 649 in Krimerman).

Goldstein (1958): Methodological individualism subsumes two claims: ontological (wholes and tendencies do not exist); and methodological ('all explanation in social science must, in the end, be reduced to individual dispositions'). 'For the most part, people are born into their kinship relationships, and it seems entirely a reversal of actual fact to say that such relations "are the product of people's *attitudes* to each other, though these are partly determined by their *beliefs* about their biological relations". It seems more reasonable to say that for the most part the proper attitudes towards one's various kin are cultivated during the enculturation process.

'The point here is that the kinds of dispositions to be found in people of any given type are socially induced dispositions. It seems odd to talk about widely recurring dispositions among Huguenot entrepreneurs and not to wonder about the coincidence of the recurrence in just this group. It was, to be sure, individual Huguenots who successfully competed in the business world of the seventeenth century. But this was presumably because the Huguenot upbringing or enculturation produced people who were adept at this sort of thing. These were people who could operate effectively within the socioeconomic framework of the time.' 'wherever Watkins talks about anonymous dispositions or the dispositions of anonymous individuals he is simply attempting to talk about non-individual characteristics of societies or parts of societies, or of socially induced ways of behaving' (p. 630 in Krimerman).

Brodbeck (1958): 'Sometimes the phrase "methodological individualism" is applied both to the view that there are no undefinable group concepts and to the view that the laws of the group sciences are in principle reducible to those about individuals. The former is a denial of descriptive emergence; the latter denies that there are any logical grounds for belief in explanatory emergence . . . The latter is a matter of fact. And matters of fact cannot be legislated into existence. In other words, the empiricist commitment to *definitional* methodological individualism does not logically imply a commitment to *explanatory* methodological individualism, that is, to reduction.' (pp. 301–2 in Brodbeck).

Watkins (1959*a*): Goldstein (1958, above) seems to want to explain some social events in terms of non-human factors. He cannot logically hold this and believe human beings are the only causal factors in history.

Goldstein (1959): The issue between individualism and non-individualism concerns the proper way to analyse concepts like 'bank teller', which cannot in fact be satisfactorily analysed without remainder into individualistic terms.

Watkins (1959*b*): No methodological individualist ever prescribed, 'Analyse all sociological concepts individualistically'.

Agassi (1960): Methodological individualism denies that social entities have motives, aims, or destinies of their own. This is perfectly compatible with the existence of social institutions and social background and leads to more fruitful investigations. The aims but not the existence of wholes should be reduced.

Scott (1961): Hayek's individualism is synthetic and about data. He is concerned about where we start and how we constitute wholes. Popper's individualism is analytic, methodological and about where we finish. Collective phenomena should be understood as due to the actions, interactions, aims, hopes and thoughts of individual men, and as due to traditions created and preserved by individual men. Laws may use other notions, explanations may not. Watkins fails to discriminate Hayek's views from Popper's; downgrades laws to half-way explanations; confuses individualism with psychologism in his 1952 paper; and fails to answer Mandelbaum's demonstration that there are sociological laws that methodological individualism prohibits yet which do not suffer from the defects that Watkins wants them prohibited for.

Lukes (1968): Methodological individualism says all attempts to explain social and individual phenomena are to be rejected unless they refer exclusively to facts about individuals. But there are many kinds of facts about individuals and some of them cannot be stated without presupposing or entailing other statements about social phenomena.

Wisdom (1970): Popper thinks institutions can never be expressed wholly in terms of individuals. Hence in the explanation of a social event there may be a distributive reduction to individuals; there cannot be a collective reduction without remainder of all social events. This is because all actions have unintended consequences which may be distributively, but are certainly not collectively, predictable. The psycho-analytic theory of sub-acute depression is testable, hence scientific; it can be applied to Great Britain's present ills; methodological individualism rules this out and thus is too limiting.

# References

## 1 The logic of the situation

1 Grateful acknowledgment to G. K. Zollschan for useful comments.
2 Those who have written on it—Popper, Hayek, Watkins, Agassi, Zollschan, Wisdom, myself—seem always to have done so either in a polemical context or very briefly. The main literature is: Popper (1945, 1957a, 1962, 1963); Hayek (1952); Watkins (1953, 1957, 1963); Agassi (1960, 1963a); Scott (1961); Zollschan (1963); Albert (1963a); Jarvie (1961, 1964a, 1965); Wisdom (1970).
3 The sections on aims and means were left out for the publication in Zollschan (1972).
4 Headline to a story in the *New York Times,* 19 October 1966, p. 50.
5 *A fortiori,* the really tough problem which faced those who sought a conspiracy explanation of President Kennedy's assassination was to explain how such a conspiracy was ever consummated. So very many things can so easily go wrong, that success, not failure, of such ventures needs explanation. On this matter too, it may be worth recalling Popper's argument that to get verifications of a theory (of conspiracy, or whatever) is the easiest thing in the world. To specify what would refute the theory, and to devise a crucial test between a theory and its competitors, these are the really serious challenges. (See Popper, 1963, chap. 1.)
6 Once the jargon is mastered, however, he can be an exciting and intriguing author. A lucid introduction to his ideas is in Devereux (1961). The section 'The Frame of Reference of Action and Inter-action' (pp. 20ff.) is a Parsonian exposition of the notion of the logic of the situation.
7 Agassi (1959) claims that methodological and philosophical discussions are a regular feature in the history of science.
8 An interesting discussion of the psychological assumptions made by Evans-Pritchard is to be found in Kennedy (1967). In her intriguing book, *Purity and Danger* (1966), Mary Douglas expounds a view that might be thought to correct that put forward by Agassi and myself. In a complex and not altogether clear argument, her main

conclusion appears to be that beliefs and practices cannot be separated, so that the former can do the job of explaining the latter. Both are institutions, or parts of single institutions, not systematically thought-out philosophies. Apparently the questions, why did the granary collapse then, why did his crops fail not mine, why did the bull gore me and not him, are (pp. 90–1)

> demands for explanation . . . focussed on an individual's concern for himself and his community . . . the primitive world view is rarely itself an object of contemplation and speculation in the primitive culture. It has evolved as the appendage of other social institutions. To this extent it is produced indirectly, and to this extent the primitive culture must be taken to be unaware of itself, unconscious of its own conditions.

Social evolution leads to social differentiation and social awareness, self-consciousness and loss of organic solidarity. No doubt all this is true and to some extent enlightening. Gardner's rules of thumb have also grown up as appendages. But the origins of attempts at rational and criticizable explanations are irrelevant. Only by treating primitive ideas as attempts at explanation does one treat them seriously. To look upon primitive ideas as appendages to more significant social institutions like kinship, for example, is decisively to relegate primitive peoples to another world. (Incidentally, systems of ideas seem to me socially and ontologically in the *same*—third world—category as kinship, etc.; see chapter 6.) Only if we critically discuss their ideas with them can they learn their strengths and weaknesses *vis-à-vis* ours.

9 See Watkins (1953), section 3 and note 17. Popper (1945, chap. 10) concedes that a truly closed society may resemble an organism. For mob psychology, see Le Bon (1895).

10 (1) is Bacon and Descartes, (2) Berkeley and Duhem. For the resolution into (3) and a discussion of (1) and (2) see Popper (1963), chap. 3.

11 There is a spirited chapter on Spencer in Medawar (1967).

12 Racial memory is currently re-entering the literature with the blessing of some biologists. See Carrighar (1967) for a critique.

13 One might call this *strictly* or *permanently* hypothetical-and-deductive explanation to distinguish it from both Descartes' hypothetico-deductive scheme which allows *a priori* and eternally true axioms, and Whewell's hypothetico-deductive method where tests are continued until the hypothesis is *finally* either rejected or 'proved by experience'. Both employ the re-transmission of falsity centrally, but they see the hypothetical character as temporary, a means to finality. I see it as permanent: there is no finality—of acceptance or of rejection.

14 For full treatment of this, see Popper (1934), section 12; and Hempel and Oppenheim (1948). The latter acknowledge a debt to Mill, which is odd—what about Galileo, etc.? For a lively review of the history of the idea in modern times, see 'Hypothesis and Imagination' in Medawar (1967).

15 Cf. in this connection a beautiful riposte devised by Lakatos (1962, p. 157) when faced with the problem of whether his rational reconstruction of the history of mathematics was a caricature of the real history: 'one might equally well say that real history is a caricature of its rational reconstruction.'

16 The example is developed from an idea in Popper (1957a), p. 62.

17 My remarks on Hobbes are based on the interpretations of Brandt (1928) and Watkins (1965), sections 20–22.

18 There is an especially effective criticism in Chomsky's 1959 review of Skinner's work (1957). Skinner's air of sophistication and hard-headed 'scientific' approach is exploded, and Chomsky argues that the behaviour Skinner studies bears little or no resemblance to language or language use at all. Cybernetician, Norbert Wiener, was less naïve; see his work (1964), where the limitations of machines and the difficulty of applying cybernetics to the social sciences are discussed.

19 Although more can be situationally explained than at first sight; panic, for example, can be seen as a defence mechanism reacting to intolerable anxiety. The trouble is its self-defeating character. A panic in a theatre fire may itself cause many deaths, whereas had there been no panic, all might have survived. See Lang and Lang (1961); Smelser (1962); and Brown (1965).

20 This notion has been current among Popper's students for some time. See Jarvie and Agassi (1967), note 4; and Agassi (1969), pp. 464–5.

21 For the relation of simplicity to testabilty, see Popper (1934), section 43.

22 See the fascinating material on these questions in Gillespie (1963).

23 This story is beautifully documented and 'set out in Moynihan (1967a); and Rainwater and Yancey (1967).

24 I have heard it similarly (and, perhaps, even more plausibly) argued against certain critics of the Vietnam War that, in their call for no compromise, total American defeat and withdrawal, they are 'objectively', possibly consciously, certainly disingenuously, prolonging the war for which they affect such hatred.

25 Since this was written I have seen the important forthcoming paper, Wisdom (1970).

26 See chapter 4, section 5. One can imagine the problems in a bureaucratic state: a quota is fixed for agricultural production, say, sanctioned by threats. Who is then going to take responsibility by reporting that it is not fulfilled?

27 See Jarvie (1967a).

28 On egoistic suicide (Durkheim, 1897, p. 209): 'When society is strongly integrated, it holds individuals under its control, considers them at its service and thus forbids them to dispose wilfully of themselves'. On altruistic suicide (p. 234): a soldier

> must be trained to set little value upon himself, since he must be prepared to sacrifice himself upon being ordered to do so . . . a soldier's principle of action is external to himself . . .

the army . . . consists of a massive, compact group providing a rigid setting for the individual and preventing any independent movement.

On anomic suicide (p. 246):

No living being can be happy or even exist unless his needs are sufficiently proportioned to his means . . . if his needs require more than can be granted, or even merely something of a different sort, they will be under continual friction and can only function painfully. Movements incapable of production without pain tend not to be reproduced. Unsatisfied tendencies atrophy, and as the impulse to live is merely the result of all the rest, it is bound to weaken as the others relax.

## 1 Understanding and explaining in the social sciences

1 Robert Brown (1963, p. 41) defines the one in terms of the other: 'Explaining away, then, is the removing of an impediment, an impediment either to someone's relationships with other people or to his intellectual understanding.'
2 For the requirements, see Popper (1934), pp. 59–62, and (1957a), pp. 24ff.; and Bartley (1962b).
3 For some further animadversions on objectivity, see Jarvie (1970a).
4 A recent critique of relativism is Nowell-Smith (1971).
5 Since Winch does not set out these relations between the narrower and broader problems explicitly, I will not take up this latter contention. But that the solution of the broader problem will flow from a solution of the narrower problem does not seem obviously true.
6 In his 1960 paper, Winch argues that there are also moral universals, especially truth-telling, integrity and justice. Winch's universals bear comparison with Malinowski's theory of basic needs (see Piddington, 1957), which were mainly biological, and with Goldschmidt's recent theory (1966) that they are socio-cultural.
7 To exclude from these universal facts food, the obtaining, preparing and consuming of it, is a little odd. But then one might have to consider water, and sleep, and defecation, and micturition, and illness, and where would it end? All of which can be derided, as in Vedic Transcendentalism, although they must be taken care of somehow.
8 Winch's ideas have already been discussed in the following: Brodbeck (1963), Gellner (1962), Louch (1963, 1965), Winch (1964a), Saran (1964), Martin (1965), MacIntyre (1967), Bell (1967), Bryant (1970). There are also three papers on Winch in Lakatos and Musgrave (1968). They are by Gellner, Cohen and Watkins. In a perceptive footnote to his 1956 (n. 10, p. 502 in Gardiner) Gellner anticipates Winch 1958.
9 There are some criticisms of Winch's book in my review in the *British Journal for the Philosophy of Science*, **12**, 1961, 73–7, and in Gellner's (1960). Agassi and I have developed our own view of

how to understand magic (see Jarvie and Agassi, 1967). The two papers by Gellner listed in the previous reference have influenced me considerably, and a certain amount of overlap was unavoidable.

10 This is the general tenor of the philosophy of K. R. Popper; it is excellently expounded in Watkins (1972).

11 Criticism of the meaning/use thesis can be found in Gellner (1951 and 1959b); and Wisdom (1963).

12 Although, incidentally, it would be a mistake to think that our scientific culture admits as rational only those views which agree with current orthodoxy. No one calls Newton's optics, or Bohr's model of the atom irrational, though they are by now superseded.

13 See p. 18 of Bertrand Russell's Introduction to Wittgenstein (1922); and Englemann (1967).

14 Agassi maintains that I concede too much here; that metaphysical or not, Evans-Pritchard is right and magic is false. Agassi wishes perhaps to maintain the possibility of rational discussion of metaphysical statements. I gladly follow him in this, but feel it is not necessary for me to maintain this in the text.

15 In a fascinating aside, Popper (1945, i, p. 177 and note) suggests that sea-communications and commerce are the most powerful cause of the breakdown of the closed society and its monolithic outlook. For Popper's reconstruction of Ionia see his work (1963), chap. 5.

16 I am referring to that part of the Einstein-Bohr debate which concerns standards of rational appraisal; see Bohr (1949).

17 See Polanyi (1952).

18 Around this point the argument draws very heavily on Gellner (1968).

19 I owe this rational reconstruction to a lecture given by Professor J. Agassi. He was discussing (in Hong Kong) the uneasy coexistence of Chinese traditional medicine and western medicine in Hong Kong.

20 Clashes over policy are still frequent nowadays, e.g. birth control. Logically, ideas which lead on to absurd or false conclusions have doubt cast on them. It seems *false* to say the world will be a better place without birth control.

21 This kind of metaphysics is what Popper calls 'essentialism' (see Popper, 1945, ii, pp. 9–21).

22 Popper nowhere suggests that it ever was actualized or even could be.

23 See the important article by Goody and Watt (1963).

24 For actual demonstrations of how alien world-views can be handled see Lawrence (1964) and Horton (1964).

25 Winch's suggestion above that 'to say of a society that it has a language is also to say that it has a concept of rationality' is a deep error. See Jarvie and Agassi (1967).

26 Martin's and Cohen's criticisms (see ref. 8) are especially pertinent here.

27 Some Popperians, e.g. Agassi (1964), might want to exclude God and witches from metaphysics.

28 Interesting recent criticism of Winch is to be found in Nielsen (1967).
29 Time and height involve no entities, putative or otherwise, only relations. For this reason I think Winch's introduction of them confuses both the discussion and himself.
30 For the term 'justification' and the main philosophical criticism of it, see Bartley (1962b). Bartley considers his work an extension of Popper's.

## 3 Between adult and child: notes on the teenage problem

1 The first draft of this chapter, no part of which has been published before, was completed in 1963. Revising it for this publication I am struck by the accuracy of a sentence like this (which has not been changed). The ensuing eight years have only seen the generation gap widen and polarize more than expected.
2 Van Gennep (1908), p. 68:
It is appropriate to distinguish between *physical puberty* and *social puberty*, just as we distinguish between *physical kinship* (consanguinity) and *social kinship,* between *physical maturity* and *social maturity* (majority).
3 *Pace,* the reactionary conclusions of Wilson's otherwise perceptive articles (1964).
4 For this notion of the influence of a prediction on a predicted effect, see Popper (1957a), p. 13.
5 Cf. the fate of the dance 'The Mule', narrated in *Newsweek,* 67, 21 March 1966, pp. 50–1. Elsewhere (Jarvie, 1970b) I have criticized the charge that films and other aspects of pop culture are undifferentiated and that choice is manipulated, not genuine.
6 Here is a sentence that does need qualification. The development of pop music in the sixties from rock-and-roll through folk-rock, hard rock, acid rock, to oratorios like 'Sergeant Pepper's Lonely Hearts Club Band' (The Beatles), 'Arthur or The Decline and Fall of the British Empire' (The Kinks), and even an opera—'Tommy' (The Who), is even more encouraging.

## 4 The idea of social class

1 A version of what was to become this chapter was read in the Comparative Social Institutions' seminar of Professors Schapera, Freedman and MacRae, at the London School of Economics in October 1959. Another version was aired in the autumn of 1964 in Professor Karl Popper's seminar on Scientific Method, at the same institution. During the substantial rewriting which has ensued it benefited greatly from discussion with Professors J. W. N. Watkins and J. Agassi.

2 I dislike this formulation because it suggests essentialism (see ch. 2, ref. 21; ch. 4, ref. 6). I do not intend to discuss and try to define the name 'social class'; and I do not believe there is something called '*the* class system' whose essential features can be encapsulated in such a definition. It would perhaps be better if I had formulated my problem as: are any of the known theories of social class true of our society? But I felt I could not open the discussion in such an untraditional way without causing worse misunderstandings than those I shall try to clear up.

3 Exploded, it is to be hoped, by Kedourie (1961), *passim*.

4 Ginsberg puts it crudely thus: (1934, p. 160): 'Class . . . operates as an instrument for keeping people "in their place" . . .'

5 I consciously ignore the suggestion that we cut off the regress by defining some words in terms of other, perfectly well-understood, words. This evades, rather than solves, the problem of the infinite regress. If, in order to be clear, we must define our terms, then this applies to well-understood terms too. If well-understood terms are special, then which ones are well-understood and which are not becomes a problem. Whatever the solution to the problem, 'social class' can hardly be well-understood since attempts to define it in well-understood terms differ.

6 For the term and a critique of essentialism, see Popper (1945), i, chap. 3, section vi; and ii, chap. 11, sections i and ii. For a criticism of essentialistic or 'what is' questions, see Popper (1957*b*). See also ch. 2, ref. 21, above.

7 Lipset and Bendix (1959) list the following 'attributes' of social class: occupation, income, education, consumption style, origin, religion. Kahl (1957, pp. 8–10) lists the 'variables': personal prestige, occupation, possessions, interaction, class consciousness, and value orientations. The later work, happily, is the better. I shall use the word 'characteristic' throughout.

8 Davis (1949), p. 367:

> If the duties associated with the various positions were all equally pleasant, . . . all equally important to social survival, and all equally dependent on the same ability or talent, it would make no difference who got into which positions . . . but actually it does make a great deal of difference . . . not only because some positions are inherently more agreeable . . . but also because some require special talents or training and some have more importance than others. . . .
>
> Social inequality is . . . an unconsciously evolved device by which societies insure that the most important positions are conscientiously filled by the most qualified persons.

9 The best I know of is Blunt (1874).

10 For religion there was the Inquisition; ignorance prevents my saying whether there was any comparable institution for decision on remote children of the upper classes, except insofar as there were definite tables of status enshrined in law and conventions; for race, South Africa and Nazi Germany did have to set up quasi-legal

tribunals, but the troubles the former has had with the classification of Asiatics—Japanese are honorary whites but Chinese are not, and Japanese sometimes get maltreated because people cannot tell them from Chinese—and the racial dubiousness of even some prominent Nazi leaders, illustrates that such institutions have an impossible job.

11 Unless I completely misread him I have an ally on this point in Professor MacRae. He says (1961, p. 77): 'there is . . . in British society . . . a considerable surviving estate or feudal component at work in the reality and, even more, the ideology of our contemporary system of ranks.' He does not go on to explain or expand this; I shall. By arguing that the reality is a product of the ideology I have only to explain the one, which I attempt on pp. 118–21.

12 See Hayek (1952); Agassi (1960), footnote 14 and text; and Jarvie (1964a), p. 191.

13 Strictly speaking, observability is a matter of degree. Ownership is an abstraction, a title deed is not. Wealth is an abstraction, cash or a bank account is less so, but only our abstract understanding of these pieces of paper makes it seem concrete. The idea that things and behaviour are observable, while relationships and meanings are not, is common sense. But in the social sciences we are entirely concerned with relationships and meanings as they give significance to things and behaviour. Hence common sense observationalism really gets us nowhere.

14 Remembering that to be probable an event must have a likelihood of appreciably more than one half.

15 'With the exception of some primitive societies where difference of status is based on age or sex all human groupings exhibit hierarchical arrangements based on less "natural" criteria.' Rumney and Maier (1953), p. 130.

16 To Professor J. Agassi, I owe the following precise definitions:
complete ordering $df.$ $(a)(b)$ $a>b$ v $a<b$ v $a=b$
A hierarchy is a weaker requirement:

$$df. (a) (b) (a>b. b>c) \supset ((a>c. a\overline{<}b) \supset a<b) \mathrm{v}((a>b. b>c) \supset (a\overline{<}c))$$

17 'The corner peanut vendor is not a member of the middle class simply because he thinks he is.' Rumney and Maier (1953), p. 145. But he will be if a sufficient number of people join him in his belief, not only those who accept him as an equal, but also those who defer to him (cf. Shils, 1968). And the sociologist will then try to find the rational core of this novelty.

18 Sprott (1949), p. 105. The paragraph preceding this sentence is incisive enough and reads as follows.

The result of this relative segregation of commensality and class endogamy is to establish markedly different ways of life and thought as one passes from one class to another, as in a spectrum, there is no clear dividing line between one 'band' and another. An attempt to enumerate the numbers of classes, therefore, meets with insuperable difficulty. The usual threefold division into 'upper', 'middle' and 'lower' has been elaborated in American studies . . . into a sixfold one: upper-upper, lower-upper, upper-middle, lower-middle, upper-lower and lower-lower, but however refined the differentiation there will always be disputes as to who belongs to which group and as to the basis of classification. A behaviouristic criterion of interpersonal treatment, gestures of respect, camaraderie, or hauteur is too difficult to apply with any hope of success. Perhaps a more 'objective' criterion might be found in terms of expenditure-patterns, as is suggested by R. G. D. Allen, . . . but here again the collection of data presents almost insuperable difficulties.

19 In a superb paper published since this chapter was drafted, Nisbet (1968) has argued along parallel lines. Starting from the same premise that contemporary sociological studies of class bear little relation to reality, he traces the origins back to Marx, and the breakdown to the fact that all the markers of class which seemed then so obvious have become widely available and distributed, and attitudes are no longer homogeneous. He concludes that status has detached itself from any clearly definable scale of ranks, and works instead in diverse scales. People's denial of class cannot be attributed to ideological distortion since the ideology is a social fact, precisely the social fact which prevents the crystallization of status distinctions into classes.

20 Parallels here are to be found in 'On the Diversity of Morals' by Ginsberg where the theme is that when we remove the debris and compare apparently different ethical systems, a clear and true 'rational ethic' will stand revealed. Ginsberg calls the debris 'accretions', a slightly historist touch. See Jarvie (1960). Modern Oxford philosophy also exaggerates the wisdom of ordinary language. See Gellner (1959b), passim.

21 MacRae (1961), p. 66. Cf. the discussion in Banton (1960).

22 So I am able, interpreting it in my sense, to agree with Rumney and Maier's statement (1953, p. 141) that, 'Except for nationalism, the existence of social classes is perhaps the cardinal reality of our society.'

23 It may be of some interest to note that the Lipset and Bendix definition, discussed above on pp. 116–17, has a distinct dispositional tendency.

24 Cf. the following. Does, ask Lipset and Bendix (1959, p. 187), the lack of social mobility in the lower levels of society indicate a shying away from the psychological stress of mobility?

25 During the discussion of the ideas that were to become this chapter in Popper's seminar at the LSE (see ref. 1), it transpired that the following was about the nearest reality ever gets to the Castle and Gate model: (1) a fairly settled population; (2) a definite number of classes; (3) an hierarchical arrangement of the classes; (4) not much overlap between the classes, they are pretty distinct; (5) some definite criteria of allocating people to classes; (6) the whole set-up somewhat unstable and problematic.

26 A similar problem is presented to us by Lipset and Bendix (1959). They show clearly that America's alleged high social mobility, compared with other industrial societies, is a myth. What they do not explain is how such a myth arose, and continued, in the face of evidence to the contrary. I find their book intellectually stimulating precisely because it presents us with this brand new open problem. (I should stress that my concern is not how the author(s) of the common sense theory of social class hit upon it: we cannot answer questions about the origin of ideas without explaining too much. A more manageable question would be tracing the theory from its earliest appearance to its rise to general acceptance.) My thesis would be that, just as pressure to conform resulted from the 'melting pot' situation in America, so the stratification of people by income was also accepted because it was a common and easily understood standard to those in the melting pot. But it did not last long as the exclusive stratifier. While it was the only criterion, perfect mobility was possible and there was a lot of movement. Once it lost its place, movement was inhibited, but the myth persisted. The inertia of social theories again. MacRae says (1961, p. 69) that he does not accept that the Lipset and Bendix thesis is true, but frankly confesses that he cannot show this. Nisbet (1968) goes further than Lipset and Bendix.

27 The argument here borrows heavily from Popper's lectures.

28 See *Novum Organum*, Book I, aphorism xlvi; I present the doctrine in section 3.5 of my paper (Jarvie, 1961).

29 For the term see Popper (1957a) and cf. Merton (1957), chap. XI, 'The Self-Fulfilling Prophecy'.

30 See MacRae (1962), p. 137:

> Of course the neglect of knowledge and areas easily enough accessible is not mere parochialism . . . it is also the product of the pernicious ghosts who haunt the sociological sensibility of British social scientists, and in particular the ghost of the mythagogue Marx . . . people, right and left in politics, yet accept definitions of what is socially significant which have been derived from Marxism. This narrow legislation which makes all reality in society which is not bound up with stratification, mere ideology, error, surface iridescence on the depths of industrial capitalism . . .

Nisbet (1968), p. 117:

> Marx, with the vivid model of the landed class and its fusion of power and prestige in front of him, made the understandable assumption that industrial society would follow, *mutatis mutandis,* the same course of class development.

However, administrative centralization, nationalism, industrialization, and mass education, took the same toll of class as of village and kindred, as Tocqueville saw (p. 118).

31 E.g. Rumney and Maier (1953), p. 141; Johnson (1961), p. 504; Mayer (1955), p. 1. The Harvard social psychologist, Roger Brown,

in his authoritative textbook (1965), argues that social classes are not real in the United States (p. 134). His argument is that interactions and life styles are governed by roles; some of the roles fall on a continuum of socio-economic status, but behaviour is prescribed in terms of roles. While sentences like 'A Brahmin should . . .' or 'A Parsee should . . .' or 'A knight should . . .' start a flow of completions, the sentence 'Members of the middle-class should . . .' leads nowhere.

32 Evans-Pritchard (1962), pp. 18–19.

33 Indeed this seems to be the implicit thesis of Glass (1954, p. 21):
    the general picture so far is of a rather stable social structure,
    and one in which social status has tended to operate within,
    so to speak, a closed circuit. Social origins have conditioned
    educational level, and both have conditioned achieved status. . . .
    See also ref. 25 above.

34 Nisbet (1968), p. 111:
    At its extreme, especially in some of the works of W. Lloyd
    Warner and his students, the class perspective has the attributes
    of a Never Never land: observations carefully sterilized of
    historical considerations, constructed of self-fulfilling interviews
    and premises, skilfully extrapolated through use of linear scales
    and multiple correlations; the whole possessing a certain
    internal consistency, even credibility, but, on over-view,
    possessing about as much relation to national American society
    as James Branch Cabell's enchanted land of Poictésme does
    to Times Square.

35 Others concern, for example, race, heredity and tradition.


## 5 The sociology of knowledge reconsidered

1 This premise of the sociology of knowledge, that people believe what serves their interests, is both naïve and unconvincing. It seems naïve in face of the plentiful counter-examples of people accepting ideas which set them at a disadvantage, or even those which are actually self-destructive. It is unconvincing because what is 'objectively' in a person's interests is not, according to the sociology of knowledge, necessarily apparent to him. If this is so, then what mechanism ensures that his opinions and beliefs are kept in line with what objectively serves his interests? This gap in the theory has led to a great deal of intellectual squirming to handle things like working class conservatism, lack of revolutionary ardour, etc. See Shils (1957).

2 Among expositions not mentioned in Berger and Luckmann is Horowitz (1961). Berger's paper (1966) is a useful summary.

3 There is some further discussion of this in Jarvie (1969) and Nowell-Smith (1971). A most valuable recent treatment using anthropological materials is Moser (1968).

4 This interpretation of Scheler is buttressed by a reading of Schutz's essay 'Max Scheler's Epistemology and Ethics' (Schutz, 1966, pp. 145–78). Although deeply respectful of Kant, Scheler nevertheless criticized his doctrines as products of their time: Nature is a kind of enlarged Prussian state, Kant's ethics a continuation of the old Protestant Lutheran and somewhat Calvinistic doctrine of the Fall. Yet Scheler was not a relativist, he believed in absolute values. As Schutz points out (p. 170):

> The normative ought-to-do changes from group to group and from one historical period to the other. How is this fact compatible with the assumed objectivity and immutability of eternal values in their aprioristic order? Scheler deals at length with this objection. Not the existence of values, but their perceptibility, is relative.

5 The interest evinced in the so-called Whorf-sapir hypothesis is a case in point. As is the doctrine of Peter Winch (1964b) that there is no way in which it can be in order for a western anthropologist to adjudge the magical theories of a primitive society false (see chapter 2). Relativism is criticized in a new Addendum to the 1962 and subsequent editions of Popper's work (1945).

6 Here I am following Popper (1945), ii, pp. 213–14 and the Addendum, pp. 369–96.

7 On the problems of a sociology of science, see Musgrave (1969b).

8 This argument would make space 'coercive' too: 'The time, the place, the action.' One is reminded of Ayer's comment on existentialism: it is perverse to make a tragedy of what could not possibly be otherwise.

9 Why else do radicals feel they must organize? Perhaps because they want political success and do not believe in magic? But why do they want such success if not to endorse their reality? 'To endorse their reality' may be bad Berger and Luckmannese; perhaps our authors would grant that radicals may have some objective discontents which they wish to alleviate.

10 This applies also to their reconstruction of how human encounters began, became typified, and led to institutions. Phylogeny recapitulates ontogeny, as well as vice versa, perhaps. No man was ever, just as no baby is ever, forced to begin *ab initio*; there are always those who have been before, and we lose trace of them in the labyrinths of evolution. This is pointed out in David Martin's excellent review (1968).

11 When Berger and Luckmann allow (p. 115) that most modern societies are pluralistic, it is unclear what they mean. That myth, theology, and science coexist, possibly? They hardly tolerate each other and co-operate *intellectually,* one would think, even if they do join in a political consensus that erects a legal framework of tolerance. What do the authors mean when they write that within this pluralism there is a 'shared core universe' taken for granted, and different partial universes coexisting in mutual accommodation?

Is White's massive study (1896) of the warfare between science and religion not sufficient evidence of basic lack of agreement?

12 Agassi claims (1964) that those scientific questions are interesting which promise answers that might change our metaphysics, our whole way of looking at the whole world.

13 A chapter of Hayek's work (1967) is entitled 'The Results of Human Action but not of Human Design'. This is perhaps the most devastating of the arguments against radical change. That the social results of what we do will bear at best only some relation to our intentions gives us some reason to proceed with caution. The more attempted at any one time the greater the chances for things to get out of hand. Canvas cleaning is ruthlessly criticized by Popper (1945, pp. 167–8) as self-destructive and irrational, and elegantly sneered at by Oakeshott (1962 p. 112):

> In any generation, even the most revolutionary, the arrangements
> which are enjoyed always far exceed those which are recognized
> to stand in need of attention, and those which are being
> prepared for enjoyment are few in comparison with those which
> receive amendment: the new is an insignificant proportion
> of the whole.

14 Berger and Luckmann grant (p. 115) that pluralism itself is an accelerating factor in the process of change in modern societies. This is an addition to my stronger claim that our fundamental concern with social reality stems from a desire to change it; we may then institutionalize pluralism to galvanize that process.

## 6 Concepts and society

1 Barrie (1928), p. 32.

2 The slight shudder evoked by locutions like 'racist institutions', 'racist society' (apart from the grammatical quibble that the adjective is 'racialist', the noun 'racialism'), has to do with our notion that institutions and societies do not, except in an analogical sense, have any beliefs, racialist or otherwise. The argument is sometimes made that they are 'objectively' racialist: in their actual workings, the institutions or the society serve the interests of one race or another. But a man may serve the interests of a race without being a racialist in the important sense of believing in the virtue of racial discrimination, or the superiority of one race over another. Failure to distinguish in this way includes many more people among 'the enemy' than is necessary. (Ockham's razor applies to feuds and warfare.) A man who rejects the racialist ideology may be prevailed upon in addition to act differently, if he can be shown how his actions 'objectively' serve one race only and thus the racialism he has rejected. This move will hardly be available to use on one who embraces racial discrimination, unless by accident his actions serve the race he is concerned to discriminate against.

**191**

3 Boulding (1966), p. 103:
 . . . non-idle curiosity is that which arises out of a perception
 of the salient problems of the system, for it is only when
 problems become salient and enter the conscious awareness
 that conscious intellectual resources are devoted to their solution.
 We should expect, therefore, to find that as the dynamics
 of the social system bring one or another problem to salient
 positions, the interests of the social sciences change accordingly.

4 Rubinstein (1968), p. 24:
 Young SDS people have sought to alleviate their isolation and
 exhaustion by establishing a myth of international revolution
 and then identifying with it . . .
 Aron (1969) calls it a psychodrama.

5 Feuer (1969a), p. 462; Hook (1970), pp. 24ff.; Nisbet 1971.

6 Entities are born and die in the first and second worlds without
 the problem of reality arising. Houses are built and demolished
 and are real. People are born and die and are real. Neuroses begin
 and get cured, emotions well up and fade, and their comings and
 goings are not used as an argument to deny their real existence.
 (It is sometimes deployed as an argument to suggest the insuperable
 difficulty of studying them.) Not so with ideas. Whether Beethoven's
 fifth symphony is objectively real or not, hinges by consensus on
 the question whether it can come and go: usually, those who allow
 that it is an objectively real thing would deny that it can come and
 go (it was always there for Plato who would anchor it to a permanent form); and those who would deny its objective existence would
 insist that it can come and go.
 These are some of the puzzles which have emerged in discussion
 with Agassi of Popper's idea of the third world. (Incidentally, the
 name is unfortunate as it has already been used as a collective
 expression for developing countries of Asia, Africa and Latin
 America.)

7 This is one of the most brilliant *aperçus* of Sir Henry Maine (1861,
 Chap. V).

8 Popper (1945), ii, pp. 9ff. in the 1962 edition.

9 These ideas are central to Popper (1934).

10 Landheer (1952), p. 22:
 Society as such is a concept, an abstraction—*What exists in
 reality are individuals in whose minds society exists as a
 factor determining certain types of behaviour.* If the mental
 attitude no longer exists, society no longer exists either. If
 people were not aware of each other's existence, society would
 not exist, even if all the same people were still in existence,
 being fed and kept alive, for instance, by hitherto non-existent
 rays from the moon.

11 Nagel has argued persuasively (1955) that one can only say a
 whole is more than the sum of its parts relative to an assumed
 theory. My argument is really saying that theories which explain

192

why individuals are as they are do not explain the social relations or institutions they build.

12 After this chapter was drafted in 1969 I read Holzner (1968) where the map metaphor is introduced and used.

13 Landheer (1952), p. 36:

If society were stable and permanent, there would be little need for social theory as social processes would become subconscious and habitual as they are in the relatively stable primitive societies.

Madge (1962), p. 55:

At the archaic stage the picture of society was essentially mysterious and in the intervening stage it has been essentially moral and religious. At the contemporary stage, along with a plentiful inheritance of mystery and morality, there is an overriding tendency to look on society as a working system, which can be made to work better and better by rational-technical means. Central to this conception are, first, the idea of progress, second, the economics of the market and, third, the politics of the ballot box.

14 Boulding (1966), p. 102:

It is essenial to the understanding of the relations between the social sciences and the social system to realise that the social sciences are themselves part of the social system and are produced by it. It is of the nature of knowledge processes and evolutionary systems that they feed on themselves and that each part feeds back into the other with positive or at least disequilibrating feedback.

15 What cannot be guaranteed is that all scientists will interpret, see the same meaning in, the communications. This is the problem of the correspondence between the third world and the second, which is only a special case of the general problem of the correspondence between the different worlds. Logically, we cannot show that these correspondences obtain systematically. We can only judge by our successes and failures, and conjecture correspondence as the best explanation of what we appear to be having success at doing.

16 There is an interesting discussion in chapter 8 of Louch (1966).

# Bibliography

AGASSI, J. (1959), 'Epistemology as an Aid to Science', *British Journal for the Philosophy of Science*, **10**, 135–46.

AGASSI, J. (1960), 'Methodological Individualism', *British Journal of Sociology*, **11**, 244–70.

AGASSI, J. (1963*a*), *Towards an Historiography of Science*, The Hague: Mouton; Middletown (Ill.): Wesleyan University Press (*History and Theory*, Beiheft No. 2).

AGASSI, J. (1963*b*), 'Empiricism *versus* Inductivism', *Philosophical Studies*, **14**, 85–6.

AGASSI, J. (1964), 'The Nature of Scientific Problems and their Roots in Metaphysics', in BUNGE, ed. (1964), pp. 189–211.

AGASSI, J. (1968), 'On the Limits of Scientific Explanation: Hempel and Evans-Pritchard', *Philosophical Forum*, **1**, 171–84.

AGASSI, J. (1969), 'Unity and Diversity in Science', in COHEN and WARTOFSKY, (1969), pp. 463–522.

ALBERT, HANS, ed. (1963*a*), *Theorie und Realität*, Tübingen: J. C. B. Mohr (Paul Siebeck).

ALBERT, HANS (1963*b*), 'Probleme der Theorie Bildung', in ALBERT, ed. (1963*a*), pp. 3–70.

ARON, RAYMOND (1957), *The Opium of the Intellectuals*, London: Secker.

ARON, RAYMOND (1964), *German Sociology*, New York: Free Press.

ARON, RAYMOND (1969), *The Elusive Revolution*, New York: Praeger.

BACON, FRANCIS (1620), *Novum Organum*, London, various editions.

BANTON, MICHAEL (1960), 'Social Distance: A New Appreciation', *Sociological Review*, **8**, 169–83.

BARBU, Z. (1960), *Problems of Historical Sociology*, London: Routledge & Kegan Paul.

BARRIE, J. M. (1928), *Peter Pan or the Boy Who Would Not Grow Up*, London: Hodder & Stoughton.

BARTLEY III, W. W. (1962*a*), 'Achilles, the Tortoise, and Explanations in Science and in History', *British Journal for the Philosophy of Science*, **15**, 15–33.

BARTLEY III, W. W. (1962b), *The Retreat to Commitment*, New York: Knopf.

BAUMRIN, B., ed. (1963), *Philosophy of Science, The Delaware Seminar*, vol. 2, New York: Interscience.

BELL, D. R. (1967), 'The Idea of a Social Science', *Aristotelian Society*, Supplementary Volume, xli, 115–32.

BENDIX, R. and BERGER, B. (1959), 'Images of Society and Problems of Concept Formation in Sociology', in GROSS (1959), pp. 92–118.

BERGER, P. (1966), 'Identity as a Problem in the Sociology of Knowledge', *European Journal of Sociology*, 7, 105–15.

BERGER, P. and LUCKMANN, T. (1966), *The Social Construction of Reality*, London: Allen Lane.

BLACK, MAX (1961), *The Social Theories of Talcott Parsons*, Englewod Cliffs: Prentice-Hall.

BLAU, P. M. (1964), *Exchange and Power in Social Life*, New York: Wiley.

BLUNT, J. H. (1874), *Directionary of Sects, Heresies, Ecclesiastical Parties and Schools of Religious Thought*, London: Rivingtons.

BOHR, NIELS (1949), 'Discussion with Einstein on Epistemological Problems in Atomic Physics', in SCHILPP, ed. (1949), pp. 199–241.

BORGER, R. and CIOFFI, F., eds (1970), *Explanation in the Behavioural Sciences*, Cambridge University Press.

BOULDING, K. E. (1966), *The Impact of the Social Sciences*, New Brunswick: Rutgers University Press.

BRANDT, F. (1928), *Thomas Hobbes' Mechanical Conception of Nature*, Copenhagen: Levin & Munksgaard.

BRODBECK, MAY (1954), 'On the Philosophy of the Social Sciences', *Philosophy of Science*, 21, 140–56.

BRODBECK, MAY (1958), 'Methodological Individualisms: Definition and Reduction', *Philosophy of Science*, 25, 1–22; reprinted in DRAY, ed. (1966), pp. 297–329; and BRODBECK (1968), pp. 280–303.

BRODBECK, MAY (1963), 'Meaning and Action', *Philosophy of Science*, 30, 309–24; reprinted in BRODBECK (1968), pp. 58–78.

BRODBECK, MAY (1968), *Readings in the Philosophy of the Social Sciences*, New York: Macmillan.

BROWN, ROBERT (1963), *Explanation in Social Science*, London: Routledge & Kegan Paul.

BROWN, ROGER W. (1965), *Social Psychology*, London: Collier-Macmillan.

BRYANT, C. G. A. (1970), 'In Defence of Sociology: a reply to some contemporary philosophical criticisms', *British Journal of Sociology*, 21, 95–107.

BUNGE, M., ed. (1964), *The Critical Approach to Science and Philosophy*, London: Collier-Macmillan.

CAREW HUNT, *see* Hunt.

CARRIGHAR, S. (1967), 'War is not in Our Genes', *New York Times Magazine*, 10 September, 74ff, reprinted in MONTAGU, ed. (1968), pp. 37–50.

## BIBLIOGRAPHY

CARSTAIRS, G. M. (1962), *This Island Now*, London: Hogarth Press (also Penguin).

CHOMSKY, NOAM (1959), Review of B. F. SKINNER (1957), *Language*, **35**, 26–58.

COHEN, P. (1968), 'The Very Idea of a Social Science', in LAKATOS and MUSGRAVE, eds (1968), pp. 407–23.

COHEN, R. and WARTOFSKY, M. W., eds (1969), *Boston Studies in the Philosophy of Science*, vol. IV, New York: Humanities Press.

COLLINGWOOD, R. G. (1939), *An Autobiography*, London: Oxford University Press.

COLODNY, R. G., ed. (1965), *Beyond the Edge of Certainty*, Prentice-Hall.

CRICK, BERNARD (1969), 'The Proper Limits of Student Influence', in MARTIN (1969), pp. 155–71.

CROMBIE, A. C., ed. (1963), *Scientific Change*, London: Heinemann.

DANTO, ARTHUR (1966), *Analytical Philosophy of History*, Cambridge University Press.

DAVIS, KINGSLEY (1949), *Human Society*, New York: Macmillan.

DAVIS, KINGSLEY (1966), 'Sexual Behavior', in MERTON and NISBET, eds (1966), pp. 322–72.

DEVEREUX, JR, E. C. (1961), 'Parsons' Sociological Theory', in BLACK (1961), pp. 1–63.

DONAGAN, ALAN (1964), 'Historical Explanation: The Popper–Hempel Theory Reconsidered', *History and Theory*, **4**, 2–26; reprinted in DRAY, ed. (1966), pp. 127–59.

DOUGLAS, MARY (1966), *Purity and Danger*, London: Routledge & Kegan Paul.

DRAY, W., ed. (1966), *Philosophical Analysis and History*, New York: Harper & Row.

DURKHEIM, EMILE (1897), *Le Suicide*, Paris (English translation, *Suicide*, 1962, London: Routledge & Kegan Paul).

EISENSTADT, S. N. (1956), *From Generation to Generation*, London: Routledge & Kegan Paul.

ELLIS, L. F. (1962), *Victory in the West* (*History of the Second World War*, United Kingdom Military Series), London: HMSO.

ENGLEMANN, PAUL (1967), *Letters from Ludwig Wittgenstein: With a Memoir*, Oxford: Blackwell.

ERIKSON, E. H. (1959), *Young Man Luther*, London: Faber.

EVANS-PRITCHARD, E. E. (1937), *Witchcraft, Oracles and Magic Among the Azande*, London: Oxford University Press.

EVANS-PRITCHARD E. E. (1956), *Nuer Religion*, London: Oxford University Press.

EVANS-PRITCHARD, E. E. (1962), *Essays in Social Anthropology*, London: Faber.

FEIGL, H. and BRODBECK, M. (1953), *Readings in the Philosophy of Science*, New York: Appleton-Century-Crofts.

FEUER, LEWIS (1962), 'What is Alienation? The Career of a Concept', *New Politics*, **1**, 116–34; reprinted in FEVER (1969b), pp. 70–99.

FEUER, LEWIS (1969a), *The Conflict of Generations*, New York: Basic Books.

FEUER, LEWIS (1969*b*), *Marx and the Intellectuals*, New York: Doubleday Anchor.

FEYERABEND, P. K. (1961), *Knowledge Without Foundations*, Oberlin College.

FEYERABEND, P. K. (1963), 'How to be a Good Empiricist—A Plea for Tolerance in Matters Epistemological', in BAUMRIN, ed. (1963), pp. 3–39.

FEYERABEND, P. K. (1965), 'Problems of Empiricism', in COLODNY, ed. (1965), 145–260.

FIRTH, R. W., ed. (1957), *Man and Culture*, London: Routledge & Kegan Paul.

FIRTH, R. W. (1966), 'Twins, Birds and Vegetables: Problems of Identification in Primitive Religious Thought', *Man* (N.S.), **1**, 1–17.

GARDINER, PATRICK, ed. (1959), *Theories of History*, London: Allen & Unwin.

GELLNER, E. A. (1951), 'Use and Meaning', *Cambridge Journal*, **4**, 753–61.

GELLNER, E. A. (1956), 'Explanations in History', *Aristotelian Society*, Supplementary Volume, XXX, 157–76; reprinted with additions in GARDINER, ed. (1959), pp. 489–503; and BRODBECK (1968), pp. 254–68.

GELLNER, E. A. (1959*a*), 'Reply to Mr. Watkins', in GARDINER, ed. (1959), pp. 514–15.

GELLNER, E. A. (1959*b*), *Words and Things*, London: Gollancz; Penguin.

GELLNER, E. A. (1960), Review of WINCH (1958), *British Journal of Sociology*, **11**, 170–2.

GELLNER, E. A. (1962), 'Concepts and Society', *Transactions of the 5th World Congress of Sociology*, Louvain, vol. 1, 153–83; reprinted in WILSON, ed. (1970), pp. 18–49.

GELLNER, E. A. (1965), *Thought and Change*, London: Weidenfeld & Nicolson.

GELLNER, E. A. (1968*a*), 'The New Idealism', in LAKATOS and MUSGRAVE, eds (1968), pp. 377–406.

GELLNER, E. A. (1968*b*), 'The Entry of the Philosophers', *The Times Literary Supplement*, 5 April, 347–9.

GILL, JERRY H., ed. (1969), *Philosophy Today*, no. 2, New York: Macmillan.

GILLESPIE, C. G. (1963), 'Intellectual Factors in the Background of Analysis of Probabilities', in CROMBIE, ed. (1963), pp. 431–53.

GINSBERG, MORRIS (1934), *Sociology*, London: Oxford University Press.

GOFFMAN, ERVING (1961), *Asylums*, New York: Doubleday Anchor; Penguin.

GOLDSCHMIDT, W. (1966), *Comparative Functionalism*, Cambridge University Press.

GOLDSTEIN, LEON J. (1956), 'The Inadequacy of the Principle of Methodological Individualism', *Journal of Philosophy*, **53**, 801–13; reprinted in KRIMERMAN, ed. (1969), pp. 612–20.

GOLDSTEIN, LEON J. (1958), 'The Two Theses of Methodological Individualism', *British Journal for the Philosophy of Science*, **9**, 1–11; reprinted in KRIMERMAN, ed. (1969), pp. 625–31.

197

GOLDSTEIN, LEON J. (1959), 'Mr. Watkins on the Two Theses', *British Journal for the Philosophy of Science*, 10, 240–1.

GOODY, JACK, ed. (1986), *Literacy in Traditional Societies*, Cambridge University Press.

GOODY, JACK and WATT, IAN (1963), 'The Consequences of Literacy', *Comparative Studies in Society and History*, 5, 304–45; reprinted in GOODY, ed. (1968), pp. 27–68.

GROSS, LLEWELYN, ed. (1959), *Symposium on Sociological Theory*, New York: Harper & Row.

HAYEK, F. A. (1949), *Individualism and Economic Order*, London: Routledge & Kegan Paul.

HAYEK, F. A. (1952), *The Counter Revolution of Science*, London: Allen & Unwin.

HAYEK, F. A. (1967), *Studies in Philosophy, Politics and Economics*, London: Routledge & Kegan Paul.

HEMPEL, C. G. (1962), 'Rational Action', *Proceedings and Addresses of the American Philosophical Association*, 35, 5–23.

HEMPEL, C. G. (1965), *Aspects of Scientific Explanation*, London: Collier-Macmillan.

HEMPEL, C. G. and OPPENHEIM, P. (1948), 'Studies in the Logic of Explanation', *Philosophy of Science*, 15, 135–75; reprinted in part in FEIGL and BRODBECK (1953), pp. 319–52, in full in HEMPEL (1965), pp. 245–90.

HEYERDAHL, THOR (1950), *The Kon-Tiki Expedition*, London: Allen & Unwin; Penguin.

HEYERDAHL, THOR (1958), *Aku-Aku*, London: Allen & Unwin; Penguin.

HOLZNER, BURKART (1968), *Reality Construction in Society*, Cambridge (Mass.): Schenkman.

HOMANS, GEORGE C. (1967), *The Nature of Social Science*, New York: Harbinger (Harcourt, Brace & World).

HOOK, SYDNEY (1970), *Academic Freedom and Academic Anarchy*, New York: Cowles.

HOROWITZ, I. L. (1961), *Philosophy, Science and the Sociology of Knowledge*, Springfield (Ill.): Charles C. Thomas.

HORTON, W. R. G. (1964), 'Ritual Man in Africa', *Africa*, 34, 85–103.

HOUGH, R. (1959), *Admirals in Collision*, London: Hamish Hamilton.

HOWSON, COLIN (1969), Review of KYBURG (1968), in *British Journal for the Philosophy of Science*, 20, 359–61.

HUGHES, PENNETHORNE (1952), *Witchcraft*, London: Longmans Green.

HUNT, R. N. CAREW (1957), *A Guide to Communist Jargon*, London: Geoffrey Bles.

JACKSON, J. A., ed. (1968), *Social Stratification*, Cambridge University Press.

JARVIE, I. C. (1960), 'Ginsberg on Ethics', *Enquiry*, 2 June, 19–27.

JARVIE, I. C. (1961), 'Nadel on the Aims and Methods of Social Anthropology', *British Journal for the Philosophy of Science*, 12, 1–24.

JARVIE, I. C. (1964*a*), *The Revolution in Anthropology*, London: Routledge & Kegan Paul.

JARVIE, I. C. (1964*b*), Review of HOROWITZ (1961), in *British Journal for the Philosophy of Science*, 15, 266–8.

**198**

JARVIE, I. C. (1965), 'Limits to Functionalism and Alternatives to it in Anthropology', in MARTINDALE, ed. (1965), pp. 17–34; reprinted in MANNERS and KAPLAN, eds (1968), pp. 196–203.

JARVIE, I. C. (1967a), 'Is Technology Unnatural?', *Listener*, **77**, 322–3, 333.

JARVIE, I. C. (1967b), Review of RUDNER (1966), in *American Anthropologist*, **69**, 782–3.

JARVIE, I. C. (1968), 'The Emergence of Anthropology from Philosophy', *Philosophical Forum*, Fall, 73–84.

JARVIE, I. C. (1969), 'The Problem of Ethical Integrity in Participant Observation', *Current Anthropology*, **10**, 505–8, 521–2.

JARVIE, I. C. (1970a), 'On the Objectivity of Anthropology', in COHEN, ed. Proceedings of AAAS at Boston 1970, forthcoming.

JARVIE I. C. (1970b), *Towards a Sociology of the Cinema: Movies and Society*, London: Routledge & Kegan Paul.

JARVIE, I. C. and AGASSI, J. (1967), 'The Problem of the Rationality of Magic', *British Journal of Sociology*, **18**, 55–74; reprinted in WILSON, ed. (1970), pp. 172–93.

JOHNSON, HARRY M. (1961), *Sociology: A Systematic Introduction*, London: Routledge & Kegan Paul.

KAHL, J. A. (1957), *The American Class Structure*, New York: Holt, Rinehart & Winston.

KEDOURIE, E. (1961), *Nationalism*, London: Hutchinson.

KENNEDY, J. G. (1967), 'Psychological and Social Explanations of Witchcraft', *Man* (N.S.), **2**, 216–25.

KOESTLER, ARTHUR (1959), *The Sleepwalkers*, London: Hutchinson (also Penguin).

KRIMERMAN, LEONARD I., ed. (1969), *The Nature and Scope of Social Science*, New York: Appleton-Century-Crofts.

KUHN, THOMAS (1962), *The Structure of Scientific Revolutions*, University of Chicago Press.

KYBURG, HENRY E. (1968), *Philosophy of Science: A Formal Approach*, New York: Macmillan.

LAKATOS, IMRE (1962), 'Infinite Regress and the Foundations of Mathematics', *Aristotelian Society*, Supplementary Volume, xxxvi, 155–84.

LAKATOS, IMRE (1968), 'Criticism and the Methodology of Scientific Research Programmes', *Aristotelian Society*, **69**, 149–86.

LAKATOS, IMRE and MUSGRAVE, ALAN, eds (1968), *Problems in the Philosophy of Science, Proceedings of the International Colloquium, London, 1965*, vol. III, Amsterdam: North Holland.

LANDHEER, BART (1952), *Mind and Society*, The Hague: Mouton.

LANG, K. and LANG, G. (1961), *Collective Dynamics*, New York: Crowell.

LASLETT, P. and RUNCIMAN, W. G., eds (1962), *Philosophy, Politics and Society* (second series), Oxford: Blackwell.

LAWRENCE, PETER (1964), *Road Belong Cargo*, Manchester University Press.

LAZARSFELD, PAUL and ROSENBERG, M. (1955), *The Language of Social Research*, London: Collier-Macmillan.

LEACH, E. A. (1954), *Political Systems of Highland Burma*, London: G. Bell.

LEACH, JAMES J. (1968), 'The Logic of the Situation', *Philosophy of Science*, 35, 258–73.

LE BON, GUSTAVE (1895) (1963 ed.), *Psychologie de Foules*, Paris: F. Alcan.

LETHBRIDGE, T. C. (1962), *Witches*, London: Routledge & Kegan Paul.

LIPSET, SEYMOUR M. and BENDIX, REINHARD (1959), *Social Mobility in Industrial Society*, Cambridge University Press.

LOUCH, A. R. (1963), 'The Very Idea of a Social Science', *Inquiry*, 6, 273–86.

LOUCH, A. R. (1965), 'On Misunderstanding Mr. Winch', *Inquiry*, 8, 212–6.

LOUCH, A. R. (1966), *Explanation and Human Action*, Oxford: Blackwell.

LUKES, STEVEN (1968), 'Methodological Individualism Reconsidered', *British Journal of Sociology*, 19, 119–29.

MACINTYRE, ALASDAIR (1962), 'A Mistake About Causality in Social Science', in LASLETT and RUNCIMAN, eds (1962), pp. 48–70.

MACINTYRE, ALASDAIR (1967), 'The Idea of a Social Science', *Aristotelian Society*, Supplementary Volume, xli, 94–114; reprinted in WILSON, ed. (1970), pp. 112–30.

MACRAE, DONALD G. (1961), *Ideology and Society*, London: Heinemann.

MACRAE, DONALD G. (1962), 'Neglecting Society', *Twentieth Century*, 171, 133–7.

MADGE, CHARLES (1962), *Society in the Mind*, London: Faber.

MAINE, H. S. (1861), *Ancient Law*, London: John Murray.

MAIR, L. P. (1969), *Witchcraft*, London: Weidenfeld & Nicolson (also Penguin).

MANDELBAUM, MAURICE (1955), 'Societal Facts', *British Journal of Sociology*, 6, 305–17; reprinted in GARDINER, ed. (1959), pp. 476–88; and KRIMERMAN, ed. (1969), pp. 632–41.

MANDELBAUM, MAURICE (1957), 'Societal Laws', *British Journal for the Philosophy of Science*, 8, 211–24; reprinted in DRAY, ed. (1966), pp. 330–46; and KRIMERMAN, ed. (1969), pp. 642–50.

MANNERS, R. O. and KAPLAN, D., eds (1968), *Theory in Anthropology: A Source Book*, London: Aldine Press.

MANNHEIM, K. (1936), *Ideology and Utopia*, London: Kegan Paul.

MANNHEIM, K. (1952), *Essays on the Sociology of Knowledge*, London: Routledge & Kegan Paul.

MANNHEIM, K. (1953), *Essays on Sociology and Social Psychology*, London: Routledge & Kegan Paul.

MANNHEIM, K. (1956), *Essays on the Sociology of Culture*, London: Routledge & Kegan Paul.

MARSHALL, T. H. (1950), *Citizenship and Social Class*, Cambridge University Press.

MARTIN, DAVID (1968), 'The Sociology of Knowledge and the Nature of Social Knowledge', *British Journal of Sociology*, 19, 334–42.

MARTIN, DAVID (1969), *Anarchy and Culture*, London: Routledge & Kegan Paul.

MARTIN, MICHAEL (1965), 'Winch on Philosophy, Social Science and Explanation', *Philosophical Forum*, **23**, 29–41.

MARTIN, MICHAEL (1968), 'Situational Logic and Covering Law Explanations in History', *Inquiry*, **11**, 388–99.

MARTINDALE, DON, ed. (1965), *Functionalism in the Social Sciences* (American Academy of Social and Political Science), Philadelphia.

MAYER, K. (1955), *Class and Society*, New York: Random House.

MEAD, G. H. (1934), *Mind, Self and Society*, University of Chicago Press.

MEDAWAR, PETER (1967), *The Art of the Soluble*, London: Methuen.

MERTON, ROBERT K. (1957), *Social Theory and Social Structure*, Chicago: Free Press.

MERTON, ROBERT K. and NISBET, ROBERT A., eds (1966), *Contemporary Social Problems*, London: Hart-Davis.

MONTAGU, M. F. ASHLEY, ed. (1968), *Man and Aggression*, New York: Oxford University Press.

MORRIS, TERENCE (1963), 'The Teenage Criminal', *New Society*, **1**, 4 November, 13–15.

MOSER, SHIA (1968), *Absolutism and Relativism in Ethics*, Springfield (Ill.): Charles C. Thomas.

MOYNIHAN, DANIEL P. (1967*a*), 'The President and the Negro: The Moment Lost', *Commentary*, **43**, February, 31–45.

MOYNIHAN, DANIEL P. (1967*b*), 'Riots: Where the Liberals Went Wrong', *Boston Sunday Globe*, 8 August 1967.

MUSGRAVE, ALAN (1969*a*), 'Impersonal Knowledge: A Criticism of Subjectivism in Epistemology', unpublished Ph.D. thesis, University of London.

MUSGRAVE, ALAN (1969*b*), Review of ZIMAN (1968), in *British Journal for the Philosophy of Science*, **20**, 92–4.

NAGEL, E. (1955), 'On the Statement "The Whole is More than the Sum of its Parts" ', in LAZARSFELD and ROSENBERG (1955), pp. 519–27.

NATANSON, MAURICE, ed. (1963), *Philosophy of the Social Sciences*, New York: Random House.

NIELSEN, KAI (1967), 'Wittgensteinian Fideism', *Philosophy*, **42**, 191–209.

NISBET, ROBERT (1968), 'The Decline and Fall of Social Class', in *Tradition and Revolt, Historical and Sociological Essays*, New York: Random House, 105–27.

NISBET, ROBERT (1971), *The Degredation of the Academic Dogma*, New York: Basic Books.

NOWELL-SMITH, P. H. (1971), 'Cultural Relativism', *Philosophy of the Social Sciences*, **1**, 1–17.

OAKESHOTT, MICHAEL (1962), *Rationalism in Politics*, London: Methuen.

PAGE, BRUCE, LEITCH, DAVID and KNIGHTLY, PHILLIP (1968), *Philby: The Spy Who Betrayed a Generation*, London: Hutchinson.

PIDDINGTON, RALPH (1957), 'Malinowski's Theory of Needs', in FIRTH, ed. (1957), pp. 33–51.

PITCHER, GEORGE, (1964), *The Philosophy of Wittgenstein*, Prentice-Hall.

POLANYI, MICHAEL (1952), 'The Stability of Beliefs', *British Journal for the Philosophy of Science*, **3**, 217–37.

POPPER, K. R. (1934, 1959), *The Logic of Scientific Discovery*, Vienna; London: Hutchinson.

POPPER, K. R. (1945, 1962), *The Open Society and Its Enemies*, London: Routledge & Kegan Paul.

POPPER, K. R. (1948), 'The Trivialization of Mathematical Logic', *Proceedings of the 10th International Congress of Philosophy*, Amsterdam, vol. II, 722-7.

POPPER, K. R. (1957a), *The Poverty of Historicism*, London: Routledge & Kegan Paul.

POPPER, K. R. (1957b), 'The Aim of Science', *Ratio*, 1, 24-35.

POPPER, K. R. (1962), 'Die Logik der Sozialwissenschaften', *Kölner Zeitschrift für Soziologie und Sozialpsychologie*, 14, 233-48.

POPPER, K. R. (1963), *Conjectures and Refutations*, London: Routledge & Kegan Paul.

POPPER, K. R. (1967), 'Epistemology Without a Knowing Subject', Rootsellaar and Staal, eds *Proceedings of the Third International Congress for Logic, Methodology, and Philosophy of Science*, Amsterdam, pp. 333-73; reprinted in GILL, ed. (1969), pp. 225-77

POPPER, K. R. (1968), 'On the Theory of the Objective Mind', *Proceedings of the 14th International Congress of Philosophy*, 1, 25-53.

RADCLIFFE-BROWN, A. R. (1952), *Structure and Function in Primitive Society*, London: Cohen & West.

RAINWATER, LEE and YANCEY, WILLIAM L. (1967), *The Moynihan Report and the Politics of Controversy*, Cambridge (Mass.): M.I.T. Press.

ROTH, PHILIP (1969), *Portnoy's Complaint*, London: Cape (also Corgi).

RUBINSTEIN, JONATHAN (1968), 'SDS Against the World', *New York*, 1, 14 October, 24ff.

RUDNER, RICHARD (1966), *Philosophy of Social Science*, Prentice-Hall.

RUMNEY, JAY and MAIER, J. (1953), *The Science of Society*, London: Duckworth.

RUSSELL, BERTRAND (1955), *Human Society in Ethics and Politics*, London: Allen & Unwin.

SARAN, A. K. (1964), 'A Wittgensteinian Sociology?', *Ethics*, 75, 195-200

SCHELER, MAX (1925), 'Probleme einer Soziologie des Wissens', in *Die Wissenformen und die Gesellschaft*, Bern.

SCHILPP, P. A., ed. (1949), *Albert Einstein: Philosopher-Scientist*, New York: Open Court.

SCHILPP, P. A., ed. (1972), *The Philosophy of Karl Popper*, New York.

SCHUTZ, ALFRED (1966), *Collected Papers*, Vol. III, The Hague: Mouton.

SCOTT, K. J. (1961), 'Methodological and Epistemological Individualism', *British Journal for the Philosophy of Science*, 11, 331-6.

SHILS, EDWARD (1957), 'Daydreams and Nightmares! Reflections on the Criticism of Mass Culture', *Sewanee Review*, 65, 587-608.

SHILS, EDWARD (1968), 'Deference', in JACKSON, ed. (1968), pp. 104-32.

SIMMEL, GEORG (1959a), *Sociology of Religion*, New York: Philosophical Library.

SIMMEL, GEORG (1959b, 1965), *Essays on Sociology, Philosophy and Aesthetics*, New York: Harper Torchbooks.

SKINNER, B. F. (1957), *Verbal Behavior*, New York: Appleton-Century-Crofts.

SMELSER, NEIL J. (1962), *Theory of Collective Behaviour*, London: Routledge & Kegan Paul.

SPENCER, HERBERT (1900), *First Principles* (6th ed.), London: Watts.

SPROTT, W. J. H. (1949, 1957), *Sociology*, London: Hutchinson.

STARK, WERNER (1958), *The Sociology of Knowledge*, London: Routledge & Kegan Paul.

THOMAS, W. I. (1928), *The Child in America*, University of Chicago Press.

VAN GENNEP, ARNOLD (1908, 1960), *The Rites of Passage*, London: Routledge & Kegan Paul.

WALSH, W. H. (1970), 'Pride, Shame and Responsibility', *Philosophical Quarterly*, **20**, 1-13.

WALTON, PAUL (1970), 'From Surplus Value to Surplus Theories: Marx, Marcuse and MacIntyre', *Social Research*, **37**, 644-55.

WATKINS, J. W. N. (1952, 1953), 'Ideal Types and Historical Explanation', *British Journal for the Philosophy of Science*, **3**, 1952, 22-43; an improved version appeared in FEIGL and BRODBECK (1953), pp. 723-43; and KRIMERMAN, ed. (1969), pp. 457-72.

WATKINS, J. W. N. (1955), 'Methodological Individualism: A Reply', *Philosophy of Science*, **22**, 58-62.

WATKINS, J. W. N. (1957), 'Historical Explanation in the Social Sciences', *British Journal for the Philosophy of Science*, **8**, 104-17; reprinted in GARDINER, ed. (1959), pp. 503-14; KRIMERMAN, ed. (1969), pp. 603-11; and BRODBECK (1968), pp. 269-80.

WATKINS, J. W. N. (1958), 'The Alleged Inadequacy of Methodological Individualism', *Journal of Philosophy*, **55**, 390-5; reprinted in KRIMERMAN, ed. (1969), pp. 621-4.

WATKINS, J. W. N. (1959*a*), 'The Two Theses of Methodological Individualism', *British Journal for the Philosophy of Science*, **9**, 319-20.

WATKINS, J. W. N. (1959*b*), 'Third Reply to Mr. Goldstein', *British Journal for the Philosophy of Science*, **10**, 242-4.

WATKINS, J. W. N. (1963), 'On Explaining Disaster', *Listener*, 10 January, 69-70.

WATKINS, J. W. N. (1965), *Hobbes's System of Ideas*, London: Hutchinson.

WATKINS, J. W. N. (1968), 'Anthropomorphism in Social Science', in LAKATOS and MUSGRAVE, eds (1968), pp. 432-6.

WATKINS, J. W. N. (1970), 'Imperfect Rationality', in BORGER and CIOFFI, eds (1970), pp. 167-217.

WATKINS, J. W. N. (1972), 'Popper's Systematic Philosophy', in SCHILPP, ed. (1972).

WEBER, MAX (1925, 1964), *The Theory of Social and Economic Organization*, Tübingen; London: Collier-Macmillan.

WHITE, A. D. (1896), *A History of the Warfare of Science with Theology*, New York: Dover Books.

WHITE, MORTON (1965), *The Foundations of Historical Knowledge*, New York: Harper & Row.

BIBLIOGRAPHY

WHITE, ROBERT L. (1970), 'Little Lord Fauntleroy as Hero', paper delivered to the American Studies Association.

WIENER, NORBERT (1964), *God and Golem Inc.*, Cambridge (Mass.): M.I.T. Press.

WILSON, BRYAN (1964), 'War of the Generations, I and II', *Daily Telegraph*, 24 and 25 August.

WILSON, BRYAN, ed. (1970), *Rationality*, Oxford: Blackwell.

WINCH, PETER (1958), *The Idea of a Social Science*, London: Routledge & Kegan Paul.

WINCH, PETER (1960), 'Nature and Convention', *Proceedings of the Aristotelian Society*, 60, 231–52.

WINCH, PETER (1964a), 'Mr. Louch's Idea of a Social Science', *Inquiry*, 7, 202–8.

WINCH, PETER (1964b), 'Understanding a Primitive Society', *American Philosophical Quarterly*, 1, 307–24; reprinted in WILSON, ed. (1970), pp. 78–111.

WISDOM, J. O. (1963), 'Metamorphoses of the Verifiability Theory of Meaning', *Mind*, 72, 335–47.

WISDOM, J. O. (1970), 'Situational Individualism and the Emergent Group Properties', in BORGER and CIOFFI, eds (1970), pp. 271–96.

WISDOM, J. O. (1971), 'Science *versus* the Scientific Revolution', *Philosophy of the Social Sciences*, 1, 123–44.

WITTGENSTEIN, L. (1922), *Tractatus logico-philosophicus*, London: Kegan Paul; reprinted 1962.

WITTGENSTEIN, L. (1954), *Philosophical Investigations*, Oxford: Blackwell.

ZIMAN, J. D. (1968), *Public Knowledge: An Essay Concerning the Social Dimension of Science*, Cambridge University Press.

ZOLLSCHAN, G. K. ed. (1963), *Explorations in Social Change*, London: Routledge & Kegan Paul.

ZOLLSCHAN, G. K. ed. (1972), *Essays on Sociological Explanation*, Santa Barbara: Glendessary Press.

# Name index

Agassi, Joseph 11, 12, 16, 27, 66, 122, 124, 136, 142, 152, 155, 156, 157, 158, 178, 179, 181, 182, 183, 184, 186, 191, 192
Albert, Hans 179
Alexander, Mrs C. F. 95, 114
Allen, R. G. D. 187
Ardrey, Robert 20
Aristotle 99, 104
Aron, Raymond 91, 134, 192
Artful Dodger, the 87
Ayer, A. J. 190

Bacon, Sir Francis 13, 27, 124, 180
Banton, Michael 187
Barbu, Z. 122
Barrett-Brown, Michael 116
Barrie, Sir James 152, 153, 154, 191
Bartley III, W. W. 14, 54, 182, 184
Beatles, the 184
Beethoven, Ludwig van 192
Bell, D. R. 182
Bendix, Reinhard 92, 116, 119, 185, 187, 188
Berger, Bennett 119
Berger, Peter 32, 131-46 *passim*, 150, 155, 165, 189, 190, 191
Berkeley, Bishop George 180
Blau, Peter M. 124
Blunt, Rev. J. H. 185
Bohr, Niels 48, 63, 183
Boulding, Kenneth 192, 193
Brandt, F. 181

Brodbeck, May 174, 177, 182
Brown, Robert 182
Brown, Roger 12, 181, 188-9
Bryant, C. G. A. 182

Cabell, James Branch 189
Carew Hunt, *see* Hunt
Carrighar, Sally 180
Carstairs, G. M. 73, 82
Chamberlain, Neville 4
Charles I of England 15
Chomsky, Noam 181
Cohen, Percy S. 46, 182, 183
Collingwood, R. G. 24, 28, 29
Cooley, C. H. 3

Danto, Arthur 14
Davis, Kingsley 11, 92, 105, 185
De Gaulle, General Charles 175
Descartes, René 13, 180
De Tocqueville, A. 188
Devereux, Eugène 179
Donagan, Alan 12
Douglas, Mary 179-80
Duhem, Pierre 180
Durkheim, Émile 35, 109, 123, 125, 142, 152, 181

Einstein, Albert 48, 63, 183
Eisenstadt, S. N. 83, 85
Eliot, T. S. 46
Ellis, L. F. 25
Englemann, Paul 183

205

# Subject index

# International Library of Sociology

Edited by
## John Rex
*University of Warwick*

Founded by
## Karl Mannheim

as The International Library of Sociology
and Social Reconstruction

*This Catalogue also contains other Social Science
series published by Routledge*

Routledge & Kegan Paul   London and Boston

68-74 Carter Lane  London EC4V 5EL
9 Park Street  Boston  Mass 02108

# Contents

● *Books so marked are available in paperback*
*All books are in Metric Demy 8vo format (216 × 138mm approx.)*

# GENERAL SOCIOLOGY

**Belshaw, Cyril.** The Conditions of Social Performance. *An Exploratory Theory. 144 pp.*

**Brown, Robert.** Explanation in Social Science. *208 pp.*

**Cain, Maureen E.** Society and the Policeman's Role. *About 300 pp.*

**Gibson, Quentin.** The Logic of Social Enquiry. *240 pp.*

**Homans, George C.** Sentiments and Activities: *Essays in Social Science. 336 pp.*

**Isajiw, Wsevold W.** Causation and Functionalism in Sociology. *165 pp.*

**Johnson, Harry M.** Sociology: *a Systematic Introduction. Foreword by Robert K. Merton. 710 pp.*

**Mannheim, Karl.** Essays on Sociology and Social Psychology. *Edited by Paul Keckskemeti. With Editorial Note by Adolph Lowe. 344 pp.*

Systematic Sociology: *An Introduction to the Study of Society. Edited by J. S. Erös and Professor W. A. C. Stewart. 220 pp.*

**Martindale, Don.** The Nature and Types of Sociological Theory. *292 pp.*

**Maus, Heinz.** A Short History of Sociology. *234 pp.*

**Mey, Harald.** Field-Theory. *A Study of its Application in the Social Sciences. 352 pp.*

**Myrdal, Gunnar.** Value in Social Theory: *A Collection of Essays on Methodology. Edited by Paul Streeten. 332 pp.*

**Ogburn, William F.,** and **Nimkoff, Meyer F.** A Handbook of Sociology. *Preface by Karl Mannheim. 656 pp. 46 figures. 35 tables.*

**Parsons, Talcott,** and **Smelser, Neil J.** Economy and Society: *A Study in the Integration of Economic and Social Theory. 362 pp.*

**Rex, John.** Key Problems of Sociological Theory. *220 pp.*

**Stark, Werner.** The Fundamental Forms of Social Thought. *280 pp.*

# FOREIGN CLASSICS OF SOCIOLOGY

**Durkheim, Emile.** Suicide. *A Study in Sociology. Edited and with an Introduction by George Simpson. 404 pp.*

Professional Ethics and Civic Morals. *Translated by Cornelia Brookfield. 288 pp.*

**Gerth, H. H.,** and **Mills, C. Wright.** From Max Weber: *Essays in Sociology. 502 pp.*

**Tönnies, Ferdinand.** Community and Association. *(Gemeinschaft und Gesellschaft.) Translated and Supplemented by Charles P. Loomis. Foreword by Pitirim A. Sorokin. 334 pp.*

# SOCIAL STRUCTURE

**Andreski, Stanislav.** Military Organization and Society. *Foreword by Professor A. R. Radcliffe-Brown. 226 pp. 1 folder.*

● **Cole, G. D. H.** Studies in Class Structure. *220 p.*

**Coontz, Sydney H.** Population Theories and the Economic Interpretation. *202 pp.*

**Coser, Lewis.** The Functions of Social Conflict. *204 pp.*

**Dickie-Clark, H. F.** Marginal Situation: *A Sociological Study of a Coloured Group. 240 pp. 11 tables.*

**Glass, D. V.** (Ed.). Social Mobility in Britain. *Contributions by J. Berent, T. Bottomore, R. C. Chambers, J. Floud, D. V. Glass, J. R. Hall, H. T. Himmelweit, R. K. Kelsall, F. M. Martin, C. A. Moser, R. Mukherjee, and W. Ziegel. 420 pp.*

**Glaser, Barney,** and **Strauss, Anselm L.** Status Passage. *A Formal Theory. 208 pp.*

**Jones, Garth N.** Planned Organizational Change: *An Exploratory Study Using an Empirical Approach. 268 pp.*

**Kelsall, R. K.** Higher Civil Servants in Britain: *From 1870 to the Present Day. 268 pp. 31 tables.*

**König, René.** The Community. *232 pp. Illustrated.*

● **Lawton, Denis.** Social Class, Language and Education. *192 pp.*

**McLeish, John.** The Theory of Social Change: *Four Views Considered. 128 pp.*

**Marsh, David C.** The Changing Social Structure in England and Wales, 1871-1961. *272 pp.*

**Mouzelis, Nicos.** Organization and Bureaucracy. *An Analysis of Modern Theories. 240 pp.*

**Mulkay, M. J.** Functionalism, Exchange and Theoretical Strategy. *272 pp.*

**Ossowski, Stanislaw.** Class Structure in the Social Consciousness. *210 pp.*

## SOCIOLOGY AND POLITICS

**Crick, Bernard.** The American Science of Politics: *Its Origins and Conditions. 284 pp.*

**Hertz, Frederick.** Nationality in History and Politics: *A Psychology and Sociology of National Sentiment and Nationalism. 432 pp.*

**Kornhauser, William.** The Politics of Mass Society. *272 pp. 20 tables.*

**Laidler, Harry W.** History of Socialism. *Social-Economic Movements: An Historical and Comparative Survey of Socialism, Communism, Co-operation, Utopianism; and other Systems of Reform and Reconstruction. 992 pp.*

**Mannheim, Karl.** Freedom, Power and Democratic Planning. *Edited by Hans Gerth and Ernest K. Bramstedt. 424 pp.*

**Mansur, Fatma.** Process of Independence. *Foreword by A. H. Hanson. 208 pp.*

**Martin, David A.** Pacificism: *an Historical and Sociological Study. 262 pp.*

**Myrdal, Gunnar.** The Political Element in the Development of Economic Theory. *Translated from the German by Paul Streeten. 282 pp.*

**Verney, Douglas V.** The Analysis of Political Systems. *264 pp.*

**Wootton, Graham.** Workers, Unions and the State. *188 pp.*

## FOREIGN AFFAIRS: THEIR SOCIAL, POLITICAL AND ECONOMIC FOUNDATIONS

**Bonné, Alfred.** State and Economics in the Middle East: *A Society in Transition. 482 pp.*
Studies in Economic Development: *with special reference to Conditions in the Under-developed Areas of Western Asia and India. 322 pp. 84 tables.*
**Mayer, J. P.** Political Thought in France from the Revolution to the Fifth Republic. *164 pp.*

## CRIMINOLOGY

**Ancel, Marc.** Social Defence: *A Modern Approach to Criminal Problems. Foreword by Leon Radzinowicz. 240 pp.*
**Cloward, Richard A.,** and **Ohlin, Lloyd E.** Delinquency and Opportunity: *A Theory of Delinquent Gangs. 248 pp.*
**Downes, David M.** The Delinquent Solution. *A Study in Subcultural Theory. 296 pp.*
**Dunlop, A. B.,** and **McCabe, S.** Young Men in Detention Centres. *192 pp.*
**Friedlander, Kate.** The Psycho-Analytical Approach to Juvenile Delinquency: *Theory, Case Studies, Treatment. 320 pp.*
**Glueck, Sheldon,** and **Eleanor.** Family Environment and Delinquency. *With the statistical assistance of Rose W. Kneznek. 340 pp.*
**Lopez-Rey, Manuel.** Crime. *An Analytical Appraisal. 288 pp.*
**Mannheim, Hermann.** Comparative Criminology: *a Text Book. Two volumes. 442 pp. and 380 pp.*
**Morris, Terence.** The Criminal Area: *A Study in Social Ecology. Foreword by Hermann Mannheim. 232 pp. 25 tables. 4 maps.*
**Trasler, Gordon.** The Explanation of Criminality. *144 pp.*

## SOCIAL PSYCHOLOGY

**Bagley, Christopher.** The Social Psychology of the Child with Epilepsy. *320 pp.*
**Barbu, Zevedei.** Problems of Historical Psychology. *248 pp.*
**Blackburn, Julian.** Psychology and the Social Pattern. *184 pp.*
**Fleming, C. M.** Adolescence: *Its Social Psychology: With an Introduction to recent findings from the fields of Anthropology, Physiology, Medicine, Psychometrics and Sociometry. 288 pp.*
The Social Psychology of Education: *An Introduction and Guide to Its Study. 136 pp.*
**Homans, George C.** The Human Group. *Foreword by Bernard DeVoto. Introduction by Robert K. Merton. 526 pp.*
Social Behaviour: *its Elementary Forms. 416 pp.*

**Klein, Josephine.** The Study of Groups. *226 pp. 31 figures. 5 tables.*
**Linton, Ralph.** The Cultural Background of Personality. *132 pp.*
**Mayo, Elton.** The Social Problems of an Industrial Civilization. *With an appendix on the Political Problem. 180 pp.*
**Ottaway, A. K. C.** Learning Through Group Experience. *176 pp.*
**Ridder, J. C. de.** The Personality of the Urban African in South Africa. *A Thematic Apperception Test Study. 196 pp. 12 plates.*
● **Rose, Arnold M.** (Ed.). Human Behaviour and Social Processes: *an Interactionist Approach. Contributions by Arnold M. Rose, Ralph H. Turner, Anselm Strauss, Everett C. Hughes, E. Franklin Frazier, Howard S. Becker, et al. 696 pp.*
**Smelser, Neil J.** Theory of Collective Behaviour. *448 pp.*
**Stephenson, Geoffrey M.** The Development of Conscience. *128 pp.*
**Young, Kimball.** Handbook of Social Psychology. *658 pp. 16 figures. 10 tables.*

## SOCIOLOGY OF THE FAMILY

**Banks, J. A.** Prosperity and Parenthood: *A Study of Family Planning among The Victorian Middle Classes. 262 pp.*
**Bell, Colin R.** Middle Class Families: *Social and Geographical Mobility. 224 pp.*
**Burton, Lindy.** Vulnerable Children. *272 pp.*
**Gavron, Hannah.** The Captive Wife: *Conflicts of Household Mothers. 190 pp.*
**George, Victor,** and **Wilding, Paul.** Motherless Families. *220 pp.*
**Klein, Josephine.** Samples from English Cultures.
　1. Three Preliminary Studies and Aspects of Adult Life in England. *447 pp.*
　2. Child-Rearing Practices and Index. *247 pp.*
**Klein, Viola.** Britain's Married Women Workers. *180 pp.*
　The Feminine Character. *History of an Ideology. 244 pp.*
**McWhinnie, Alexina M.** Adopted Children. *How They Grow Up. 304 pp.*
**Myrdal, Alva,** and **Klein, Viola.** Women's Two Roles: *Home and Work. 238 pp. 27 tables.*
**Parsons, Talcott,** and **Bales, Robert F.** Family: *Socialization and Interaction Process. In collaboration with James Olds, Morris Zelditch and Philip E. Slater. 456 pp. 50 figures and tables.*

## SOCIAL SERVICES

**Bastide, Roger.** The Sociology of Mental Disorder. *Translated from the French by Jean McNeil. 264 pp.*
**Carlebach, Julius.** Caring For Children in Trouble. *266 pp.*
**Forder, R. A.** (Ed.). Penelope Hall's Social Services of Modern England. *352 pp.*
**George, Victor.** Foster Care. *Theory and Practice. 234 pp.*
　Social Security: *Beveridge and After. 258 pp.*

● **Goetschius, George W.** Working with Community Groups. *256 pp.*

**Goetschius, George W.,** and **Tash, Joan.** Working with Unattached Youth. *416 pp.*

**Hall, M. P.,** and **Howes, I. V.** The Church in Social Work. *A Study of Moral Welfare Work undertaken by the Church of England. 320 pp.*

**Heywood, Jean S.** Children in Care: *the Development of the Service for the Deprived Child. 264 pp.*

**Hoenig, J.,** and **Hamilton, Marian W.** The De-Segration of the Mentally Ill. *284 pp.*

**Jones, Kathleen.** Lunacy, Law and Conscience, *1744-1845: the Social History of the Care of the Insane. 268 pp.*

Mental Health and Social Policy, 1845-1959. *264 pp.*

**King, Roy D., Raynes, Norma V.,** and **Tizard, Jack.** Patterns of Residential Care. *356 pp.*

**Leigh, John.** Young People and Leisure. *256 pp.*

**Morris, Pauline.** Put Away: *A Sociological Study of Institutions for the Mentally Retarded. 364 pp.*

**Nokes, P. L.** The Professional Task in Welfare Practice. *152 pp.*

**Timms, Noel.** Psychiatric Social Work in Great Britain (1939-1962). *280 pp.*

● Social Casework: *Principles and Practice. 256 pp.*

**Trasler, Gordon.** In Place of Parents: *A Study in Foster Care. 272 pp.*

**Young, A. F.,** and **Ashton, E. T.** British Social Work in the Nineteenth Century. *288 pp.*

**Young, A. F.** Social Services in British Industry. *272 pp.*


## SOCIOLOGY OF EDUCATION

**Banks, Olive.** Parity and Prestige in English Secondary Education: a Study in Educational Sociology. *272 pp.*

**Bentwich, Joseph.** Education in Israel. *224 pp. 8 pp. plates.*

● **Blyth, W. A. L.** English Primary Education. *A Sociological Description.*
  1. Schools. *232 pp.*
  2. Background. *168 pp.*

**Collier, K. G.** The Social Purposes of Education: *Personal and Social Values in Education. 268 pp.*

**Dale, R. R.,** and **Griffith, S.** Down Stream: *Failure in the Grammar School. 108 pp.*

**Dore, R. P.** Education in Tokugawa Japan. *356 pp. 9 pp. plates*

**Evans, K. M.** Sociometry and Education. *158 pp.*

**Foster, P. J.** Education and Social Change in Ghana. *336 pp. 3 maps.*

**Fraser, W. R.** Education and Society in Modern France. *150 pp.*

**Grace, Gerald R.** Role Conflict and the Teacher. *About 200 pp.*

**Hans, Nicholas.** New Trends in Education in the Eighteenth Century. *278 pp. 19 tables.*

● Comparative Education: *A Study of Educational Factors and Traditions. 360 pp.*

**Hargreaves, David.** Interpersonal Relations and Education. *432 pp.*
● Social Relations in a Secondary School. *240 pp.*
**Holmes, Brian.** Problems in Education. *A Comparative Approach. 336 pp.*
**King, Ronald.** Values and Involvement in a Grammar School. *164 pp.*
● **Mannheim, Karl,** and **Stewart, W. A. C.** An Introduction to the Sociology of Education. *206 pp.*
**Morris, Raymond N.** The Sixth Form and College Entrance. *231 pp.*
● **Musgrove, F.** Youth and the Social Order. *176 pp.*
● **Ottaway, A. K. C.** Education and Society: *An Introduction to the Sociology of Education. With an Introduction by W. O. Lester Smith. 212 pp.*
**Peers, Robert.** Adult Education: *A Comparative Study. 398 pp.*
**Pritchard, D. G.** Education and the Handicapped: *1760 to 1960. 258 pp.*
**Richardson, Helen.** Adolescent Girls in Approved Schools. *308 pp.*
**Simon, Brian,** and **Joan** (Eds.). Educational Psychology in the U.S.S.R. *Introduction by Brian and Joan Simon. Translation by Joan Simon. Papers by D. N. Bogoiavlenski and N. A. Menchinskaia, D. B. Elkonin, E. A. Fleshner, Z. I. Kalmykova, G. S. Kostiuk, V. A. Krutetski, A. N. Leontiev, A. R. Luria, E. A. Milerian, R. G. Natadze, B. M. Teplov, L. S. Vygotski, L. V. Zankov. 296 pp.*
**Stratta, Erica.** The Education of Borstal Boys. *A Study of their Educational Experiences prior to, and during Borstal Training. 256 pp.*

## SOCIOLOGY OF CULTURE

**Eppel, E. M.,** and **M.** Adolescents and Morality: *A Study of some Moral Values and Dilemmas of Working Adolescents in the Context of a changing Climate of Opinion. Foreword by W. J. H. Sprott. 268 pp. 39 tables.*
● **Fromm, Erich.** The Fear of Freedom. *286 pp.*
The Sane Society. *400 pp.*
● **Mannheim, Karl.** Diagnosis of Our Time: *Wartime Essays of a Sociologist. 208 pp.*
Essays on the Sociology of Culture. *Edited by Ernst Mannheim in co-operation with Paul Kecskemeti. Editorial Note by Adolph Lowe. 280 pp.*
**Weber, Alfred.** Farewell to European History: *or The Conquest of Nihilism. Translated from the German by R. F. C. Hull. 224 pp.*

## SOCIOLOGY OF RELIGION

**Argyle, Michael.** Religious Behaviour. *224 pp. 8 figures. 41 tables.*
**Nelson, G. K.** Spiritualism and Society. *313 pp.*

**Stark, Werner.** The Sociology of Religion. *A Study of Christendom.*
Volume I. *Established Religion. 248 pp.*
Volume II. *Sectarian Religion. 368 pp.*
Volume III. *The Universal Church. 464 pp.*
Volume IV. *Types of Religious Man. 352 pp.*
Volume V. *Types of Religious Culture. 464 pp.*
**Watt, W. Montgomery.** Islam and the Integration of Society. *320 pp.*

## SOCIOLOGY OF ART AND LITERATURE

**Beljame, Alexandre.** Men of Letters and the English Public in the Eighteenth
Century: *1660-1744, Dryden, Addison, Pope. Edited with an Introduction
and Notes by Bonamy Dobrée. Translated by E. O. Lorimer. 532 pp.*
**Jarvie, Ian C.** Towards a Sociology of the Cinema. *A Comparative Essay
on the Structure and Functioning of a Major Entertainment Industry.
405 pp.*
**Rust, Frances S.** Dance in Society. *An Analysis of the Relationships between
the Social Dance and Society in England from the Middle Ages to the
Present Day. 256 pp. 8 pp. of plates.*
**Schücking, L. L.** The Sociology of Literary Taste. *112 pp.*
**Silbermann, Alphons.** The Sociology of Music. *Translated from the German
by Corbet Stewart. 222 pp.*

## SOCIOLOGY OF KNOWLEDGE

**Mannheim, Karl.** Essays on the Sociology of Knowledge. *Edited by Paul
Kecskemeti. Editorial note by Adolph Lowe. 353 pp.*
**Stark, Werner.** The Sociology of Knowledge: *An Essay in Aid of a Deeper
Understanding of the History of Ideas. 384 pp.*

## URBAN SOCIOLOGY

**Ashworth, William.** The Genesis of Modern British Town Planning: *A Study
in Economic and Social History of the Nineteenth and Twentieth Centuries.
288 pp.*
**Cullingworth, J. B.** Housing Needs and Planning Policy: *A Restatement of
the Problems of Housing Need and 'Overspill' in England and Wales.
232 pp. 44 tables. 8 maps.*
**Dickinson, Robert E.** City and Region: *A Geographical Interpretation.
608 pp. 125 figures.*
The West European City: *A Geographical Interpretation. 600 pp. 129 maps.
29 plates.*
● The City Region in Western Europe. *320 pp. Maps.*

**Humphreys, Alexander J.** New Dubliners: *Urbanization and the Irish Family. Foreword by George C. Homans. 304 pp.*

**Jackson, Brian.** Working Class Community: *Some General Notions raised by a Series of Studies in Northern England. 192 pp.*

**Jennings, Hilda.** Societies in the Making: *a Study of Development and Re-development within a County Borough. Foreword by D. A. Clark. 286 pp.*

**Kerr, Madeline.** The People of Ship Street. *240 pp.*

● **Mann, P. H.** An Approach to Urban Sociology. *240 pp.*

**Morris, R. N.,** and **Mogey, J.** The Sociology of Housing. *Studies at Berins-field. 232 pp. 4 pp. plates.*

**Rosser, C.,** and **Harris, C.** The Family and Social Change. *A Study of Family and Kinship in a South Wales Town. 352 pp. 8 maps.*

## RURAL SOCIOLOGY

**Chambers, R. J. H.** Settlement Schemes in Africa: *A Selective Study. 268 pp.*

**Haswell, M. R.** The Economics of Development in Village India. *120 pp.*

**Littlejohn, James.** Westrigg: *the Sociology of a Cheviot Parish. 172 pp. 5 figures.*

**Williams, W. M.** The Country Craftsman: *A Study of Some Rural Crafts and the Rural Industries Organization in England. 248 pp. 9 figures. (Dartington Hall Studies in Rural Sociology.)*

The Sociology of an English Village: *Gosforth. 272 pp. 12 figures. 13 tables.*

## SOCIOLOGY OF INDUSTRY AND DISTRIBUTION

**Anderson, Nels.** Work and Leisure. *280 pp.*

● **Blau, Peter M.,** and **Scott, W. Richard.** Formal Organizations: *a Comparative approach. Introduction and Additional Bibliography by J. H. Smith. 326 pp.*

**Eldridge, J. E. T.** Industrial Disputes. *Essays in the Sociology of Industrial Relations. 288 pp.*

**Hetzler, Stanley.** Technological Growth and Social Change. *Achieving Modernization. 269 pp.*

**Hollowell, Peter G.** The Lorry Driver. *272 pp.*

**Jefferys, Margot,** *with the assistance of Winifred Moss.* Mobility in the Labour Market: *Employment Changes in Battersea and Dagenham. Preface by Barbara Wootton. 186 pp. 51 tables.*

**Millerson, Geoffrey.** The Qualifying Associations: *a Study in Professionaliza-tion. 320 pp.*

**Smelser, Neil J.** Social Change in the Industrial Revolution: *An Application of Theory to the Lancashire Cotton Industry, 1770-1840. 468 pp. 12 figures. 14 tables.*

**Williams, Gertrude.** Recruitment to Skilled Trades. *240 pp.*

**Young, A. F.** Industrial Injuries Insurance: *an Examination of British Policy.* *192 pp.*

## ANTHROPOLOGY

**Ammar, Hamed.** Growing up in an Egyptian Village: *Silwa, Province of Aswan. 336 pp.*
**Brandel-Syrier, Mia.** Reeftown Elite. *A Study of Social Mobility in a Modern African Community on the Reef. 376 pp.*
**Crook, David,** and **Isabel.** Revolution in a Chinese Village: *Ten Mile Inn. 230 pp. 8 plates. 1 map.*
The First Years of Yangyi Commune. *302 pp. 12 plates.*
**Dickie-Clark, H. F.** The Marginal Situation. *A Sociological Study of a Coloured Group. 236 pp.*
**Dube, S. C.** Indian Village. *Foreword by Morris Edward Opler. 276 pp. 4 plates.*
India's Changing Villages: *Human Factors in Community Development. 260 pp. 8 plates. 1 map.*
**Firth, Raymond.** Malay Fishermen. *Their Peasant Economy. 420 pp. 17 pp. plates.*
**Gulliver, P. H.** Social Control in an African Society: a Study of the Arusha, Agricultural Masai of Northern Tanganyika. *320 pp. 8 plates. 10 figures.*
**Ishwaran, K.** Shivapur. *A South Indian Village. 216 pp.*
Tradition and Economy in Village India: *An Interactionist Approach. Foreword by Conrad Arensburg. 176 pp.*
**Jarvie, Ian C.** The Revolution in Anthropology. *268 pp.*
**Jarvie, Ian C.,** and **Agassi, Joseph.** Hong Kong. *A Society in Transition. 396 pp. Illustrated with plates and maps.*
**Little, Kenneth L.** Mende of Sierra Leone. *308 pp. and folder.*
Negroes in Britain. *With a New Introduction and Contemporary Study by Leonard Bloom. 320 pp.*
**Lowie, Robert H.** Social Organization. *494 pp.*
**Mayer, Adrian C.** Caste and Kinship in Central India: *A Village and its Region. 328 pp. 16 plates. 15 figures. 16 tables.*
**Smith, Raymond T.** The Negro Family in British Guiana: *Family Structure and Social Status in the Villages. With a Foreword by Meyer Fortes. 314 pp. 8 plates. 1 figure. 4 maps.*

## DOCUMENTARY

**Meek, Dorothea L.** (Ed.). Soviet Youth: *Some Achievements and Problems. Excerpts from the Soviet Press, translated by the editor. 280 pp.*
**Schlesinger, Rudolf** (Ed.). Changing Attitudes in Soviet Russia.
2. *The Nationalities Problem and Soviet Administration. Selected Readings on the Development of Soviet Nationalities Policies. Introduced by the editor. Translated by W. W. Gottlieb. 324 pp.*

## SOCIOLOGY AND PHILOSOPHY

**Barnsley, John H.** The Social Reality of Ethics. *A Comparative Analysis of Moral Codes. 448 pp.*

**Douglas, Jack D.** (Ed.). Understanding Everyday Life. *Toward the Reconstruction of Sociological Knowledge. Contributions by Alan F. Blum. Aaron W. Cicourel, Norman K. Denzin, Jack D. Douglas, John Heeren, Peter McHugh, Peter K. Manning, Melvin Power, Matthew Speier, Roy Turner, D. Lawrence Wieder, Thomas P. Wilson and Don H. Zimmerman. 358 pp.*

**Jarvie, Ian C.** Concepts and Society. *216 pp.*

**Roche, Maurice.** Phenomenology, Language and the Social Sciences. *About 400 pp.*

**Sklair, Leslie.** The Sociology of Progress. *320 pp.*

# International Library of Social Policy

*General Editor* Kathleen Janes

**Jones, Kathleen.** Mental Health Services. *A history, 1744-1971. About 500 pp.*

**Thomas, J. E.** The English Prison Officer since 1850: *A Study in Conflict. 258 pp.*

# Primary Socialization, Language and Education

*General Editor* Basil Bernstein

**Bernstein, Basil.** Class, Codes and Control. *2 volumes.*
   1. *Theoretical Studies Towards a Sociology of Language. 254 pp.*
   2. *Applied Studies Towards a Sociology of Language. About 400 pp.*

**Brandis, Walter,** and **Henderson, Dorothy.** Social Class, Language and Communication. *288 pp.*

**Cook, Jenny.** Socialization and Social Control. *About 300 pp.*

**Gahagan, D. M.,** and **G. A.** Talk Reform. *Exploration in Language for Infant School Children. 160 pp.*

**Robinson, W. P.,** and **Rackstraw, Susan, D. A.** A Question of Answers. *2 volumes. 192 pp. and 180 pp.*

**Turner, Geoffrey, J.,** and **Mohan, Bernard, A.** A Linguistic Description and Computer Programme for Children's Speech. *208 pp.*

# Reports of the Institute of Community Studies and the Institute of Social Studies in Medical Care

**Cartwright, Ann.** Human Relations and Hospital Care. *272 pp.*
Parents and Family Planning Services. *306 pp.*
Patients and their Doctors. *A Study of General Practice. 304 pp.*
**Dunnell, Karen,** and **Cartwright, Ann.** Medicine Takers, Prescribers and Hoarders. *About 140 pp.*
● **Jackson, Brian.** Streaming: *an Education System in Miniature. 168 pp.*
**Jackson, Brian,** and **Marsden, Dennis.** Education and the Working Class: *Some General Themes raised by a Study of 88 Working-class Children in a Northern Industrial City. 268 pp. 2 folders.*
**Marris, Peter.** Widows and their Families. *Foreword by Dr. John Bowlby. 184 pp. 18 tables. Statistical Summary.*
Family and Social Change in an African City. *A Study of Rehousing in Lagos. 196 pp. 1 map. 4 plates. 53 tables.*
The Experience of Higher Education. *232 pp. 27 tables.*
**Marris, Peter,** and **Rein, Martin.** Dilemmas of Social Reform. *Poverty and Community Action in the United States. 256 pp.*
**Marris, Peter,** and **Somerset, Anthony.** African Businessmen. *A Study of Entrepreneurship and Development in Kenya. 256 pp.*
**Runciman, W. G.** Relative Deprivation and Social Justice. *A Study of Attitudes to Social Inequality in Twentieth Century England. 352 pp.*
**Townsend, Peter.** The Family Life of Old People: *An Inquiry in East London. Foreword by J. H. Sheldon. 300 pp. 3 figures. 63 tables.*
**Willmott, Peter.** Adolescent Boys in East London. *230 pp.*
The Evolution of a Community: *a study of Dagenham after forty years. 168 pp. 2 maps.*
**Willmott, Peter,** and **Young, Michael.** Family and Class in a London Suburb. *202 pp. 47 tables.*
**Young, Michael.** Innovation and Research in Education. *192 pp.*
● **Young, Michael,** and **McGeeney, Patrick.** Learning Begins at Home. *A Study of a Junior School and its Parents. 128 pp.*
**Young, Michael,** and **Willmott, Peter.** Family and Kinship in East London. *Foreword by Richard M. Titmuss. 252 pp. 39 tables.*

# Medicine, Illness and Society
*General Editor* W. M. Williams

**Robinson, David.** The Process of Becoming Ill.
**Stacey, Margaret.** *et al.* Hospitals, Children and Their Families. *The Report of a Pilot Study. 202 pp.*

# Routledge Social Science Journals

**The British Journal of Sociology.** *Edited by Terence P. Morris. Vol. 1, No. 1, March 1950 and Quarterly. Roy. 8vo. Back numbers available. An international journal with articles on all aspects of sociology.*

**Economy and Society.** *Vol. 1, No. 1. February 1972 and Quarterly. Metric Roy. 8vo. A journal for all social scientists covering sociology, philosophy, anthropology, economics and history.*

Printed in Great Britain by Lewis Reprints Limited
Brown Knight & Truscott Group, London and Tonbridge          21972